From STOREBOUGHT to HOMEMADE

• • • • SECRETS FOR COOKING EASY, FABULOUS FOOD IN MINUTES

Emyl Jenkins

foreword by Jan Karon

TAYLOR TRADE PUBLISHING
Lanham • New York • Dallas • Boulder • Toronto • Oxford

Published by Taylor Trade Publishing
An imprint of The Rowman & Littlefield Publishing Group, Inc.
4501 Forbes Boulevard, Suite 200
Lanham, Maryland 20706

Distributed by National Book Network

ISBN 1-58979-218-1 (pbk.: alk. paper)

♾™ The paper used in this publication meets the minimum requirements of American National Standard for Information Sciences—Permanence of Paper for Printed Library Materials, ANSI/NISO Z39.48–1992.
Manufactured in the United States of America.

To all who, down through the years, have shared their families'
treasured recipes for the enjoyment of others.

*If a man be gracious to strangers, it shows that he is a citizen
of the world, and his heart is no island, cut off from
other islands, but a continent that joins them.*

—SIR FRANCIS BACON, 1561-1626

And to Charlotte Sizer. Thank you for your diligence,
good nature, and winning smile.
And to Benjamin and Matthew Hultzapple, the newest
generation at our family's dinner table.

Contents

Acknowledgments

Untold numbers of people contributed ideas, suggestions, and recommendations for this book—especially those who sent me recipes from their personal archives, and the patient grocery store managers and workers who listened to my questions and helped me track down products. Thank you, each and every one.

Thank you to those who helped to uncover much needed information, especially Joan Jacobsen and Dick Pretty, Jan Harris, Bill Satterfield, and Laura Wiletsky, and the very cooperative folks at Ragú, including Jim Stringfield and Helena Tregubov.

Thank you, Jackie Legg, food writer, hostess extraordinaire, and a very capable vice-president of Ukrops, that great food chain in Richmond, Virginia.

Thank you Larry Aaron, Cyndee Moore, Danny Vaden, Kim Demont, Nina Klinkenberg, and of course, my dear husband, Bob Sexton, for your patience and help in making it possible for me to have the time to pursue this project.

And thank you, especially, Jeanne Fredericks, my agent; photographer Monica Buck; Sarah Butterworth, who actually came up with the title, *From Store-bought to Homemade*; the book's designers at Vertigo Design, NYC; and my helpful and good friends at QVC, Jill Cohen, whose brainchild this was, Cassandra Reynolds, Rebecca Helmeczi, and most of all, Karen Murgolo.

A Note on Reduced Carbohydrate and Reduced Fat Products

With everyone seemingly counting every gram of carbohydrate and fat consumed these days, you may be wondering how to make quick and easy storebought to homemade recipes that are "healthy" and also affordable. Unfortunately, specialty carb products are often hard to find and expensive. But there is good news. A new brand, Carb Focus™, retailed by Wal-Mart, has brought out several soups great for including in casseroles. Two in particular, Tuscan Style Tomato and Chicken Pot Pie Style, are excellent.

Tuscan Style Tomato soup can be used anytime tomato soup is included—the recipes for Zesty Tomato Starter and Love Apple Fromage Soup are examples. And the Chicken Pot Pie Style soup is great for Chicken Chowder and Mexican Chicken Casserole. If you're the sort of cook who likes to try a different taste or to tinker around with recipes, you may even consider occasionally using it in place of a cream of mushroom or cream of potato soup.

Another way to reduce carbs is to choose a pasta alternative—especially Mueller's Reduced Carb Penne Rigate. Keep this in mind when preparing recipes such as You-Take-the-Credit Caramelized Onion and Blue Cheese Rissoni or 10-Minute Baked Ziti.

Then there's the high fat content in cheese that we're always trying to avoid. For recipes calling for cream cheese, in addition to the low or no-fat varieties, Neufchatel cheese is an especially well-suited alternative. For cheddar, I've been delighted to learn that Cabot Vermont's 50% Light Cheddar is now available in shredded form. However, since its "shreds" packaging is primarily available in the Northeast, I find it worth my time to shred a lot of this flavorful block cheese myself, and store packages of it in the freezer. Remember, frozen pizzas have cheese on them, so why not freeze cheese?

When shopping for reduced or fat-free items, another product worth keeping in mind is I Can't Believe It's Not Butter!™ Original Buttery Spray. It's like Pam™ and the other brands of sprays, but it gives a buttery taste as well.

Try to experiment with even more of the healthier convenience items that seem to be cropping up on grocery store shelves almost daily. Part of the fun of making homemade dishes from storebought ingredients is using your imagination.

Foreword

Thoughts on Cooking
—and Not Cooking

WHEN you've put one of Emyl's sensational dishes on the table, and after you've asked the blessing (you'll be amazed how this improves everyone's disposition), try doing what the Europeans have always done far better than we: Talk! Tell jokes! Ask questions! (If you were going to be shot for treason in the morning, what would you request for your last meal?) Recite a poem! Tell your favorite experience of the day! Tell the one seated to your right what you love most about them. Then tell the one on your left, and ask the others to do the same. Focus on the food too—is it good? What do you like about it? Compliment the cook!

The next thing you know, dinner will be more than the same old blue-plate special. You may even find it well seasoned with laughter.

"Laughter doeth good like a medicine," Scripture tells us. In truth, I've found laughter to be the loveliest of all the aids to good digestion!

I haven't really "cooked" cooked in years. That's because I can make so many wonderful things by hardly cooking at all.

A great favorite with my family is Simple Roast Chicken:

Rinse a whole fryer and pat it dry.

Rub it with a good olive oil and season well with salt, cracked pepper, rosemary, and paprika.

Stuff the cavity with half a lemon and several cloves of garlic.

Put the chicken on its back in a well-seasoned black skillet, and set it on the middle rack of your oven, which you've turned to 450 degrees.

Roast at 450 degrees for 30 minutes and at 350 degrees for one hour.

This simple recipe has a great bonus:

It roasts while I write!

See? That's not cooking, that's just a little fooling around in the kitchen.

So what would *you* request as your last meal if you were to be shot for treason in the morning?

Make mine fresh lobster with drawn butter and a glass of very dry, very fine Champagne from Champagne!

Failing that, how about fried chicken, mashed potatoes, gravy, and short, flaky biscuits?

Failing that, how about liver mush? Fried crisp and golden, thanks.

When in the world are you going on a picnic again? You talk about doing it, you occasionally daydream about doing it, but you don't do it! Right? This summer, take your kids and go on a picnic. *Please!*

Spread a quilt or a blanket.

Don't worry about ants.

Lie on your back. Look up at the branches of trees. Find faces in the clouds.

Tell your kids what kind of kid you were at their age. Find out what they really, really, really want to be or do someday—what are their dreams?

And don't just take peanut-butter-and-jelly sandwiches, take something special. Like cold roast chicken (see above recipe) and really good bread (how about some Incredibly Quick Cheese Biscuits on page 224) and butter and cookies (try cooking up a batch of young Allison's Vanilla Crisps on page 264) and sweet tea.

After you eat, get out a sketchbook and colored pencils and draw your children. Then, let them draw you. This will make everyone roll with laughter, and they will say,

"Let's go on a picnic again really soon."

—JAN KARON
AUTHOR OF *THE MITFORD YEARS*

Introduction

The real art in food is flavor and not labor.

—GEORGES SPUNT,
*MEMOIRS & MENUS: THE CONFESSIONS
OF A CULINARY SNOB,* 1967

I LOVE TO COOK, but when I'm reading a recipe and I see the words "double boiler," my eyes glaze over. Mention a sieve, and I turn the page. Begin a recipe, "In a square of cheesecloth place a bouquet of herbs..." and I put the book down.

I love to cook, but I don't love the aggravation that comes with cooking. Never have. It's just not worth it, especially now that there are so many fabulous convenience foods to make the cook's job so much easier.

Still, who wants to lose the flavor and goodness of homemade cooking? Not I. Nor anybody else I know. Take my friendly UPS delivery man, for example. The other day, while he was putting an unusually large box inside for me, he said, "Don't know what you're cooking, but it sure smells good. Like when I was a little boy."

You see, I'm an old-fashioned cook, but with newfangled ways. With life so busy, I see no reason not to take advantage of the timesaving foods that are available to us. That's what our ancestors did.

Back in the nineteenth century, when women began clamoring for cookbooks, the cookbook writers took eighteenth-century recipes and modernized them to utilize new, nineteenth-century ingredients, equipment, and ways.

Same thing happened in the early twentieth century. Favorite family recipes that had once called for "a large legg of mutton," suddenly read, "take a 5-lb. leg of lamb."

Cookbooks no longer instructed the cook to "gather a peck of tomatoes," or my favorite, found scribbled in a late nineteenth-century cookbook, "buy 5 ct. worth of lemon extract." Instead, recipes now read, "Simmer 10 peeled and seeded tomatoes," or "use 1 teaspoon of lemon extract." And you better believe that once canned tomatoes were readily available from the local grocer, the recipes were changed to read, "Take a large can (16 oz.) of tomatoes...."

Trouble is, these days everyone is so anxious to cook everything *from scratch* that we've turned out a generation of frustrated cooks. It can take so long to prepare even the most basic meal that halfway through the process the weary cook asks, "Who wants pizza tonight?" or pulls out the remains of last night's Chinese takeout.

Somewhere along the way, we seem to have forgotten that it's okay to use storebought products to cook up delicious meals. That's what our mothers and grandmothers were doing in the 1950s and '60s when they made those mouthwatering dishes we still remember today.

Those mid-twentieth-century cooks had seen *their* mothers and grandmothers slaving in the kitchen, and they didn't want to follow suit. Anyway, by then, most of our mothers and grandmothers had jobs, just as we have today. Our mothers and grandmothers wanted maximum time with their families, and minimum time in the kitchen. It's time we learned what they knew.

Truth is, be it a family meal, a birthday party, a holiday gathering, or a special dinner party, family and friends and laughter are much more important than a homemade cake or a "from scratch" home-cooked meal, especially when you can turn so many ready-made storebought foods into delicious dishes with just a little doctoring.

That's what this book is all about—how to turn storebought food into delicious, easy to prepare, fun, and quick-to-make homemade dishes and meals.

Best of all, by using these recipes you'll end up having more time to spend as you wish, and fewer kitchen worries—a combination we can all use today. To top it all off, like the ice cream on pie à la mode, lots of these dishes bring back wonderful memories of bygone days. They tickle our nostalgic tastebuds.

"Cookbooks are not just for cooking...Cookbooks are for inspiration, for lifting the spirit and freeing the mind, for brightening your outlook as well as your parties and table conversation...for the understanding of people and places, for the revelation of the past and for the interpretation of the present...for culture, education, for inviting the soul, reviving memories, reliving experiences."

—"HOW, WHERE AND WHY TO READ A COOKBOOK"
HOUSE BEAUTIFUL, FEBRUARY 1957

"The culinary science is a progressive one, and many important discoveries are made every day, and new processes devised that add a new spice to life's enjoyments. This book is up with the times, and the experienced housewife will find in it many new ideas which will greatly add to her already charming methods of cooking."

—MRS. GRACE TOWNSEND, *THE STAR COOK BOOK,*
REVISED EDITION, 1895

Unfortunately, though, preparing the food isn't the hostess's only aggravation. There are menus to be worked out—a task that can be more complicated than putting together a thousand-piece jigsaw puzzle. Then there's trying to figure out what to serve the food in—a task that is sometimes reason enough to call the whole thing off. And when you add thinking up and then arranging a centerpiece to the mix—well, no wonder you don't entertain more often.

That's why, in addition to these great, easy-to-prepare dishes, I've included menu suggestions, *The Finishing Touch* hints, *Sage Advice,* and even a guide to tell you *before you start,* the type of pots and pans you'll need to cook each dish. (How many times have you had the cake batter ready to go when suddenly you read, "pour the mixture into a bundt pan," and you haven't a clue where your bundt pan is, or if you even have one?)

So toss your kitchen aggravation to one side. Grind it up in the garbage disposal. Throw it out with the moldy cheese you never got around to grating. It's time to put frustrations away and to take the easy way out.

Your family will thank you.

Your friends will rave about your delicious fare.

And you'll look and feel better while enjoying your own meal or party—all with the absolute minimum of aggravation.

"Flower decorations on the table are to be in flat designs, so as not to obscure the view of the guests."

—*THE WHITE HOUSE COOK BOOK* BY HUGO ZIEMANN AND MRS. F. L. GILLETTE, 1926

This cook's words of comfort or You don't need a designer kitchen

I thoroughly enjoy watching the food programs on TV. Those shows are my soap operas—entertaining and fanciful. When I turn on the Food Network, I become a peeping Tom in someone else's kitchen. But my kitchen and cuisine bear no resemblance to what I'm watching.

I can assure you that my kitchen looks much more like your kitchen than it does any kitchen you'll see on TV, unless it's on a rerun of the 1960's *The Donna Reed Show*. For starters, our house was built in 1941, and the last (and probably only) time the kitchen was remodeled was in the early 1970s by a former owner. When I'm feeling defensive, I smugly say I have a "retro" kitchen. In truth, the poor thing's in desperate need of a face-lift *and* a makeover.

Like most kitchens of that era, my kitchen has practically no counter space. Or at least not enough for the type of cook that I am—the spread and clutter type.

It doesn't bother me one bit that I have to balance the cookie sheet (with the cookies still on it) on the edge of the old porcelain sink that is filled to overflowing with the measuring cups and mixing bowls I used to make the casserole that came out of the oven two hours ago.

You see, I come by my habits honestly. My mother was a messy cook too. But my fastidious father put everything into perspective for me.

"Your mother's mother kept the neatest kitchen I'd ever seen," he once told me, while surveying my own disaster of a kitchen. "She'd dirty a bowl and wash it before she went on to doing anything else. Your mother, on the other hand, started tearing the kitchen apart the moment she crossed the threshold to fix breakfast. But at the end of the day your grandmother's meals were as bland as her kitchen was clean. Your mother—well, she never cooked a bad meal in her life."

I assure you, I've cooked more than my share of bad meals, but Daddy's left-handed compliment is very comforting when I'm trying to keep a well-intended guest from taking the dirty dishes into my less-than-picture-perfect kitchen.

But, back to the kitchen itself.

I cook on a normal, kitchen-size, grill-less, electric stove. (I admit that it does have a convection oven, but I haven't figured out how to use it yet.) My only "gadgets" are the essential ones—microwave, toaster (for toasting toast, not bagels), food processor, Crock-Pot, and handheld mixer. Though I keep vowing to replace my parents' 1938 countertop Sunbeam Automatic Mixmaster (it has had an electrical short since 1989 that no one seems to know how to repair), I really don't need it. I've learned how to turn storebought goodies into homemade delicacies with a minimum of equipment.

So take comfort. You, too, can turn out great-tasting dishes in your own kitchen, no matter how old or new it, and your equipment, is. Today's fabulous food folks have made it possible. How big a mess you make in the process is up to you.

Restaurant Quality…
Restaurant Recipes…

In today's "let's eat out" mind-set, even grocery store products and cookbooks are cashing in on our love for restaurant fare. Have you noticed how many frozen foods are labeled "restaurant quality"? Even magazines and cookbooks are beginning to feature "restaurant" recipes.

I'll admit that I often say, "Bob, let's eat out tonight," even when I have the makings of a perfectly fine meal in my own kitchen. But that's more for a change of scenery than for a change of food.

Think about it. Do you know what you are getting when you're eating out?

Of course, if you live in L.A. and have reservations for Wolfgang Puck's famous restaurant, Spago, you can expect the sky to be the limit. Or, if you live in a large metropolitan area where neighborhood restaurants have innovative chefs who take great pride in their creations, you're probably in for a dining treat.

On the other hand, if you're going to one of the many chain restaurants that are the staples of American family life, chances are you will be eating preprepared food you could have served up at home—and made even tastier by adding your own "homemade" touch.

I found this out one night when I ordered a bowl of Tomato Florentine soup at one of the chain restaurants. In my mind's eye I saw a chef in the kitchen stirring up a steaming, aromatic pot of hearty stock, succulent onions, fresh tomatoes, secret herbs, and baby spinach leaves.

My dream came to an abrupt end when our young waiter said, "You're really going to like that. We just got in a new brand of soup and this one's a lot better than the Tomato Florentine soup we were serving last week." He was right. It was good. And it was right out of the can.

Want more evidence? Jackie Legg, the author of many cookbooks, once told me that one of the greatest marketing coups she'd ever seen pulled off was in one of America's famous restaurants where the customers lined up for bowls of hot corn. Hot *canned* corn, drained, to which butter had been added.

So, the next time you're thinking "restaurant," remember, you already have restaurant food in your own pantry, fridge, and freezer. And with the help of these recipes, you can come up with *improved* restaurant dishes—without the hassle of waiting in line, sending the wrong order back, and having to leave a tip.

"People sometimes praise a restaurant by saying it makes them feel at home.... I don't want to feel at home in a restaurant. I want to feel that I'm having a night out."

—ALVIN KERR, *GOURMET*, OCTOBER, 1960

From STOREBOUGHT to HOMEMADE

How and When to Use This Book

The Well-Stocked Kitchen

MOTHER always said, "If you're going to be a good cook, first you have to have a good cookbook."

Really good cookbooks begin where every meal or party begins—in the kitchen, by which I mean the pantry, the fridge, even the cupboard shelves where you keep your china and glassware. That's why these next few pages are filled with suggestions for items you should keep on hand to help speed along the preparation of fast, fabulous food at home.

L et's begin with the pots and pans.

The day I tried to cook my first live lobster I learned that any meal can turn into a disaster if you don't have the right equipment.

There I was, a twenty-two-year-old bride, with a beady-eyed crustacean crawling around our Pullman-size apartment kitchen while I went running from door to door begging for a big pot. (I'd stupidly unleashed his claws before I began looking for the pot.) These days I'd know that just a large stock or pasta pot would do, but back then, we were eating spaghetti out of a can.

To avoid such culinary mishaps, here's a list of the basic cooking and baking equipment you'll need to prepare the recipes in this book:

BASIC COOKWARE

baking or casserole dishes—square and rectangular (Pyrex)

set of graduated glass mixing bowls that are also microwave/oven safe

cake, pie, and loaf pans

cookie sheet (the air-insulated variety goes a long way toward preventing burnt foods)

Crock-Pot

knives: a good set of kitchen knives, including a sharp paring knife and a serrated knife for slicing breads

one good set of measuring cups and spoons

molds: ring, individual

platter: at least one big enough to hold the holiday turkey or cut meats for a buffet

deep stock or pasta pot (8-quart)

pizza stone

saucepans: small (1-quart), medium (2-quart), and large (4 ½-quart), with lids

sauté pans: small and large

skillet, with lid

stovetop or oven roaster

The Well-Stocked Shelf

As important as the pots and pans are the staples you have in the pantry, refrigerator, freezer, and on your spice shelves.

Every well-stocked pantry should have an extra can or two of those foods that can dress up ordinary fare. These ready-made products are invaluable in two ways. Either they are used in the recipes as essential ingredients, or they help you make a great presentation.

In the essential ingredients category are the old standbys—cream of mushroom soup, chicken and beef broth, tomato paste, canned tomatoes.... Seasoned cooks find that their grocery carts go on automatic pilot when approaching the shelves where these staples are located.

But I also find some of the fancier, if not truly "gourmet" prepared foods are absolutely indispensable. When my children are coming home, I wouldn't dream of leaving the grocery store without picking up a couple of cans of artichoke hearts and at least one spare can of cilantro and lime juice–flavored chopped tomatoes—both ingredients in their favorite dishes.

Equally important to fast, fabulous food at home are wonderful pickles, jellies, and relishes. These not only add a sparkling flavor to ordinary foods, they also dress up a plate or platter, because you don't expect them to be there. And they add a bright splash of color to dishes that might otherwise look dull even though they are very tasty. Remember, we eat with our eyes as well as our taste buds.

You probably won't keep all these fancier ingredients on hand all the time. Yet, having a well-stocked larder really does make it possible to turn the mundane into something special on a moment's notice.

Now, if you never have more than four to six people (including yourself) at the table, one can or jar should suffice. But for larger groups, you should have a couple of cans or jars on hand.

(Though the following items are found on the grocery shelves, many need to be refrigerated after they are opened. Check the labels for instructions.)

IN YOUR PANTRY

bread crumbs—one canister

ketchup, mustard, and mayonnaise

crackers

> basic crackers such as Saltines or Triscuits
> more delicate crackers such as Carr's Table Water crackers

Melba toast (offered in many flavors)

cheese straws (the traditional Cheddar is now offered in an extra-spicy version, or try the blue cheese variety, if you're partial to that flavor)

salad dressings

a bottle each of Italian, Caesar, and Russian salad dressing

a few vinaigrettes (try these varieties: sun-dried tomato and red wine, balsamic, orange, garlic and herb)

fish (canned)

black caviar

minced clams

lump crab

shrimp

lump tuna

salmon

flour (self-rising) and/or Bisquick

fruits

a variety of canned fruits such as pears, peaches, mandarin oranges, and a mixed tropical fruit blend (Note: many fruits are now coming already flavored in the can, such as raspberry-flavored pears and cinnamon-flavored peaches)

Jell-O

What can I say? Jell-O, Jell-O, Jell-O in all sorts of flavors, for salads and desserts; and a box of instant vanilla and chocolate pudding mix too

meats

jar of dried beef

tin of deviled ham

nuts

sliced or slivered almonds

cashews

macadamia nuts

pecans

peanuts

pine nuts

sauces (see more on the varieties offered under convenience foods,
but keep the following on hand)

a good barbeque sauce, sweet or vinegary, to your taste

Alfredo (which can be used when a basic white sauce is called for)

Cheddar cheese sauce

roasted garlic Parmesan cheese sauce

basic spaghetti sauce (tomato-based)

soups/stews

chicken broth and beef consommé

bouillon cubes (or Wyler's Shakers) in vegetable, chicken, beef,
   and ham flavors

cream of celery soup

cream of chicken soup

cream of mushroom soup

cream of shrimp soup

onion soup, both dried and canned

tomato soup

vegetable soup or stew

herbs and spices

dried basil

dried bay leaves

cinnamon

curry powder

Italian seasoning

If You're Just Beginning to Stock Your Spice Cabinet

THERE is seemingly no end to the number of herb and spice blends that are available today. But how often do you really use these specialty blends—Mediterranean, Eastern European, Cajun, Seafood Seasoning, Poultry Seasoning, Soul Seasoning, Garlic and Herb, All-Purpose Herb and Garlic, etc.? And do you have enough space to store several jars?

If you answered, "not often" and "not really" to those questions, here's my suggestion for a basic blend. Buy individual jars of dried thyme, basil, and bay leaf (crumbled). You'll use these herbs individually.

Then, buy an empty container and combine equal amounts of these three herbs to have on hand when you want a quick mixture.

About Pepper

I BELIEVE in cooking short-cuts and take them every chance I get. Still, there's a "closet" wanna-be chef lurking somewhere in me, and, I bet, in you. In truth, I haven't the time or the inclination, to make my own pie crust or learn how to handle phyllo dough, but there has to be a compromise.

The answer? The peppermill. I get great satisfaction from giving the fancy pepper mill a few bold turns, just the way all the great chefs do on TV!

Add to that the flavor freshly ground pepper gives to even the most mundane food and I wonder how we used to get through a meal shaking a few pitiful pepper grains from a paltry shaker.

So, when the recipes herein say, "Pepper to taste," and does not designate how much pepper to measure out, use this opportunity to become the chef you want to be and crank away to your heart's content. But, for your information, 1/4 teaspoon of pepper equals approximately 12 to 15 robust grinds of the peppermill (the results will vary according to each pepper mill and your individual enthusiasm while turning).

My *Sage Advice* is to add pepper to stews and meats and vegetables early in the cooking process so the flavors will have time to blend. But, if your taste buds dictate, don't hesitate to add an extra twist of freshly ground pepper just before serving, or eating, as well.

squeeze bottle of lemon juice

at least one of the lemon-pepper blends mentioned under convenience foods

nutmeg

oregano

peppercorns

teriyaki and soy sauces

Tabasco or other hot sauce

thyme

vanilla and almond extract (real—not imitation—please)

Worcestershire sauce

spirits

bourbon

brandy

Madeira

sherry, dry

wine—a bottle of red and white for cooking (of as good a quality as if you were drinking it)

"What are the two drinks that can be served at any time of day and with any food?"

SHERRY AND CHAMPAGNE

sugar

> brown
>
> confectioners'
>
> granulated

sweets

> a box of yellow cake mix
>
> chocolate, shortbread, and graham-cracker pie crusts
>
> a box or two of fancy cookies (Pirouettes are good)
>
> ice-cream toppings/sauces, such as chocolate or butterscotch
>
> > maple and/or a flavored syrup for pancakes

V-8 juice (canned), regular and spicy

vegetables

> French's Taste Toppers in the French Fried Onions flavor
>
> artichoke hearts, both marinated (jar) and in water (canned)
>
> prepared garlic
>
> can or jar of mushrooms
>
> can or jar of olives, ripe and Spanish (whole and sliced)

About Garlic

WHO says our taste buds can't change?

Garlic, once scorned, is now adored. It was so shied away from when I was growing up that *The Joy of Cooking*, the Bible for my generation of cooks, instructed us to "Learn to rest slivers of garlic clove on meat before cooking it."

These days we can't get enough of it—on our food or on our natural-remedy medicine shelves! We shamelessly order baked garlic in fancy restaurants (remember when you wouldn't go out in public if you'd had one slice of mild garlic bread?) and we are drawn by its delicious aroma into Asian restaurants, where we order garlic shrimp and broccoli.

Even the busiest cook can easily take the moment to tear away a couple of cloves from a plump garlic bulb, peel off the outer skin, and chop or press that now highly esteemed and oh-so-good-for-you herb into whatever dish she is preparing.

But there are times when prepared garlic will come in perfectly handy—especially if you don't cook very often, or if you've used up all your fresh garlic and haven't the time to dash to the store.

That's why you should always keep a jar of ready-to-use garlic in your pantry or, if opened, in the fridge. The basic exchange rule is: 1 garlic clove equals ¼ teaspoon garlic powder, 1 teaspoon garlic salt, or ½ teaspoon prepared garlic.

pesto, prepared (jar) and mix (envelope)

pimiento (small jar)

sun-dried tomatoes

canned whole and stewed tomatoes, plain and flavored or spicy
   varieties

sliced water chestnuts

to add color and spice...

apple rings (red, in jar)

pickled beets

capers

chutney

pickled okra

olives (the "party" varieties, stuffed with almonds or cocktail onions)

spiced, pickled peaches (jar)

baby whole pickles in various flavors (sweet and/or dill)

relish

watermelon rind pickles

FROM THE FRIDGE

refrigerator biscuits and crescent rolls

cheeses

appetizer and/or party cheese such as Gouda, goat's milk, brie,
   or a bag of Old Wisconsin Party Bites

bag of shredded Cheddar or blended cheeses

feta or blue cheese to sprinkle on salads

meat

long-life products such as Hormel already-cooked beef and pork,
   Louis Rich Chicken Time Trimmers

FROM THE FREEZER

frozen meats you plan to use frequently, especially chicken, both
fresh and the ready-to-serve varieties like grilled breasts and breaded
and flavored strips

bag of frozen, cleaned, and cooked shrimp

diced or chopped onions

peppers: green, yellow, orange, and red strips, plus the diced
   green variety

pizza crust, or a single-topping pizza

spinach soufflé

baked apples (for a side or dessert)

bruschetta (for instant hor d'oeuvres or appetizers)

vanilla ice cream

a couple of bags of the mixed vegetables listed under
convenience foods

(Note: peep ahead to pages 14–18 under the Convenience Foods:
A Boon or a Boondoggle heading for other
ideas and suggestions.)

GARNISHES

Knowing that we eat with our eyes as well as our mouths, remember to include garnishes for both beauty and flavor. This final touch can turn "a bite to eat" into a "dining experience."

Herbs: The packaged herbs available today are a real boon to the cook who doesn't have an herb garden. But most don't keep very long, so buy them as near to using as possible. Dried herbs are usually called for in food preparation. If you are going to use fresh herbs, remember that they are not as strong or concentrated as dried. A general rule of thumb is to use 3 times as much fresh as dried.

The following are some ideas for garnishes that add flavor for the palate, as well as a touch of color for the eye:

slivered almonds

fresh basil leaves

fresh cilantro

eggs

lemons, limes, and oranges for decorative slices

fresh mint

sliced or diced onion or pepper, especially the colorful varieties

fresh parsley

fresh rosemary sprigs

To get ideas for unusual garnishes, study the photographs in the gourmet and lifestyle magazines. Often, you will see a single nasturtium blossom or marigold petals sprinkled on a dinner plate, or a soufflé topped with a spray of violets or violas. These are all edible flowers, so when thinking garnishes, remember to pluck a few fresh, edible flowers from your own garden and rinse them, or buy them as needed (read more about using garnishes in The Finishing Touch boxes).

Measurements

Did you know that the first cookbook to give exact measurements for recipes was the *Fannie Farmer Cookbook* published in 1895? Even back then, I'd wager that once the novice cook had tried a recipe a couple of times, she (most cooks were women in those days) would add a little here, take away a little there, and even toss some ingredients out while adding others—to please her family's tastes.

That's the wonderful thing about recipes. They aren't written in stone, only on paper. So take my *Sage Advice* based on years and years of cooking and entertaining. Use the measurements provided when first preparing a recipe. But once you've tried it, be ready to add your own very special touch.

A Tough Shell to Crack

NOPE. I'm not talking about walnuts or pecans, but hard-boiled eggs. I have never been very successful at removing that outer shell and coming up with a beautiful, unblemished white egg.

Rather, I manage to pull parts of the white away with the shell until the poor thing looks as if it has had a bad case of chicken pox and is permanently scarred.

However, thanks to that new kitchen gadget, the Egg Wave, I, and apparently millions of others, now break the egg directly into the microwave-safe container and turn out a boiled egg suitable for using as a garnish.

Even experienced cookbook writers have a difficult time with the many different products on the shelves these days. No longer can you instruct the reader to "open a can of tomato soup." Not only are there many different brands and varieties of tomato soup, but to complicate matters further, cans come in various sizes. Why, just the other day, when I was checking the ounces in a bag of tortilla chips, I had to decide whether to buy a 9-ounce, 12-ounce, 14-ounce, or 20-ounce bag.

Keeping this in mind, I have decided to round off most sizes in the recipes. Can sizes are meant to be guides—approximations. This means that when you read: "1 (14-ounce can)," it's okay to use a 13-ounce can, a 14.5-ounce can, or even a 16-ounce can. What you do not want to use is a 20-ounce can, or a 6-ounce can.

Along these same lines, generally I find it more convenient to purchase re-sealable *bags*, rather than boxes of frozen vegetables. Oftentimes I want to add a handful of lima beans to a soup or casserole. No reason to open a full box for that small quantity when I can reach into a bag, grab a few, reseal the bag, and save the rest for next time.

For that reason, many of these recipes will call for ½ cup frozen spinach, or ¾ cup yellow squash or zucchini, rather than ½ a 10-ounce box of frozen spinach, or 6 ounces of yellow squash or zucchini.

Equivalents and Conversions

No matter how carefully you plan, there isn't a cook—or even a chef—alive who hasn't scratched his head and wondered, "Now how many tablespoons are in a quarter of a cup," or "How many pounds of potatoes will it take to make two cups?"

Because *From Storebought to Homemade* is intended to provide a starting point for you to learn how to put together a meal at home easily and quickly, so that once you've seen how easy it is, you can venture out on your own, here are some charts you can refer to throughout your cooking adventures when you need to convert a measurement or determine an equivalent.

EQUIVALENTS

dash	less than ⅛ teaspoon
3 teaspoons	1 tablespoon
4 tablespoons	¼ cup
5 tablespoons plus 1 teaspoon	⅓ cup
8 tablespoons	½ cup
10 tablespoons plus 2 teaspoons	⅔ cup
12 tablespoons	¾ cup
16 tablespoons	1 cup
2 tablespoons	1 fluid ounce
1 cup	½ pint or 8 fluid ounces
2 cups	pint or 16 fluid ounces
4 cups	2 pints or 1 quart or 32 fluid ounces
4 quarts	1 gallon or 128 fluid ounces

THOSE PESKY POUND EQUIVALENTS

1 pound	equals approximately
brown sugar	3 cups
cheese	4 cups, shredded
confectioners' sugar	2 ½ cups
flour	4 cups
macaroni	4 cups
meat	2 cups, chopped
potatoes	2 cups, diced, or 2 large whole
rice, uncooked	8 cups, cooked
sugar	2 cups

HANDY SUBSTITUTIONS

1 slice bread	¼ cup dry bread crumbs
	½ cup soft bread crumbs
14 graham cracker squares	1 cup fine graham cracker crumbs
1 tablespoon fresh herbs	1 teaspoon dried herbs
1 cup honey	1 ¼ cups sugar
1 garlic clove	¼ teaspoon garlic powder
	1 teaspoon garlic salt
	⅛ teaspoon prepared garlic
1 medium lemon	2–3 tablespoons juice
	2 teaspoons grated rind
1 tablespoon prepared mustard	1 teaspoon dried mustard
1 medium orange	⅓ cup juice
	2 tablespoons grated rind
1 pound peanuts	2–3 cups nutmeats
22 vanilla wafers	1 cup fine vanilla wafer crumbs
⅓ onion	1 teaspoon onion powder
1 cup sour cream	3 tablespoons butter plus ⅞ cup buttermilk or yogurt
¼ cup soy sauce	3 tablespoons Worcestershire plus 1 tablespoon water
1 quart whole strawberries	4 cups sliced strawberries
1 ⅓ cups chopped fresh tomatoes	1 cup canned tomatoes

Convenience Foods:
A Boon or a Boondoggle?

Another problem we face these days is the *names* products are given.

For example, almost every store brand and major frozen food company puts out a "mixed vegetable" product. But what a mixture! There's a broccoli, cauliflower, and red pepper mixture. There's a corn, onion, okra, celery, and tomato mixture. There's a 3-pepper mixture. The list goes on and on and on.

In fact, I long ago concluded that one reason more people aren't using today's fabulous convenience foods is because they simply have *too many choices.* Faced with too many choices, you turn away.

That's one way *From Storebought to Homemade* can be a real help to you. By guiding you to some of the best ready-made or convenience foods for these home-tested recipes, I hope to encourage you to try a few and become more adventuresome yourself.

But this book is in no way intended to be an endorsement of just one brand or series of products. For example, you may read in one recipe, "Bird's Eye Gourmet Potato Blend" (white potatoes, broccoli florets, petite carrots, baby cob corn, red pepper). Or you may read a more generic description in another recipe, "frozen, diced combo of onion and green pepper." The point is, if you can't find the exact product, don't give up. Simply make your own mix from individual packages of frozen, or even fresh, veggies you already have on hand.

Coping with GSVO (Grocery Store Visual Overload)

This brings up the question of how to deal with the overload, even panic, you experience when you're faced with so many choices.

I know that a trip to the grocery store these days can be absolutely daunting. New products are appearing not just monthly, it seems, but weekly. The food folks are learning that fast, fabulous food at home is the way to go.

How many times have you noticed, as I have, a package of beautifully trimmed, nice pink fresh pork chops lying in the grocery store cooler where the smoked pork chops are displayed, dropped by someone who didn't want to walk over and put the fresh ones back where they belonged.

Once the shopper spied the smoked ones, she no longer wanted the fresh chops. Not only do smoked chops have a stronger, more distinctive flavor, they have a longer shelf life, and can be turned into a meal more quickly than the fresh ones.

And what happens when you get to the chicken section? The choices are seemingly limitless. Just one quick run down the frozen chicken aisle will turn up Southwestern Glazed Chicken Breasts, Breaded Strips—crispy or regular—Barbecued Wings, Grilled Breast Fillets, Country Fried Chicken Nuggets, Chicken Tenderloins, even Diced Chicken Breast, which could be the harried cook's shortcut to distinctive, almost homemade chicken salad! And those are just a few of the selections!

These days, many of those fabulous specialties we love to order when we're eating out are now as close as our home freezer. What a boon! We can combine these familiar "name brand" convenience foods with home-cooked dishes when we're craving the taste of fast food, or when we want a quick meal but don't have time to stand in line waiting for a table at a restaurant.

These foods have become a real staple in my kitchen. Today's selections of already prepared foods have made it possible to bring back dishes I stopped preparing long ago because they were just too much trouble and too time-consuming.

For example, I used to spend hours slaving over a particular favorite of mine, stuffed pasta. When the kids were young we had it on weekends because that was when I could steal enough time to boil the pasta, prepare the stuffing, and tackle the tedious task of trying to fill the shells without splitting or tearing them. Once the kids left home, I no longer bothered.

These days I buy cheese-stuffed manicotti or meat-stuffed shells, smother them with my favorite already prepared sauce—to which I've added a few extra ingredients—and I've saved hours while enjoying the process.

Although some of you know that these twenty-first-century time-savers exist, many of you may shy away from such newfangled foods simply because there are just too many of them to decide which ones to buy.

Or, maybe you haven't tried them because you're spending hours at a time trying to prepare gourmet dishes from scratch. Or, you may be stuck in the old rut of roast beef on Monday, pork chops on Tuesday, leftover roast on Wednesday, chicken pot pies on Thursday, and fish sticks on Friday. Whatever the reason, don't feel bad. I've been in your shoes, but then I saw the light. That's why I've written this book—to help you.

For starters, here's a quick guide to a *few* (just the tip of the iceberg) of the untold numbers of shortcut products to look for and use in your cooking. These products are ones that can be found in small towns and large metropolitan areas alike, and in no way does the list begin to cover all the brand names or varieties available.

generic brands offered in the following combinations:

Italian veggies	zucchini, broccoli, carrots, green beans, limas
California	broccoli, carrots, cauliflower
winter	broccoli, cauliflower
stir-fry	sugar snap peas, broccoli, green beans, carrots, celery, onion, peppers, water chestnuts
Oriental style	green beans, broccoli, onion, mushrooms
fiesta blend	broccoli, carrots, Italian green beans, white beans, kidney beans, garbanzo beans, red pepper
stew veggies	potato, carrots, onions, celery
veggie soup mix	carrots, potato, green peas, green beans, corn, limas, okra, celery, onion
gumbo soup mix	okra, corn, onions, celery, red pepper

Bird's Eye

gourmet potato blend	white potatoes, broccoli florets, petite carrots, baby cob corn, red pepper
corn blend	white corn, broccoli, baby cob corn, Parisian carrots
mixed	corn, carrots, green beans, green peas
broccoli stir-fry	broccoli, carrots, onions, red pepper, celery, water chestnuts, mushrooms

broccoli, carrots, cauliflower

broccoli, corn, red pepper

broccoli, carrots, water chestnuts

cauliflower, carrots, pea pods

three-pepper combination

Green Giant "Create A Meal" (Green Giant also offers a "Complete Skillet Meal" with meat added)

Parmesan herb chicken

Szechwan

teriyaki

sweet and sour

garlic herb chicken

cheesy pasta and herbs

lo mein

lemon pepper

Stouffer's "Skillet Sensations" (Stouffer's also offers "Oven Sensations" with meat added, but I always seem to add more meat to these)

teriyaki chicken

grilled chicken and vegetables

beef fajita

frozen meats

meatballs

Armour and Tyson offer 18-ounce bags of chicken pieces in the following varieties:

southwestern glazed chicken breasts

breaded strips

barbecued wings

grilled breast fillets

country fried chicken nuggets

chicken tenderloins

diced chicken breast

ready-to-serve sauces

Ragú® "Cheese Creations!"™

Roasted Garlic Parmesan

Parmesan and Mozzarella

Double Cheddar

Classic Alfredo

Light Parmesan Alfredo

Ragú® "Robusto!"™

Classic Italian Meat

Chopped Tomato, Olive Oil, and Garlic

Six Cheese

Parmesan and Romano

Sautéed Onion and Garlic

Sweet Italian Sausage and Cheese

Sautéed Onion and Mushroom

seasonings

Lawry's Seasoning Salt

flavor packs such as Knorr's Peppercorn Gravy or fajita and meat loaf varieties

dried lemon seasonings made by Knorr, Sun Bird, and McCormick

flavored cheeses

Philadelphia Cream Cheese blends, offered in regular, whipped, fat-free, light, and soft—and in flavors such as strawberry, honey nut (with pecans), chive, onion, and cheesecake

preblended juices

Welch's

grape (both white and red varieties)

strawberry breeze (5-juice blend)

wild raspberry (3-juice blend)

tropical carrot (carrot plus 5 juices)

Dole

pineapple-orange

orange-strawberry-banana

pineapple-orange-banana

Minute Maid

fruit punch (grape, pear)

tropical punch (pineapple, grape, passion fruit)

Tropicana

orange-tangerine

orange-strawberry

orange-pineapple

white grape-peach

Excuse Me!

I'LL ALWAYS remember the conversation I had with a very well-known cookbook author and food critic. She didn't like my use of convenience foods one bit and told me so in no uncertain terms.

But, later in the day, when in the company of several other fine cooks, chefs, and writers, she said this: "I always chop my onions first, and then freeze them so I'll have them on hand."

I was dying to ask her what she did when chopping her onions that made them so much better than the already frozen chopped onions I use! But, having been raised always to be respectful of my elders, I demurred.

When you are considering frozen and convenience foods, think about it this way: We've been using frozen vegetables for years. But it's a new cooking day out there. So for those meals when time's at a premium, the choices listed earlier are there to help you out.

And here, to get you in the right mind-set, are just a few shortcuts to keep in mind as you begin to prepare fast, fabulous food at home.

TIME-CONSUMING	TIME-SAVING
peeling and chopping onions	frozen, chopped onions
peeling and chopping green peppers	frozen, chopped peppers
washing and slicing mushrooms	frozen, or canned, sliced mushrooms; or sliced mushrooms from the produce section or salad bar
washing and preparing lettuce	ready-to-eat, bagged lettuce
washing and shredding cabbage	shredded, bagged cabbage for slaw
washing and cleaning celery for chopping	already washed, bagged celery, or salad-bar celery
mincing and pressing garlic	prepared garlic in jars
washing, peeling, and preparing fruit	salad-bar fruits or jarred fresh fruits
washing, peeling, and preparing carrots, cauliflower, and broccoli	bagged or salad-bar veggies
preparing and baking a whole chicken	ready-to-eat rotisserie chicken
preparing and cooking chicken strips and pieces	frozen, or ready-to-eat chicken strips and cubes
cooking bacon	ready-to-serve bacon
preparing, slicing, or cubing ham	fully cooked ham slices and cubes
cubing or grating cheese	ready-to-use or -serve grated or cubed cheeses
cooking, shelling, deveining shrimp	ready-to-use shrimp
preparing custards	ready-to-eat individual servings
cooking and stuffing pastas	prestuffed manicotti and shells
mixing, shaping, and browning meatballs	cooked and frozen meatballs
removing, then dicing leftover turkey	ready-to-prepare turkey breast steaks or small turkey roasts
peeling, dicing, slicing, shredding, even mashing potatoes	ready-to-prepare potatoes, frozen or from the deli or refrigerator section

Ingredients

When Fresh Is Best—and When It Isn't

"Use only the freshest ingredients." How often do you hear these words of advice from today's leading chefs? I would agree, except for a few basic problems. Fresh vegetables do not grow everywhere yearround.

In my part of the world—Virginia—local tomatoes do not come in until the very end of June or the first of July. This means that in December most of the tomatoes in the grocery store have been shipped in from Mexico—a trip that takes days of hard, bruising travel. Tomatoes that have been picked at their prime (when they're the most flavorful) have only a two or three-day shelf-life. By the time tomatoes picked in their prime are shipped halfway across the country, they're already mushy and overripe.

Of course, climate and weather conditions make every growing season slightly different as you move from South to North and from East to West. I remember how amazed a Yankee friend of mine was when she ate freshly picked, plump, succulent strawberries in Florida in February. She thought you had to wait until June for such a rich culinary treat. So you don't miss the best of what nature has to offer, here's a quick guide to the best fruits and vegetables of each season.

winter

the citrus fruits: grapefruit, oranges, tangerines

greens: the kale, collards, mustard, and turnip greens that
Southerners love and the rest of the world passes by

spring

fruit: strawberries and blueberries

vegetables: early peas, asparagus, fresh lettuces

root vegetables: beets, carrots, potatoes, turnips

summer

beans: every variety of beans, from pole and green beans to lima
beans…even October beans come in the summer!

fruit: blackberries, melons, peaches, apricots

vegetables: eggplant, peppers, zucchini, and tomatoes, of course—
you might try growing them yourself, even if just one or two
patio-variety plants

autumn

fruit: apples, grapes, pears, apricots

vegetables: pumpkins, winter squash

Presentation: The Magic Ingredient

If you think the two main ingredients that go into a successful meal, be it a special Wednesday night family meal or a Saturday night company dinner, are color and flavor, you're right. *But*, a stressed-out cook can ruin even the prettiest, most flavorful event.

It takes more than a trip to the grocery store to turn storebought food into a homemade meal. The shopping list helps take care of the first "p" in cooking—"preparation,"—but there's the second "p" in cooking, and I've already hinted at it—"presentation."

Think about it. Your eyes linger over beautifully set tables. You watch in amazement as the chefs on the Food Network flick confetti-like slivers of pimiento and green peppers around an entrée, or top a dessert with a thin layer of lacy chocolate.

"I could never do that," you're already protesting.

Oh yes you can...*if* the rest of the meal is made in just minutes with already prepared food products, or even purchased at a local restaurant, café, or deli.

You see, a great meal can be remarkably simple. Often it takes only two steps:

1. Add a surprise ingredient to an already, or very easily, prepared food.
2. Add your own finishing touch to its presentation.

Throughout this book, you'll find side notes labeled *The Finishing Touch*. These contain short, quick suggestions for giving a special flair to your food's presentation. I've said it before, I'll say it again: Always remember, we also eat with our eyes.

A Word on Tomatoes

ONE of the saddest food days at our house comes some time in October when the first frost nips at the still-green tomatoes hanging on for dear life on the spindly tomato vine.

Of course, it's time for the plants to be yanked up and for the soil to rest. But what is a sandwich without a tomato?

These days, new and improved storebought cherry, grape, and Roma varieties add flavor and color to sandwiches and salads the rest of the year...until the homegrown summertime tomatoes come in.

When to Use This Book

"You don't eat like this every day do you?" I was asked when explaining the concept of *From Storebought to Homemade*.

Of course I don't. I like to eat out just as much as the next person. Further, there are those days when I roll up my sleeves to make some exotic concoction from scratch. And I don't expect you to cook this way every day either.

A Word about *The Finishing Touch*

WHEN IT COMES to creating your own finishing touches, let your imagination run away with you—especially when you're standing in front of a beautiful display of colorful fruits and vegetables in the grocery store or farmer's market.

Literally any fruit or vegetable that can be hollowed out can be used to enhance the presentation of your meal, and, in many instances, be eaten as well. A perfect example of this are the recipes, Peas in a Boat (page 168) and Peas in Tomatoes (page 169), and Shrimp-Filled Avocado Salad (page138).

To help get you started thinking creatively, here are some suggestions, many already familiar to you, but others that I hope you'll find a little more imaginative and different.

Fill the cavity of a pear or peach with cottage cheese or a flavored cream cheese and top it with a cherry, fresh berries, or mint sprig.

Pineapple halves, or even canned pineapple rings, are perfect "containers" for any variety of fruits or cheese.

Lemons, limes, and oranges make great "cups," either cut crosswise or lengthwise. What could be more colorful and spirit-lifting than seeing a scooped-out lemon shell filled with mint jelly or a scooped-out lime shell filled to the brim with salsa? Try putting apple sauce in an orange or tangerine shell to delight the children in your family.

Bake acorn squash in the microwave (5 to 6 minutes) or oven (350 degrees for 25 to 30 minutes) by cutting it in half, scooping out the seeds, and placing it in a baking dish with enough water to cover the bottom third of the vegetable. When done, fill it with ready-to-serve mashed potatoes, stovetop dressing, or flavored rice.

Here's another idea. Scoop out a thick-skinned small, uncooked pumpkin and use it as an individual soup bowl. Or use a much larger one as a tureen.

Tomatoes, either the cherry or grape varieties, or the traditional, beefsteak variety, can be topped with any number of fillings, from a single small shrimp placed fancifully in a large cherry tomato, to crabmeat salad in a large, round one.

Boats made from yellow or green squash can be filled with anything from rice to cooked sausage. A head of cabbage filled with slaw...a small cantaloupe filled with ice cream...the possibilities are almost limitless.

The one drawback is that these presentations do take a little time. But I think of it

But when you want to bring the family or friends together at home, over a kitchen or dining-room table, but you haven't the time (or the energy) to make a true, homecooked meal from scratch, these recipes and suggestions can turn a laborious chore into a pleasant task.

this way. These are unexpected touches, gifts, so to speak, that tell volumes about you as a hostess. They say that you're witty, caring, and imaginative.

Presentation isn't just the decorative touches added to plates and serving dishes. The plates, platters, and bowls themselves can also enhance the total dining experience. Never fear. You don't have to dash out and buy a new set of china or serving dishes, but you can add, one by one, the pieces that will complement what you already have.

So let's peek inside the china and crystal cabinet for some versatile pieces you can use at an individual place setting or on a buffet table to add charm and distinction to any meal or party.

You may not have all these pieces right now, but I assure you that, as you accumulate them over time, they will pay for themselves in convenience and appearance.

Individual ramekin dishes can be used for everything from rich desserts to spoon bread to minisoufflés to fruit garnish to nuts. *Individual seafood shells* are an alternative to ramekins, but they aren't quite as versatile. Both are inexpensive and make a nice showing.

A pretty crystal bowl can be used for the basic tossed salad, the incomparable holiday trifle, or any range of dishes in between, from potato salad to jelled salads.

Platters are indispensable for serving meats surrounded by garnish or accompanying fruits and vegetables. But small servings get lost on an oversized platter, so try to have various sizes to fit various needs.

Attractive casserole dishes that can go from the oven or microwave to the table are a staple in these days of casual entertaining. Though the highly decorated ones are ex-

tremely attractive, if you change your china pattern or even the wallpaper in your dining room, you may find that your favorite casserole dishes suddenly clash with the surroundings. I recommend basic white dishes that will go with everything. That way you can spiff up your presentation with an imaginative centerpiece of flowers or fruit, or with the food itself.

Young cooks who are just beginning to collect their "party essentials," and even more experienced folk, can come up lacking the perfect serving utensil at the last minute. So, before settling on the menu for a party or company dinner, think what you will need to serve each dish—fork, spoon, slotted spoon, etc. If you love antiques, you'll have fun searching for the proper cold meat fork or pastry server as you rummage through yard sales, flea markets, antique shops, even your grandmother's silver chest!

I say this more than once...if you will just take the time to do a little menu planning, the way you do when you're planning your shopping list, and figure out *where* you want to put your emphasis—on the entrée, the dessert, an interesting salad—you can turn out a meal with a minimum of effort that will bring in the maximum of compliments. By making just one special, or signature, dish you can tilt the tables. If you make a simple ice cream pie (page 257), that fantastic finale can turn your storebought rotisserie chicken garnished

For the Love of Food

BEFORE serving any meal, for company, or to your family, ask yourself three simple questions:

Does it look good?

Does it smell good?

Does it taste good?

Does it look good? If it doesn't, no one will want to eat it. Think about it. Why does mush look so uninviting? Because it looks like mush!

To make the food you are serving look good, arrange it prettily on the plate or platter. Don't just plop the food on the plate at random. Arrange it to show off the colors and textures of the food to their best advantage.

If the food is colorless—and even delicious items like chicken, pork, rice, and potatoes can be colorless and boring to look at—brighten it up with an eye-catching garnish.

How? Well, even if you aren't serving carrots, if you have a handheld grater and a fresh carrot (remember, you can buy just one carrot or a handful of presliced carrots from the salad bar), you can create a colorful garnish that will bring the whole plate or platter to life.

Or how about keeping a jar of sliced olives with pimientos in the fridge? Use them as garnish, or take thirty seconds and dice a couple of them into smaller pieces to create red and green "confetti." Use it alone or in combination with the carrots.

And what brings the chicken to life in the Cranberry-Sauce Chicken recipe? The red cranberry sauce, of course.

You'll find other items that can be used as garnish listed on page 9. Let your eyes, taste buds, and imagination

be your guide.

Does it smell good? What makes you begin to salivate when your neighbor is grilling outside? The aroma, of course. What makes pumpkin pie, pumpkin pie? It isn't just the pumpkin. It's the aroma of the fabulous spices mixed with the pumpkin custard.

You can't bottle the delicious smells that come from the kitchen. The lesson here is that heating up or baking just one dish for your meal can fill your whole home with that "homemade" feeling (even if you've just doctored up a storebought product with one added ingredient).

But a word of warning! Don't overwhelm those rich kitchen smells by lighting scented candles. Nothing is worse than the rich beef-and-tomato aroma of a stew with pickled peach slices, deli potato wedges, and salad-bar salad into a special meal indeed.

And for those of you who are watching sodium and sugar and cholesterol, using storebought items at home actually can give you *greater* control over your choices and diet than eating at a restaurant or fast-food chain.

When to use this book? When you're looking for a quick and easy way to gather everyone together, enjoy your kitchen, and share your best.

combined with a light, sweet, gardenia-scented candle. Conversely, a heavily scented Christmas bay candle will completely smother the smell of delicate lemon zest.

The rule is simple. Use unscented candles on your dining table to create ambiance, not fragrance. Unscented votives are best because they don't cut off the across-the-table view of the diners, and they send out a low, romantic glow that relaxes everyone.

Does it taste good? Taste, after all, is what food is all about. But our tastes and taste buds vary. That's surely how the old saying "too many cooks spoil the broth" came into being. Mix together too many individual likes and dislikes, and you end up with a hodgepodge instead of a well-flavored delicacy.

Just as individual taste buds are different, so are the tastes of different brand-name foods. Simply put, not all canned tomatoes taste alike. And not everyone likes the same brand.

Throughout these pages I've suggested some specific products because they provide a quick and easy way to get around those time-consuming steps that might keep you from trying a recipe in the first place. Though I've tried to use products that are easily found, not all brands are available in every store.

If you can't find a product, speak to your grocery store manager. He or she should be able to help you locate it if it is available in that store, or even in the region, or to help you find an acceptable substitute.

I live in a small town, an hour's drive from the closest "big city." If you're in my situation, you've probably learned to keep a shopping list of specialty items to pick up when you're somewhere that has more choices than you can find at home. I anticipate those grocery store trips with as much enthusiasm as I do shopping trips for a special dress, a pair of shoes, or even toys for the grandkids.

Whether or not you have the perfect ingredient, or a good substitute, to make every dish taste its best, you still must do some tasting yourself. As you taste, make adjustments if necessary. If you think a dish needs more pepper, start grinding. If thyme is your favorite herb, toss in an extra ¼ teaspoon. If a dish calling for cream of mushroom soup seems a little dry to you, add ¼ or ⅓ cup of milk.

And all the time you're tasting, remember these words of wisdom: "Cooking is like love. It should be entered into with abandon, or not at all."

Menus
That Work

*In America, even your menus have the gift of language…
"The Chef's own Vienna Roast. A hearty, rich meatloaf,
gently seasoned to perfection and served in a creamy nest of
mashed farm potatoes and strictly fresh garden vegetables."
Of course, what you get is cole slaw and a slab of meat, but
that doesn't matter because the menu has already started your
juices going. Oh, those menus. In America, they are poetry.*

—LAURIE LEE, BRITISH AUTHOR, *NEWSWEEK*, OCTOBER 24, 1960

THINK ABOUT IT. Take any shelf of cookbooks. Pick a book. Turn to the index. Look under "M." What do you find? "Meat…Meatballs…Meatloaf…Melon…Meringue…Minestrone…Mocha…Mousse…Muffins…Mushrooms…Mustard…." There's everything from Mamaliga (a Romanian cornmeal dish similar to Mexico's polenta) to Mixed Grill. All the "M" food words, but seldom *Menu*.

But what do you have to have before you can begin cooking a meal, be it supper for two or a buffet for twenty? A plan. A menu.

Without a menu that provides complementary tastes, colors, and food groups, even the fanciest meal will fall short. No matter how delicious each individual dish may be, a menu consisting of two cream of mushroom soup vegetable casseroles, a chicken dish, white rice, and a vanilla ice cream dessert will be...*boring*...from taste to color.

Of course, today's great "salad in a bag" selections make it much easier to add color and nutrition to any meal. But who wants to eat a mixed green salad twice a day, every day?

All in all, putting together easy, time efficient, and delicious complementary dishes can be difficult. Yet, I really can't overemphasize how important it is to match up foods properly. It's so important that food stylists are paid huge salaries to put together eye-appealing displays for magazines, books, and television shows.

As a quick rule of thumb, a mixture of colors will provide variety in taste and nutrition while pleasing the eye. You see this rule put into practice on your favorite television cooking show when a white fish and rice entree is brought to life by arranging strips of yellow and red peppers on top and green baby Brussels sprouts all around, or when a few blueberries are sprinkled around a vanilla pudding or ice cream dish.

Once you have chosen the food fare, there's yet another consideration—the pots and pans you'll need to prepare each course, and where each item needs to be cooked. A menu that calls for three casseroles to be cooked at different oven temperatures is useless to the young New York bride who owns only two baking dishes and cooks on an apartment-size ministove. That's why I've included a list of cookware needed at the end of the ingredients list for each recipe. In this menu section, if there's more than one item that requires an oven, I've made sure they can be cooked together.

Here, now, are menu suggestions to lighten up your kitchen duties while turning storebought items into homemade meals. As you read through these menus, note that there are two symbols to help you with your planning. A white box (□) denotes ready-to-serve selections that involve no more than opening a can or cello bag or microwaving a frozen item. A green box (■) denotes a *From Storebought to Homemade* recipe that can be easily and quickly prepared.

Here's another tip to keep in mind. The addition of a simple relish, a favorite pickle, or even a raw vegetable dish such as chow-chow, pickled peaches, watermelon rind pickles, or marinated carrots, can be a real pick-me-up at any table. They add unexpected flavor, they're filled with vitamins, and they add the splash of color that cooks are always looking for. What more could you ask?

Sage Advice

When planning a menu, write it out. Next, visualize it in your mind, making sure you have a pleasing blend of colors, tastes, and textures. Finally, think about what equipment you'll need to cook each item in and how you will serve it. These steps only take a few seconds and can keep you from last minute panic attacks.

Family Dinner Menus

The
Finishing Touch

You'll save so much time using the menus, recipes, and ideas in this book, that you'll have time to add a distinctive finishing touch to special dinners and parties. Why not write out the menu on a heavy stock card that fits the occasion's mood, or that matches your décor. To save even more time, do it on your computer, using a whimsical font. You might even take a hint from Laurie Lee's quote at the beginning of the chapter and give your dishes a fancy name and elaborate description.

I'm a great proponent of the old-fashioned family meal. These days, when the kids have soccer practice and music lessons and the parents find themselves getting home later and later from work or civic meetings or volunteer activities, we're losing more than just the family dinner, or supper (depending on what your family calls it), time. Families are losing the art of conversation, lessons in manners, and the chance to get to know one another—yes, even your own family—better. They are missing out on the wonderful joie de vivre that comes from sitting around the family dinner table and having fun.

I've never seen any studies done on the subject, but I'd wager that children whose families converse during the evening meal do better in school. When I was a little girl, the evening meal was when we talked about what I had learned in school that day. It's a tradition that was continued when my children were young too. We discussed their history, literature, science, and current events topics, and suddenly school lessons became fun and were reinforced as part of a relaxed dinnertime conversation.

But, back to the food. It's always easy to settle for pasta. Everyone likes it and it's so quick and effortless to prepare that you can have it every night. But it doesn't have to be that way, as these family dinner menus testify. The suggestions I make don't involve hours of preparation, and the menus combine ready-to-serve selections with quickly pulled together courses eveyone will enjoy.

And then there's yet another bonus. I promise that the delicious aroma of just one *From Storebought to Homemade* dish will whet everyone's appetite and make the entire meal special.

Family Menus

☐ Denotes ready-to-serve selections that involve no more than opening a can or cello bag or microwaving a frozen item.

■ Denotes a *From Storebought to Homemade* recipe that can be easily and quickly prepared.

■ Orange-Pineapple Mold (page 147)

☐ Simple buttered broccoli

☐ Rotisserie roasted chicken

■ Bouillon Rice (page 179)

☐ Parker House dinner rolls

■ Brown Sugar Pie (page 255)

☐ Tossed salad (your favorite packaged, ready-to-serve salad and salad dressing.)

■ Chicken Marsala (page 90)

☐ Mashed potatoes

☐ Peas

■ Fruit Pizza (page 247)

■ Quick Chicken Pie (page 204)

■ Cheerful Green Beans (page 165)

☐ Sliced tomatoes

■ Marmalade Muffins (page 222)

☐ Chocolate chip or butter pecan ice cream

■ Quickly Assembled Chicken Meal-in-One (page 203)

☐ Garlic bread

■ Cake Mix Cookies (pages 276–277) and fruit

Sage Advice

Smart cooks perfect 3 or 4 dishes in every category—appetizers, soups, salads, entrees, accompaniments, desserts—and mix and match these when they need to serve up a spectacular meal at a moment's notice.

■ Everybody's Mother's Pork Chop Casserole (page 114)

☐ Rice

☐ Le Seur peas

☐ Applesauce (one of the flavored varieties)

☐ Carrot cake

☐ Tossed salad

■ Mexican Chicken Casserole (page 199)

■ Mango Soufflé (page 146)

■ Old-Fashioned Pot Roast (page 103)

■ Bouillon Rice (page 179)

■ Green Bean Casserole (page 164)

☐ Apple turnovers

■ Sweet and Sour Pork, American-Style (page 112)

☐ Rice

☐ Vegetable sauté

☐ Caramel frosted cake

■ Tangy Tomato Aspic (page 148)

■ The Picky Eater's Beef Stew (page 209)

☐ Noodles

☐ French bread

☐ Raspberry sherbet and cookies

- Lime Yogurt Salad (page 145)
- Quick-Quick Brunswick Stew (pages 210–211)
- ☐ Biscuits
- Serendipity Pumpkin Cake (pages 268–269)

- Pickled Cole Slaw (page 131)
- ☐ Your favorite storebought fried chicken
- Jalapeño Corn Bread (page 230)
- A Side of Beans (page 281)
- You'll-Never-Guess-It's-Made-with-Cookies Ice Box Dessert (page 275)

When it comes to having a family dinner, and there are children in the house, don't forget the leftovers from an adult dinner party—casual or formal. This is a great way to begin to introduce children to fancier dishes without going to the trouble to specially prepare them.

- ☐ Tossed salad
- Pork and Cherry Supreme (page 113)
- Vidalia Onion Casserole (pages 166–167)
- Peas in Tomatoes (page 169)
- ☐ Chocolate cake (as a reward for trying the fancy dishes)

- Pepper and Mushroom Chicken Delight (page 96)
- ☐ Mashed potatoes
- ☐ Peas and carrots
- Bread Pudding (pages 270–271)

- Corned Beef (page 102)
- No-Fail Potatoes (page 184)
- ☐ Applesauce (perhaps one of the flavored ones)
- ☐ Green beans
- Allison's Vanilla Crisps (page 264)

- ☐ Tossed salad
- Old-Fashioned Pot Roast (page 103)
- Dressed-Up Noodles (page 189)
- Green Bean Casserole (page 164)
- Chinese Chews (page 265)

Company Dinner Parties, Served Formally or Informally

"I hadn't realized that throwing a party was quite so much hard work. Perhaps that's why Mummy and Gran never throw parties in London."

—LUCY, IN *WINTER SOLSTICE* BY ROSAMUNDE PILCHER

Hard work aside, I decided a long time ago that one of the reasons people may be hesitant to entertain at home these days is that we've all been spoiled by cafeterias and buffet lines. They provide such abundance and variety that the poor hostess feels she just can't prepare enough food for her guests. (If, perchance, you are a Southerner, as I am, and are used to the three-meat, five-vegetable spread associated with Southern hospitality, the problem is compounded.)

In truth, however, your guests don't *care* how many items you're serving! They're coming to your home for the friendship and fellowship (and the chance to get out of their own kitchens). So rather than burden yourself with four appetizers, two entrées, and three vegetables, keep it simple. In these calorie-conscious days, many of your guests will secretly thank you!

Try any of the following easy-to-prepare, timesaving menus for a memorable dinner party. You can serve the meal yourself, but that might make you a disgruntled host or hostess—heaven forbid! So relax. Have a buffet. Or prepare a simple meal you can serve up on a plate and keep warm in the oven, or on a warming tray, while you fix the other plates. Or even serve the food in pretty bowls and on nice platters...family style.

With a little planning, and the use of prepared foods as a starting point, you'll find that throwing a party really doesn't have to be such hard work after all.

Just one more word of *sage advice* that my mother gave me. She'd say, "You know all your friends who lead such exciting lives? They're always busy going here and there and doing such interesting things in faraway places? Well, dear, invite them to dinner—and I bet they can all come!"

A SAMPLE MENU AND HOW TO THINK IT THROUGH.

Pretend it's a nice late-spring or early-summer Saturday and you decide you'd like to have some friends over for an early night, light Sunday supper. You don't have much time to plan, but you can still prepare an impressive and delicious, but almost effortless get-together. This is how.

Menu:
- Anything Goes Fruit Soup (page 83)
- Shrimp-Filled Avocado (page 135)
- ☐ Petite peas on a small leaf lettuce
- ☐ Sliced Roma tomatoes garnished with fresh basil leaves
- ☐ Dainty buttered biscuits from the frozen section served with butter and crab-apple jelly
- English Trifle (page 266)

The shrimp filling takes all of 5 minutes to stir together and should be prepared the night before. It's best if you mix the pudding and sherry together so the tastes have time to blend. But do not assemble the trifle yet.

The morning of the supper, whip the cream, cut the pound cake, and assemble the trifle. Place it in the refrigerator. The peas can be cooked in the microwave in 3 to 4 minutes while you're dishing the shrimp into the avocados or putting the lettuce to hold the peas on the plates.

The delicious combination of hot buttery biscuits served with storebought crab-apple jelly on individual bread and butter plates is always a hit, so plan to have plenty of biscuits on hand.

Company Menus

☐ Assorted nuts (from a can)

■ Cream Cheese and Olive Spread with crackers and celery stalks (page 43)

■ Lamb Chops in Sherry Marinade (page 124)

☐ Instant long grain and wild rice

■ Celery Casserole (page 159)

☐ Tomato with Mozarella and Basil Salad

☐ Peach sherbet and cookies

☐ Cocktail olives stuffed with almonds or jalapeño, kalamata olives, and caper berries

■ Pimiento Surprise with crackers and celery sticks (page 51)

■ Lettuce, Orange, and Almond Salad (page 129)

■ Timeless Chicken (page 97)

☐ Herb-flavored rice

☐ Green beans and almonds

■ Incredibly Quick Cheese Biscuits (page 224)

☐ Vanilla ice cream with Grand Marnier drizzled on top

■ Zesty Tomato Starter with Incredibly Quick Cheese Biscuits (pages 76)

■ Cranberry Sauce Chicken (page 92)

■ No-Fail Potatoes (page 184)

☐ Broccoli

■ Sinful Butter Brickle Ice Cream Pie (page 257)

- Avocado and Tomato Salad (page 137)
- Chicken à la Simon and Garfunkle, served over rice (page 89)
- ☐ Petite whole green beans
- Glazed Carrots with Onions (page 158)
- ☐ Apple pie à la mode

- Antipasto American Style (page 61)
- Garlic Roasted Pork Tenderloin (page 118)
- Pecan Rice (page 180)
- Peas in Tomatoes (page 169)
- Baked Tipsy Apples with ice cream (page 242)

- Chilled Strawberry Soup Number 1 (page 81)
- Champagne Chicken (page 88)
- ☐ Rice
- ☐ Broccoli topped with buttered bread crumbs
- Old-Fashioned Lemon Chess Pie (page 250)

- ☐ Spinach salad
- Easy Beef Stroganoff (page 105)
- Dressed-Up Noodles (page 189)
- Tomato Puddin' (page 173)
- Sour Cream Biscuits (page 227)
- ☐ Fresh melon and fruit cup with Cointreau drizzled on top

- Virginia Cream of Peanut Soup (page 80)
- Beef Tenderloin (pages 106–107)
- Pureed Artichokes (page 151)
- Carrot Surprise (page 156)
- ☐ Whole string beans, buttered and garnished with pimiento
- Frozen Oranges and assorted chocolates (page 243)

From Storebought to Fabulous Retro-Modern Party

CAROL CARLISH was in a pickle of a mess. It was December 26th—enough to put anyone in a tizzy. A combination of Christmas traffic, long family good-byes, and nasty weather had delayed Carol and her husband, Robert, from getting back to their home in Danville until 3 P.M. Company was coming for supper at 7 P.M. What to do?

In her usual ingenious way, Carol headed for the grocery store while Robert helped on the home front.

While Carol was buying Knorr's Vegetable Soup Mix and Russian dressing, Cheese Whiz, and Moon Pies, Robert was gathering together recycled Christmas bows, half-burned candles, and a long-out-of-style Christmas tablecloth and napkins stored up in the attic.

By the time the company arrived, everything was cooked, and the decorations were in place.

Now, this was not your usual fancy party, but it was a night to remember, and it just goes to show what a little imagination can do. As Carol laughingly admits, her friends not only are still talking about the night, they are also copying her idea—now that they've gotten over their initial shock.

Here it is for you, too, to copy exactly what she did.

But first you have to know that behind her idea is a seldom-admitted, but very true food fact: *Foods have fads, and if you haven't eaten something in a while, you'll be amazed how good it is.* Or, in Carol's own words, "It's not that the foods taste bad, it's that they've gone out of fashion. Try them again, and they actually taste pretty good."

It's a fact I adhere to and often put to work myself. It's also why my kids are always asking me for their grand-

- Artichoke and Oyster Soup with cheese crackers (page 69)
- Pork and Cherry Supreme (page 113)
- ☐ Roasted potato wedges
- Green Bean Casserole (page 164)
- Flan, with whipped cream and raspberries (page 240)

mothers' recipes. And it's why I've updated so many "old-timey" recipes in these pages.

Now, this is what Carol's friends saw when they walked into her house.

In the living room the hors d'oeuvres were set out on the table for everyone to help themselves: Cheese Whiz in the jar, Saltines in the box, Vienna sausages and deviled ham in the tins, and a big bowl of veggie dip made by combining sour cream and Knorr's Vegetable Soup Mix surrounded by crudités—carrots, celery, broccoli, cauliflower...straight from the cello bags.

When they moved into the dining space, there on the once-stunning, but now-tacky Christmas tablecloth was quite a spread.

There was Spam—scored, glazed, and decorated with cloves; meatloaf; iceberg lettuce cut in quarters and "dressed" with bottled Russian dressing; green beans straight out of the can (which, Carol remembers, "Somebody actually said were good"); a broccoli casserole she had whipped up in no time with mushroom soup; a pretty, ready-to-serve jelled red fruit salad; mashed potatoes made straight from the box; as well as a casserole of Kraft's boxed macaroni and cheese (Carol's favorite "closet food"); and a loaf of white bread, still in its wrapper.

And for dessert...that Southern favorite—Moon Pies served with RC Cola and peanuts. (For those of you who don't know, you put the peanuts in the RC bottle and the salt makes the soda fizz up.)

Needless to say, everyone is now wondering what Carol will do next. She's confided that she's thinking about offering everyone a choice of different microwaveable meals.

The moral of this story is that imagination can make any meal a joyful, memorable time—for who can live without friends and food!

■ Gazpacho Plus (page 84)

■ Easy Chicken Tetrazzini (page 91)

■ Peas in a Boat (page 168)

■ Cornmeal Biscuits (page 228)

□ Butter pecan ice cream over angel food cake

□ Biscotti

■ Spanish Pork Chops (page 115)

□ Wild Rice

□ Broccoli

□ Bread and preserves

■ English Trifle (page 266)

■ Love Apple Fromage Soup (page 77)

■ Baked Rainbow or Brook Trout (page 98)

■ Portobello Deluxe (page 170)

□ Asparagus

□ Dinner rolls

■ The Basic Poached Pear (pages 244–245)

■ Avocado and Tomato Salad (page 137)

■ Garlic Roasted Pork Tenderloin (page 118)

□ Peas and almonds

■ Very Good Winter Squash (page 172)

□ Cheese straws

□ Raspberry ice cream and hazelnut pirouettes

"Civilized man cannot live without cooks."

—BULWER-LYTTON, 19TH-CENTURY ENGLISH POET AND NOVELIST

Appetizers and Hors d'oeuvres

WHICH IS IT? An appetizer or an hors d'oeuvre? Check any dozen cookbooks and you'll find that half of them call cocktail meatballs an "appetizer," while the other half call them an "hors d'oeuvre." Does it really matter? The recipes are the same.

Further, the particular recipe (whether it's for cocktail meatballs or hot crab dip) is intended to whet your appetite, to make you want more.

So the difference between an appetizer and an hors d'oeuvre really comes down to this: *When* are you going to serve it?

An appetizer is traditionally served before a full meal. It's supposed to provide a nibble or two—something to stave off your hunger, but not so much that it fills you up while you are anticipating the main event.

On the other hand, an hors d'oeuvre is traditionally served at a cocktail party or before sitting down at the dinner table.

In reality, any of the selections given here can be served either as an appetizer before a real meal, or as part of a larger "cocktail spread."

Here's an interesting sidenote, though. The term "hors d'oeuvre" literally translates to "out of (the) work," meaning that these goodies are outside of the "work" required to prepare the rest of the meal. But wait. That means that hors d'oeuvres add more work to the cook's duties.

With that in mind, I've tried to assemble recipes for appetizers or hors d'oeuvres that are practically no work at all.

"At the moment of dining, the assembled group stands for a little while as a safe unit, under a safe roof, against the perils and enmities of the world. The group will break up and scatter, later. For this short time, let them eat, drink and be merry."

—MARJORIE KINNAN RAWLINGS, *CROSS CREEK COOKERY*, 1942

Hors d'oeuvres Aren't Just for Cocktail Parties

Setting the tone for a meal can be just as important as the food you serve. That's why there's no better way to begin a special family or company meal than with a fabulous (but easy) first course, leisurely presented. All the appetizer (and most hors d'oeuvre) recipes included in this chapter can be easily adapted to serving as a first course at a dinner party.

These days, a casual first course, served in the living room, den, or even the kitchen, is a great way to keep everyone occupied until all the guests or family members have arrived.

Further, the first course can be the cook's best friend. A tray of nibbles can be an instant icebreaker when all your guests don't know one another well. (Everyone loves to talk about food these days!)

Sage Advice

The thing about cocktail party food is that it's made up of all those foods you never fix for yourself at home, so everything tastes delicious. Here's another comforting thought. The cocktail hour conveniently arrives just as your guests' stomachs begin to grumble. And when you're hungry, everything tastes delicious. Remember that and your next cocktail party will be much easier. The way I see it, the preparations for a cocktail party—getting glasses and napkins together, putting flowers or seasonal decorations all around, seeing about ice—can be sufficiently time-consuming, so my rule for cocktail food is, keep it as simple as possible.

Or, a soup course served at the table can give the cook time to assemble the entrée plates, or even to make last-minute dessert preparations. (Suggestions for a variety of delicious and unusual soups suitable for serving as a light first course follow in the *Soups* chapter.)

To my way of thinking, a first course is very important.

A fabulous first course is the host or hostess's way of extending warm hospitality. It's something extra. Something special. Something unnecessary. Something that you took the time to do.

Whichever direction you choose—a finger-food appetizer or a soup served at the table—remember that the first course sets the tone of the meal to come.

An appetizer should be like a pretty bow on a nicely wrapped package that is yet to be opened.

Only you will know that the preparation took almost no time at all!

Sage Advice
A note on servings. There's really no way to figure out how many servings a dip or spread will yield. Dieters in the crowd will put a tiny morsel on the corner of a cracker, while those who are craving cream cheese and olives will dig deep into the bowl and heap the cracker high. So when preparing appetizers, ask yourself, how much would I eat and then remember, it is better to have too much than too little.

A Word about Time

TO HELP YOU conserve your valuable time, approximate preparation and total time guides are given for each recipe, except in the case where a "variation" creates no appreciable time difference.

Needless to say, the exact time it will take you to make any of the recipes will vary according to how many times your phone (or doorbell) rings (or you remember a call you forgot to make); how many times your kids, pets, friends, or other family members interrupt you; how long it takes you to put your hands on the ingredient you're looking for; and whatever other of life's little distractions come along.

But when you're reading through a recipe and checking the time it requires, remember this: The PREPARATION TIME given in *From Storebought to Homemade* is based on using convenience foods. If you decide to peel potatoes, dice onions, and grate a pound of cheese, my estimated times will be far off. Further, the preparation times are the minutes required to prepare the food *prior* to its cooking (or serving, if no cooking is required.) Cooking or chilling (in the case of several jelled salads and desserts) time is added to the preparation time to arrive at the approximate TOTAL TIME.

I've included these time gauges because I'm the type who likes to know what to expect. The fewer surprises, the better! I hope they will be helpful to you.

In short, I like my kitchen time to be pleasurable, and I'd like for yours to be too.

Cream Cheese: Better Than Sliced Bread

As any seasoned host or hostess will tell you, the 8-ounce package of cream cheese is a cocktail party lifesaver.

It doesn't matter whether you decide to use traditional cream cheese, one of the lighter varieties, or, my personal favorite, Neufchâtel (it has few calories but rich flavor). Tubs of whipped or soft cream cheese make these tasty treats easier than ever to stir up. Whichever variety you choose, this staple makes it possible to turn out any number of flavorful appetizers quickly and easily.

The secret to preparing any of the following recipes in no time is simple. Keep some cream cheese in the fridge and several toppings and items to combine with it in the pantry.

So, the next time you need a quick appetizer, just flip through these recipes, match the ingredients in the recipes with those you have on hand, and you're set to go. But don't stop there. While gathering those ingredients, use your imagination.

Roquefort Cheese Spread

BLEND the cheeses together. For a creamier consistency, you can add a tablespoon of heavy cream or a teaspoon or so of milk. Or, for variety, add 2 tablespoons of good cognac or brandy in place of the cream or milk.

YIELDS APPROXIMATELY 1¾ CUPS

1 (8-ounce) package soft cream cheese

4 ounces Roquefort cheese

1 tablespoon heavy cream or a teaspoon milk (optional)

2 tablespoons cognac or brandy (optional)

Cookware needed: mixing bowl

PREPARATION TIME: *3 to 5 minutes*
TOTAL TIME: *3 to 5 minutes*

Cream Cheese and Olive Spread

READY-TO-ADD and highly flavorful diced olive spreads make this delicious treat a cinch. But if you're using a jar of olives rather than a prepared olive spread, add just enough of the liquid from the olives to give the spread the consistency you desire. Also remember it will take longer to prepare, since you have to dice the olives.

YIELDS APPROXIMATELY 1 CUP

1 (8-ounce) package soft cream cheese

½ cup diced olive product such as Vine Country Food's garlic and herb olive spread, or a tapenade (or, use a 4-ounce jar of sliced olives with pimiento)

Cookware needed: mixing bowl

Blend the cheese and olives together.

PREPARATION TIME: *5 minutes*
TOTAL TIME: *5 minutes*

"The great thing about entertaining is being with the people you have invited. It is a bit discomfiting for your guests if you are slaving over the stove, and emerge, hot and rather martyred, just in time to sit down at the table with your guests!"

—CLAIRE MACDONALD,
THE HARRODS BOOK OF ENTERTAINING, 1986

Sage Advice

The Cream Cheese and Olive, and Pimiento Surprise (pages 48 and 51) spreads aren't for cocktail parties only. They also make delicious lunchtime or picnic sandwiches.

Date Cheese Ball

WHEN I BEGAN writing this book, I had no idea what a sentimental journey it would be. But I've learned that just the mention of a particular food can bring on a flood of memories of a meal, a trip, and very often of friends, family, and loved ones. This, of course, speaks volumes about what is really important in life.

Imagine going on like this just because the moment I began to type out "1 (8-ounce) box chopped dates" I remembered how much my father liked dates, especially around Christmas time.

Years ago, Christmas was the only time you could find dates in the stores. Today, they are available year-round, which makes this easy appetizer a perennial favorite at my house—and it always brings back precious memories.

YIELDS 1 LARGE, OR 2 SMALL BALLS

2 (8-ounce) packages soft cream cheese

1 (8-ounce) box chopped dates

1 cup chopped pecans

Cookware needed: mixing bowl

The Finishing Touch

Serve this with ginger snaps and Ritz crackers.

Combine the cream cheese and chopped dates.

Shape the mixture into one or two balls and roll each one in the chopped pecans.

Chill at least 24 hours before serving. The longer this spread has to "mellow," the better it tastes.

PREPARATION TIME: *15 minutes*
TOTAL TIME: *15 minutes, plus the chilling time*

Russian Delight

TO SERVE this for a cocktail party, you simply put the cream cheese on a plate, gently spread it with the caviar taken straight from the jar (being careful not to break the bubbly eggs), and sprinkle the onions on top. But to make individual appetizers, follow the directions below. For a variation on Russian Delight, try the next recipe.

The Finishing Touch

Add yet another color and texture by garnishing with a curly parsley leaf. Put a few small crackers on each plate, or pass them.

SERVES 8

- 1 or 2 tablespoons frozen, diced onions
- 1 (8-ounce package) soft cream cheese
- 1 (2-ounce) jar red caviar

Spread a handful of frozen, diced onions on a paper towel to defrost.

Put a dollop of the soft cream cheese on each of 8 plates.

Cover the cheese with a liberal helping of caviar and top each serving with a sprinkling of the now-defrosted diced onions.

PREPARATION TIME: *10 minutes*
TOTAL TIME: *10 minutes*

Caviar Pâté

YIELDS APPROXIMATELY 1¾ CUPS

- 1 (8-ounce) package soft cream cheese
- ½ cup sour cream
- 1 teaspoon onion flakes or finely diced, frozen onions
- ⅛ teaspoon prepared garlic, or one small clove minced
- 1 (2-ounce) jar red caviar
- **Cookware needed:** mixing bowl

Combine all the ingredients in a small bowl and chill well before serving with your favorite crackers or cocktail bread.

PREPARATION TIME: *10 minutes*
TOTAL TIME: *10 minutes plus chilling time*

Instant, No-Mixing-Required Cheese Spreads

WHAT COULD BE simpler than unwrapping a block of cream cheese, or turning it out of the tub, and topping it with a flavorful addition? I've already suggested you do that in the Russian Delight recipe given earlier, but not everyone is going to serve caviar. If you're one of those who won't, consider using one of these alternatives.

YIELDS VARY ACCORDING TO GUESTS

1 (8-ounce) package soft cream cheese

1 jar of your favorite chutney, preserves, or marmalade

or

1 medium-size bar creamy goat cheese (chèvre)

1 jar sun-dried tomato tapenade, with olive oil added for taste and consistency

or

1 medium wedge brie

1 jar fruit salsa (raspberry is good)

To serve any of these instant, no-mixing-required cheese spreads, just take the wrapping off the cheese, place it on a pretty plate or in a bowl, and spoon the topping gently over the top.

PREPARATION TIME: *4 to 5 minutes*
TOTAL TIME: *4 to 5 minutes*

"You should never think of a recipe as more than the basic foundation upon which you can build a dish which is exactly right for yourself and your family. Imagination, originality, experimentation, all these play a part in the kitchen."

—PAMELA FRY, *THE GOOD COOK'S ENCYCLOPEDIA*, 1962

Cheddar Cheese Comes to the Rescue

Though cream cheese may be the staple of the cocktail party buffet, Cheddar cheese runs a close second. There may be times when you have either a block of trusty "rat" cheese on hand, or even a resealable, already grated cheese mixture on hand, but no cream cheese.

For such emergencies, or to include in your menu if you're planning ahead, try these hors d'oeuvres.

Sage Advice

Too many cheese-based hors d'oeuvres or appetizers are boring and similar in taste. Unless you are preparing a true cocktail buffet to be spread through several rooms— your living room, dining room, and kitchen, for example—do not put out more than one cream cheese and one other cheese selection.

Crackers

SERVE WITH CRACKERS. But what kind of crackers? Here's a guide.

For spicy, salty, or meat or seafood spreads, try Carr's Table Water Crackers with Cracked Pepper, Rye (Wasa) crackers, and flavored Melba toast.

When serving highly flavored dips or strong cheeses (slices or cubes), serve a variety of the blander (but absolutely delicious) crackers—Saltines, Triscuits, Wheatsworth, or Pepperidge Farm Butterfly Crackers.

And don't overlook those sweet crackers. Not only can they add variety to your cocktail buffet, but they can actually take the place of a dessert. How? Try this.

Create your own instant, no-mixing-required cheese spread by topping a fruit-flavored spread (like the Philadelphia Cream Cheese varieties or Brummel and Brown Spreads) with a complementary fruit (for example, fresh strawberries or strawberry preserves atop a strawberry cream cheese), and serve it with wheat crackers (Carr's or Breton are examples) or thin ginger snaps.

Cheese and Olive Ball

YIELDS 1 LARGE BALL

¼ cup tapenade, or sliced ripe olives, or Spanish olive pieces, drained

1 (8-ounce) package sharp Cheddar cheese, grated

¼ stick soft butter

⅛ to ¼ teaspoon minced garlic

Few drops Tabasco sauce

Dash cayenne

Cookware needed: mixing bowl, food processor

The Finishing Touch

If you wish, once the mixture is thoroughly chilled, you can make small, individual cheese balls and put out party picks for serving.

If using olives (not tapenade), chop in a food processor so they will be finer in consistency.

Combine them with the other ingredients and chill the mixture in the refrigerator until it is firm enough to be formed into a ball.

Serve with a spreader and crackers.

PREPARATION TIME: *5 minutes*
TOTAL TIME: *10 minutes,*
unless you make the bite-sized balls

Say Cheese!

THE MANY, and ever increasing, varieties of already grated cheese found in the refrigerator section of grocery stores today should make you smile.

Pick up a bag of mozzarella, Parmesan, or a Colby-Jack blend to top a casserole. Buy some Cheddar—from mild to sharp according to your taste—to toss with a salad or to make a fondue. Select from a variety of seasoned cheeses when preparing Mexican or Italian dishes. In addition, there are low-fat options and both finely and coarsely grated cheeses.

When figuring out how much of an already grated cheese to buy, remember that 4 ounces of grated cheese equals 1 cup. Most recipes found in these pages call for either 8- or 16-ounce packages of cheese. Sometimes the packages give cup measurements. In that case, a 2-cup bag will yield 8 ounces of grated cheese, and a 4-cup bag 16 ounces. So just pick up a 2- or 4-cup resealable bag and you're done. Another storebought convenience to take home.

Cheese Dip in the Round

IF YOU LIKE my suggestions about using fruits and vegetables as "containers" in *A Word about The Finishing Touch* on page 22, you'll enjoy fixing and serving this imaginative and very tasty Cheddar cheese dip.

YIELDS APPROXIMATELY 3 CUPS

1 loaf round bread—white, dark, or rye, from the bakery

1 (16-ounce) package sharp Cheddar cheese, grated

4 ounces blue cheese (or Roquefort)

½ teaspoon dry mustard

1 teaspoon butter, softened or whipped

2 teaspoons frozen, diced onion

⅛ to ¾ teaspoon Worcestershire sauce

1 (8-ounce) bottle beer

Cookware needed: mixing bowl

Cut the top off the round loaf of bread the way you would cut the top off a pumpkin. Hollow out the interior, saving as much of the bread as possible to use for dipping (as in a fondue).

Blend the cheeses, mustard, butter, onion, and Worcestershire sauce in a mixing bowl, and allow the mixture to stand for at least 30 minutes. (If you plan ahead, you can use this time to prepare the bread loaf.)

When you are ready to fill the bread loaf with the mixture and put it out for your guests, slowly beat the beer into the mixture, until the dip is smooth and airy.

Fill the hollowed-out bread round, and serve with the reserved bread bits, along with additional cubes of rye, wheat, or grain breads for dipping.

The
Finishing Touch

Garnish this fanciful spread with chopped chives, paprika, or parsley.

PREPARATION TIME: *15 minutes*
TOTAL TIME: *approximately 45 minutes*

Cheddar Cheese with Strawberry Preserves

SURPRISE. That's what gives zing to a recipe. Like serving a dip in a round of bread. Or serving strawberry preserves with a cheese appetizer. That unexpected combination seems to have originated around Augusta, Georgia, the home of the famed Master's Tournament. That's where I had it the first time.

The tasty combination was probably thought up by some desperate hostess who found out she was having last-minute guests drop by after a day on the golf course. Don't wait for that to happen to you to prepare it. It's a great appetizer to serve while you're getting dinner on the table, or as part of a cocktail party spread.

YIELDS APPROXIMATELY 3 CUPS

1 (16-ounce) package sharp, grated Cheddar cheese

1 cup chopped pecans

½ cup mayonnaise

¼ cup frozen, minced onion

1 clove garlic, or 1 teaspoon prepared garlic

½ teaspoon Tabasco sauce

1 cup strawberry preserves (your favorite brand)

Cookware needed: mixing bowl

Combine all the ingredients except the strawberry preserves. Mix well and chill for 2 to 3 hours.

Shape the mixture into a ball, or put it in an attractive serving dish. Or, if you have time, press it into a lightly greased ring mold.

If served as a cheese ball or spread, surround it with the strawberry preserves or put the preserves on the side. If served as a mold, fill the center with the preserves.

Serve with crackers. Melba toast rounds or Triscuits are good choices.

PREPARATION TIME: *15 minutes*
TOTAL TIME: *2 to 3 hours*

Pimiento Surprise

BOBBYE INGRAM used her imagination one day when she was putting out a tray of pimiento cheese and crackers. "What would happen if I added a little horseradish to dress up my storebought pimiento cheese," she wondered. She tried it and had an instant success on her hands.

Keeping this story in mind, read on.

YIELDS APPROXIMATELY 1 CUP

8 ounces pimiento cheese, from the deli

4 tablespoons prepared horseradish

Cookware needed: a mixing bowl

Stir together, adjusting the amount of horseradish to your taste. Serve with your favorite crackers or bread.

PREPARATION TIME: *2 to 3 minutes*
TOTAL TIME: *2 to 3 minutes*

"'What about using that great recipe of yours for a parsley dip as a sandwich filing?' she asked.

...And what about that stuff you do with chopped ripe olives and garlic?'"

—VIRGINIA RICH,
THE NANTUCKET DIET MURDERS, 1985

Hot Cheese Pie

LOOKING for a simple Cheddar cheese appetizer that's hot? This will fill the bill. It is hot both temperature- and taste-wise. Though this recipe will serve a crowd, you can easily halve or quarter it to meet your needs.

SERVES 8 TO 12

3 (4-ounce) cans diced or sliced jalapeño peppers, mild or hot to your taste

1 (16-ounce) package sharp Cheddar cheese, grated

8 eggs

Cookware needed: pizza pan, mixing bowl

Sage Advice

To make this a heartier appetizer, add a layer of cooked ground beef (1/2 to 1 pound) after the cheese and before the eggs.

Preheat the oven to 350 degrees.

Drain the jalapeño peppers and spread them out on paper towels. Be sure to pick out any remaining seeds.

Spread the peppers in a shallow, throwaway aluminum pizza pan.

Top the peppers with a layer of cheese.

Beat the eggs until foamy and pour them over the cheese and peppers.

Bake in the preheated oven for 35 minutes.

PREPARATION TIME: *10 minutes,*
if you don't add the meat (see Sage Advice)
TOTAL TIME: *45 minutes*

Dressed-up English Muffin Appetizers

Sage Advice

Use plain, wheat, or sourdough muffins, but not any of the sweeter varieties.

HERE'S another Cheddar cheese appetizer you can easily prepare in the twinkling of an eye. In fact, it takes more time to grab up the necessary ingredients at the grocery store than it does to assemble the mixture.

True, the spreading and cutting may take a little while, but once that's done, these appetizers are easily frozen. Then you'll have a "homemade" appetizer that can be served as quickly as a minipizza or any other snack you could have bought at the store and stashed in your freezer.

These are guaranteed to come in handy for a spur-of-the-moment casual evening with friends, if someone drops by unexpectedly, or if you happen to crave a salty snack while watching late-night TV.

MAKES 72 APPETIZERS

2 cups olive spread or tapenade

1 (8-ounce) package sharp Cheddar cheese, grated

¼ cup diced onion, fresh or frozen

½ cup mayonnaise

1 teaspoon curry powder

6 English muffins, halved

Cookware needed: mixing bowl, cookie sheet

Preheat the oven to 375 degrees.

Combine the olive spread, cheese, onion, mayonnaise, and curry powder.

Spoon an ample amount onto each muffin half and cut each half into 6 pie-shaped wedges.

Put these on a cookie sheet, cover, and freeze. Once frozen, transfer them to freezer baggies until needed.

When ready to serve, bake them, still frozen, at 375 degrees for 10 to 12 minutes, or until bubbly.

PREPARATION TIME: *30 minutes*
TOTAL TIME: *45 minutes*

Sausage-Cheese Balls

IF YOU HAVE the time to make them, it is nice to serve bite-sized appetizers (in addition to nuts—which guests actually seem to eat by the fistful, rather than one by one).

I like these three-ingredient, quick-cooking sausage-cheese balls because the ingredients can be sort of "mixed or matched" according to what you have on hand—hot or mild sausage, mild or highly seasoned cheese. I'll give you the basic recipe first, and then show how you can alter it.

MAKES 10 TO 12 DOZEN

16 ounces hot sausage, uncooked
1 (16-ounce) package mild
    Cheddar cheese, shredded

3 cups biscuit mix
Cookware needed: mixing bowl,
    cookie sheet

Sage Advice

Even though these take some time to prepare, after baking, they can be frozen in moisture-proof containers. To serve, remove them from the freezer and heat at 350 degrees until warm.

Preheat the oven to 350 degrees.

Crumble the sausage into a large bowl.

Add the cheese and mix well.

Blend the biscuit mix into the sausage and cheese.

Shape the mixture into walnut-sized balls and place them on an ungreased, air insulated cookie sheet.

Bake for 10 to 12 minutes.

Options: If you have mild sausage on hand, use a jalapeño cheese in place of the mild Cheddar; or if you have only mild sausage and mild cheese on hand, add paprika or even chili powder to taste.

PREPARATION TIME: *approximately 30 minutes*
TOTAL TIME: *approximately 1 hour*

Parsley, Sage, Rosemary, and Wine

SEASONED butters are a treat often associated with fine restaurant dining, but they can also add a special touch to your own dining or buffet table, especially for a first course or appetizer.

Try serving honey-flavored butter (Land O Lakes makes a good one) with wedges of good dark pumpernickle or marble rye bread for a sweet savory.

YIELDS 1 CUP

If you are unable to find a ready-to-serve honey-flavored butter, simply stir 3 to 5 tablespoons of honey into 8 ounces of softened butter and mix well.

To make your own herbed butter, soak 2 tablespoons of mixed herbs (McCormick makes many blends) in 2 tablespoons of dry white wine for 2 hours. The herbs will absorb the wine flavor. Then mix the herb mixture with an 8-ounce tub of whipped butter or spread.

Served with crackers or bread, just as you would offer cream cheese with bagels, these flavored butters make a nice addition to an individual appetizer plate. Or, used in place of mayonnaise or mustard, they can dress up any sandwich.

PREPARATION TIME: *5 minutes*
TOTAL TIME: *5 minutes to 2 hours,*
depending on the blend

"There is so much wine made all over Italy that I wouldn't have been surprised if I had turned on a faucet in a particularly luxurious hotel, and found a luscious red wine coming out!"

—MORRISON WOOD.
THROUGH EUROPE WITH A JUG OF WINE, 1964

Cheddar-Crab Spread

RANKING right up there with cheese as a favorite appetizer is crabmeat. Add the cheese to the crabmeat and you have a spread that's sure to please.

Many crab appetizers are intended to be served hot—which can be a drawback. But this one can be served at room temperature immediately after you've stirred it together, or it can be made earlier in the day and served chilled.

Sage Advice

Don't forget the horseradish. That's what gives this its zip!

YIELDS APPROXIMATELY 2 CUPS

1 ¼ cups mayonnaise

1 (6 ½-ounce) can crabmeat

4 ounces sharp Cheddar cheese, grated

1 teaspoon prepared horseradish

4 tablespoons French dressing

¼ cup frozen diced onion, or to taste

1 tablespoon dried parsley

1 teaspoon dried dill

1 teaspoon Durkee's seasoned salt

Cookware needed: mixing bowl

Combine all the ingredients and stir until well blended. Serve at once, or refrigerate.

PREPARATION TIME: *5 to 10 minutes*

TOTAL TIME: *5 to 10 minutes*

Crabmeat Spread

WHAT *is* it about seafood that makes it so appealing as an appetizer?

Well, in the days before it was possible to ship fresh fish, or freshly frozen fish, to inland locations, canned fish—shrimp, crab, minced clams, even sardines— was often the only fish available. These selections were much better suited for preparing a delicious appetizer than they were for making a full entrée.

Times and food availability may have changed, but crab and shrimp and clam appetizers are just as good as ever. The trick is to serve them in a snazzy way. You've read some ideas in *Hints and Tips* and *A Word about The Finishing Touch* in Chapter 1, but check *The Finishing Touch* to this recipe for yet another.

YIELDS APPROXIMATELY 2 CUPS

1 (8-ounce) package cream cheese

½ (10-ounce) can cream of chicken soup

2 teaspoons Wyler's Shakers, chicken flavored

1 (6-ounce) can crabmeat, drained

Cookware needed: mixing bowl

Stir all the ingredients together to blend well.

Serve with cracker rounds or crinkled potato chips.

PREPARATION TIME: *5 minutes*
TOTAL TIME: *5 minutes*

The
Finishing Touch

This is a perfect time to put into practice my suggestion for using a vegetable in place of a ceramic or glass serving bowl. How about using a pepper—yellow, orange, red, green, or purple—whatever complements your party's décor—to hold the Crabmeat Spread.

Yummy Shrimp Spread

YIELDS APPROXIMATELY 1 CUP

1 (8-ounce) package cream cheese

½ cup frozen salad-size shrimp, defrosted or 1 (6-ounce) can shrimp, drained

2 tablespoons cocktail sauce

or

1 (8-ounce) package cream cheese

½ cup frozen salad-size shrimp, defrosted or 1 (6-ounce) can shrimp, drained

2 tablespoons ketchup plus ¼ teaspoon Worcestershire sauce, 1 teaspoon lemon juice, and ⅛ teaspoon prepared garlic

or

1 (8-ounce) package cream cheese

1 individual jar ready-to-eat shrimp cocktail

Cookware needed: food processor or blender

Toss all the ingredients into your food processor or blender and mix to a pastelike consistency.

Chill and serve with crackers.

PREPARATION TIME: *about 5 minutes*
TOTAL TIME: *5 minutes, plus time to chill*

Never Underestimate the Power of Celery

VIRTUALLY any of the spreads or balls in this chapter can be spread in celery stalks and passed as an extra treat before or even during dinner. Remember this when you have leftovers after a cocktail party.

Smoky Salmon Ball

THE EVIDENCE is in and the verdict is salmon is *really* good for you. So why not serve it as an appetizer when you're having beef for an entrée?

Actually, it isn't the salmon, but rather the liquid smoke that turns this inexpensive and otherwise pretty bland food combination into a recipe that will have everyone clamoring for more.

YIELDS 2 CUPS

¼ teaspoon salt

1 teaspoon liquid smoke, or to taste

Cookware needed: mixing bowl

Prepare the salmon by removing any bones or discolored flesh. (FYI, the bones are very good for you and the discolored flesh is natural, but you don't want to include these in the ball. Personally, I always gobble these up on the spot.)

Combine all the ingredients until totally blended. Let the mixture sit for a while at room temperature and then taste to check the flavoring. The liquid smoke taste should be present but not overpowering.

Shape it into a ball for serving. (Cover and refrigerate if not serving at once.)

PREPARATION TIME: *10 minutes*
TOTAL TIME: *10 minutes, or longer if you elect to use one of the suggestions in The Finishing Touch.*

Sage Advice

This is one of my favorite spreads so I do lots of tasting while preparing it. Fresh lemon juice is best, but the bottled type will do. And I don't like the onions to dominate or compete with the salmon, lemon, and liquid smoke flavor, so I go easy on those, depending on how potent the onion is.

The Finishing Touch

If you wish, chill the ball before serving and roll it either in finely chopped fresh parsley or in finely chopped pecans for a dressier appearance.

Pineapple-Cheese Ball

MY FORMER sister-in-law, Janet Kimsey, introduced me to this pineapple and cream cheese appetizer back in the early '70s. I don't remember anything else about her party that particular night. Probably because I never moved from my spot in front of this truly delicious and rather "different" cocktail food. From that night on, it's been standard fare in my home.

Over the years, thanks to the introduction of frozen onions and green peppers, I can make it more quickly than ever. And if I tossed the cream cheese and pineapple in the food processor or blender, it would go even more quickly. Actually, I'm sure you could make this recipe using pineapple-flavored cream cheese and that would cut the prep time down even more. But I like to use my handheld electric mixer to blend the pineapple and cream cheese, just the way I did the first time I made it...as sort of a tribute to the old days.

The Finishing Touch

Like the Smoky Salmon Ball, after chilling, when it is easier to handle, this Pineapple-Cheese Ball can be rolled in a topping— in this case either finely chopped fresh parsley or finely chopped pecans. But, it's much zippier if you serve it in a pineapple boat. To do this, slice the pineapple lengthwise (leaving the leaves attached) and scoop out the fruit. Then fill the shell to overflowing with the Pineapple-Cheese mixture. Sprinkle additional pecans and green pepper on top as a garnish, if you wish. Serve with wheat thin crackers.

YIELDS APPROXIMATELY 3 CUPS

2 (8-ounce) packages cream cheese

1 (8-ounce) can crushed pineapple, drained

or

2 (8-ounce) containers pineapple-flavored cream cheese

⅓ cup diced green pepper

2 tablespoons frozen, diced onion

2 heaping tablespoons Durkee's seasoned salt

½ cup pecans, chopped

Finely chopped parsley or pecans (see *The Finishing Touch*)

Cookware needed: mixing bowl

Either thoroughly mix the cream cheese and drained, crushed pineapple together, or begin with the pineapple-flavored cream cheese.

To this, add the green pepper, onion, seasoned salt, and pecans.

Roll into a ball, cover, and chill.

PREPARATION TIME: *5 to 10 minutes*
TOTAL TIME: *5 to 10 minutes, plus time to chill*

Antipasto Appetizers

Years ago, many fine restaurants—and they weren't necessarily Italian—served an "antipasto" appetizer. (Though it appeared to be free, the cost was hidden in the price of the entrée.)

Sometimes one large antipasto plate was presented for the table. Other times each person was treated to an individual plate of goodies. Either way, it was a delightful way to begin a meal, and much healthier and prettier than today's usual bread, a couple of crackers still in their packaging, and aluminum foil–wrapped butter or margarine pats served in a brown plastic basket.

I think it's time to bring the antipasto plate back, but this time to *your* dining table—whether for a Wednesday night family meal, a Saturday night company dinner, or a cocktail party.

If you'd like a traditional antipasto plate, see The Traditional Antipasto Plate on page 62. The one below is lighter and simpler.

The Finishing Touch

A good-sized dab of an easily spreadable flavored cheese or butter gives the antipasto platter or plates an air of elegance and your taste buds a real treat. Or, if you wish, you can fill the cavities of ready-to-serve celery stalks with some of the spreads found in this chapter. Remember, any of the spreads can be made ahead of time and kept in the refrigerator.

Antipasto American Style

FOR A QUICK, light antipasto-type appetizer course, all you need are some pickles and olives (either from jars or selected from the deli section of the grocery store), a few crudités (a French word for healthy veggies—carrot, celery, cherry or grape tomatoes, broccoli florets, even crisp, blanched green beans) from ready-to-serve packages or the salad bar, plus a few crackers (taken out of the cellophane, please) or rounds of good bread.

Arrange these items on a "commonly-shared" platter, or on individual plates.

The Traditional Antipasto Plate

THERE isn't a drop of Italian blood on either side of my family, even by marriage—a fact that I greatly regret. So to learn the ingredients for a traditional antipasto plate, I had to ask around.

In the process, I found that everyone I asked had a slightly different version of what constitutes a truly authentic antipasto. For example, both Karen Murgolo, at QVC Publishing, and my Danville friend, Pete Castiglione, have Southern Italian roots. In that warm area of Italy, the traditional antipasto plate always includes some wonderful native-grown citrus fruit, such as grapefruit or orange.

Here, as best I can determine, are the most popular ingredients used for a traditional antipasto. Make your selections from this list when preparing yours.

YIELD VARIES ACCORDING TO QUANTITY
AND NUMBER OF ITEMS INCLUDED

artichoke hearts—use the marinated ones out of a jar

olives—both Spanish and black, pitted or not

hard-boiled eggs—this is the only potentially time-consuming ingredient

slices of pepperoni or salami

sardines or anchovies

tomatoes—either whole cherry or grape tomatoes or sliced large tomatoes

green peppers

cold vegetables—green beans, celery, asparagus, even beets

a few beans—preferably chickpeas or garbanzo beans, but lentils work, too

cheese cubes

and, of course, some colorful and delicious citrus sections or slices

Cookware needed: individual plates or large platter

The Finishing Touch

After you've made your antipasto selections according to your (and your guests') tastes, you get to the fun part— arranging the plate attractively. Try beginning with either the beans or sliced hard-boiled eggs in the center. Top these with a strip or two of green peppers, or a couple of anchovies or sardines. Surround the beans or eggs with pepperoni, olives, artichoke hearts, tomatoes, cheese cubes, or whatever. Sprinkle the entire plate lightly with an oil-based (not creamy) Italian dressing and a few turns (to taste) of freshly ground pepper. I often use the marinade from the jar of artichokes as the dressing.

Curried Chicken Bits

LOOKING for a different finger food to serve as an appetizer? Try these Curried Chicken Bits accompanied by a bowl of duck sauce taken right out of the bottle.

SERVES 12 PLUS

1 cup white wine

1 teaspoon curry powder

1 teaspoon celery salt

1 to 2 tablespoons duck, or egg roll sauce, plus additional for serving

2 pounds fresh or frozen chicken cubes, strips, or tenders, unflavored and unbreaded, uncooked

Cookware needed: skillet

Combine the wine, curry powder, celery salt, and 1 or 2 tablespoons of the duck or egg roll sauce in a deep skillet, and bring the mixture to a gentle bubble.

Add the chicken to the pan and, if necessary, just enough water so that the chicken is completely covered.

Cover the pan and cook for 2 to 3 minutes. Turn the pieces over and cook another few minutes, until done.

Remove from the heat and refrigerate the chicken in the liquid for 2 to 3 hours or longer. When ready to serve, drain the chicken and cube it into bite-size pieces.

Serve it with toothpicks and duck sauce on the side.

PREPARATION TIME: *30 minutes*
TOTAL TIME: *about 3 hours, or until well chilled*

The
Finishing Touch

Wondering what to put the toothpicks in? Think fancifully. A silver cordial glass, a miniature vase, even an empty spice jar disguised with a few strands of colored raffia tied at the throat.

1, 2, 3 Appetizer

WHO says that deli meats have to be paper-thin slivers and used only for sandwiches? Not I. Especially when I need a quick and easy appetizer.

Now, if you're thinking of one of those chunky cheese-and-mystery-meat-cube platters served with toothpicks, think again.

You can present a nice appetizer by taking a hint from the way fancy restaurants do it. It's as easy as 1, 2, 3 and the key word is "presentation."

1. Ask for ⅛-inch-thick slices of specialty deli meats.

2. Select a vinaigrette that complements the flavor of the meat to give it an elegant and distinctive touch.

3. Arrange everything prettily on a salad plate for individual servings.

SERVES 4

1 pound sun-dried turkey breast, peppered beef, or other specialty deli meat, sliced ⅛ inch thick; or smoked salmon

4 ounces organic greens (mesclun) or several small lettuce leaves

1 jar tomato basil, balsamic, Dijon mustard, lime-cilantro, orange, or another bottled vinaigrette or dressing that will complement the taste of the meat

Coarsely grated Parmesan cheese, to taste

Freshly ground black pepper, to taste

Slice the deli meat into quarter pieces.

To serve, cluster some of the greens at one side of the plate. Beginning where the leaves end, layer 3 or 4 pieces of the meat so they slightly overlap. Add a few more greens at the outside edge of the meat.

Drizzle a tablespoon or so of the vinaigrette over each serving. Sprinkle with a little coarsely grated Parmesan cheese and finish off with a turn or two of fresh pepper.

PREPARATION TIME: *10 minutes*
TOTAL TIME: *10 minutes*

Everyone's Favorite...Meatballs

MY MOTHER-IN-LAW Margaret Rich eats her dessert first. "Why save the best for last?" she asks.

Maybe it was the New England influence in my childhood, but I was brought up to believe you *must* save the best for last. That's why I've saved the quickest, easiest, and absolutely no-fail best appetizer for last.

And, if you aren't at the feeding trough first when these are on the menu, I can guarantee there won't be any left for the latecomers. What are they?

Meatballs.

Already you're conjuring up visions of chopping, dicing, stirring, mixing, and oh no...sautéing.

Forget it. Hop in the car and drive to the nearest store where you can buy already cooked, ready-to-serve plain old meatballs...the type you can toss into spaghetti or, as you'll see, turn into an instant appetizer.

Sage Advice
The same jelly and ketchup formula can also be used with ready-to-eat ham cubes and cocktail franks. Also, usually plan on 3 to 5 "pieces" per person. This recipe is easily doubled.

SERVES APPROXIMATELY 20

1 (18-ounce) package fully cooked meatballs, frozen

1 (10-ounce) jar grape jelly

1 (16-ounce) bottle ketchup

Combine the grape jelly and ketchup in a large, heavy saucepan.

Stir over medium heat to blend the jelly and ketchup.

Add the meatballs and simmer for 20 to 30 minutes, so the wonderful flavors will be absorbed.

PREPARATION TIME: *5 minutes*
TOTAL TIME: *approximately 30 minutes*

Soups

"**SOUPS,**" said my friend, Jan Harris. Most everyone in town knows Jan. When she was in kindergarten her mother used to prop her up on a milk crate so she could reach the cash register and check customers out at her family's Midtown Market in Danville, Virginia. "I love soups, but I don't have time to spend hours watching over them. Please put some easy soups in your book," she begged. I promised I would, because when I'm eating out and am given the choice of soup *or* a salad, I'll take the soup, thank you very much.

And when planning a seated dinner at home, I almost always include a soup course. To my way of thinking, a flavorful soup starts the meal off on the right note and can add zest to an otherwise simple menu. It even sends a special, caring signal to your guests. (They think you've been slaving over the stove, mixing, stirring, and flavoring your magical concoction for hours—though none of mine require so much work.) Served as a first course, soup can be elegant.

Some like it hot;
Some like it cold;
Some like it
in the pot,
Nine days old.

—MOTHER GOOSE

Yet a hearty soup can be a meal in itself. Anytime there's a chill in the air, give me a bowl of soup, some bread, and sweet butter or cheese, and I'm set.

For that reason, you'll find soups in this chapter that work well as appetizers *and* heartier, full-meal soups that are perfect for serving with a salad or a sandwich.

Either way, when it comes to soup, count me in.

Dollops Don't Have to be Fattening

TIME and again in this chapter you'll read "sprinkle with Parmesan cheese," or "garnish with a teaspoon of sour cream," or " top with a small dollop of whipped cream."

If fat calories begin dancing in front of your eyes, don't dismay. You're only adding a little bit of those luscious ingredients, and that primarily for color. But if you're still concerned, use one of the reduced-fat substitutes that are available on the market.

Or, try this. Buy some sliced low-fat cheese and a couple of attractive, very small pastry or cookie cutters. A star or crescent moon, for example. Cut out a cheese shape and float it in your soup.

And remember that a thin slice of lemon or cucumber, a sprig of parsley or chives, a thin slice of pimiento-stuffed Spanish olive, even a few plain or flavored croutons, can always be used as a garnish.

2-Step Steak Soup

TRADITIONALLY, soups were made from leftovers, especially the remains of a pot roast, turkey, or ham. But unless you're cooking for a sizable group, chances are you won't have a roast around to begin with. Still, that shouldn't deter you from enjoying the hearty goodness of a meat-based soup, such as this quick and easy 2-Step Steak Soup.

SERVES 6

2 (14 ½-ounce) cans Progresso Vegetarian Vegetable soup

1 (17-ounce) package Hormel Always Tender beef tips with gravy

Dash of Tabasco or other hot sauce, to taste

Cookware needed: saucepan

Heat the soup on medium high until piping hot. Add the beef tips with their juices and hot sauce, to taste. Stir, and simmer for 10 to 15 minutes

PREPARATION TIME: *5 minutes*
TOTAL TIME: *20 to 25 minutes*

Sage Advice
If you prefer a less thick soup, toss in as much V-8 or tomato juice as you like.

"In these days, when a request on a postal card, will bring to a housekeeper the grocery catalogue of any of the great city stores, there is little excuse for the home caterer being ignorant in the matter of what is new and desirable in the line of canned goods.... An entire meal may be easily and quickly prepared, either using canned goods in connection with other materials at hand, or having the entire meal composed of food put up in glass or tin."

—*THE BUTTERICK COOK BOOK*, EDITED BY HELENA JUDSON, 1911

Artichoke and Oyster Soup

TRUST ME, my guests do. I never tell them the name of this soup until they've tasted it. By then they're hooked. Further, they don't believe me when I smile and say, oysters and artichokes. In truth, it's the garlic and the anise and the red pepper that bring the soup to life.

I first tasted this delicacy in Delaware. When I asked for the recipe, it was eagerly shared by my hostess. Though the soup is simple to make, it really does need a resting period, so don't plan to make it and dish it up immediately. Plan to let it sit in the refrigerator for at least 6 to 8 hours, or even a full day before serving. Then be ready for a real treat.

SERVES 8 TO 10

2 sticks butter

⅓ cup frozen, diced onions

3 (14-ounce) cans artichoke hearts, drained and quartered

3 tablespoons flour

4 (14-ounce) cans roasted garlic flavored chicken stock

1 teaspoon red pepper flakes

1 teaspoon anise seed, or to taste

1 teaspoon salt

1 tablespoon Worcestershire sauce

1 quart oysters

Fresh or prepared additional garlic, to taste

Cookware needed: large pot with lid, food processor

Melt the butter in a pot large enough to hold all the ingredients and sauté the onions until soft.

Add the artichokes and sprinkle the vegetables with the flour. Stir to coat everything well but do not allow the flour to brown.

Add the garlic flavored chicken stock, the red pepper flakes, anise seed, salt, and Worcestershire sauce.

Cover and simmer for about 15 minutes.

While the mixture cooks, drain the oysters, reserving their liquor, and check them for shells.

Mince the oysters in a blender or food processor. This can be done in just a whirl or two. Be sure not to overchop and turn them into puree. Add the oysters and oyster liquor to the pot and simmer for about 10 minutes longer. Do not allow the soup to boil.

Refrigerate for a minimum of 6 to 8 hours, or for a full day. (It keeps well for up to 3 days.) Reheat over medium-low to medium heat; do not allow the soup to boil. At this point, taste it and decide if you want to add a little garlic flavoring.

The Finishing Touch

To add a little color to this bland-appearing, though extremely flavorful, soup, sprinkle it with a little paprika or garnish it with some chopped parsley or chives. Or, in the center of each bowl, place a single parsley leaf or 2 chive leaves crossed to form an x.

PREPARATION TIME: *15 minutes*
TOTAL TIME: *25 minutes*

Chicken Chowder

THANKS to the availability of skinless, boneless, frozen chicken breasts and trusty cream of chicken soup, it's possible to put a filling bowl of chicken soup on the table in nothing flat.

The trick is to keep a resealable package of chicken in your freezer and, when you reach for the cream of mushroom soup at the grocery store, grab up a couple of extra cans of cream of chicken soup for your pantry, as well.

With these ingredients on hand, you only have to add a can of creamed corn and some evaporated milk and suddenly you've turned chicken soup into a delicious chowder.

SERVES 6 TO 8

The
Finishing Touch

Though you will have added pepper while the soup is cooking, add a couple of grinds to each bowl and pass peppered crackers with a mild cheese, such as Swiss or Camembert, as an accompaniment. The sharp pepper taste really sets off the creamy chicken chowder.

2 frozen (or fresh) boneless chicken breasts

1 ¼ cups water

½ cup frozen PickSweet Seasoning Blend (onion, celery, green and red pepper, and parsley mix)

2 tablespoons butter

2 (10-ounce) cans cream of chicken soup

1 (15-ounce) can creamed corn

1 (5-ounce) can evaporated milk

Freshly ground pepper, to taste

Cookware needed: large saucepan

Cook the chicken breasts in the microwave by placing them in a microwave-safe bowl and covering them with the water. Microwave on high for 4 to 5 minutes, or until they are no longer pink.

While they are cooking, sauté the Seasoning Blend in the butter in a heavy saucepan over medium heat.

Stir in the soup, corn, milk, and pepper.

While the soup is heating and the flavors are blending, remove the chicken from the microwave. Pour the cooking water into the soup mixture and stir well.

Dice the chicken breasts and add them to the pan.

Bring the soup to a gentle bubble, stir, and then reduce the heat.

Simmer for 10 to 15 minutes.

PREPARATION TIME: *20 minutes*
TOTAL TIME: *30 to 40 minutes*

Cioppino

MANHATTAN clam chowder is good, but the presence of the shrimp and the absence of the potatoes and vegetables in this tomato-based clam soup make it a delicious, light alternative. The availability of shelled, cooked frozen shrimp and the convenience of canned minced clams make it possible to mix it up in nothing flat.

SERVES 6

- 2 tablespoons olive oil
- ⅔ cup frozen, diced combo of onion and green pepper
- 1 clove garlic, minced, or 1 teaspoon prepared garlic
- 3 (7 ½-ounce) cans minced clams with their juice
- 1 (14-ounce) can Italian-flavored diced tomatoes
- ½ cup dry white wine
- 1 (8-ounce) package raw shrimp
- Salt, pepper, dried basil, and dried oregano, to taste
- **Cookware needed:** large pot with lid

Heat the olive oil in a large, heavy pot.

Add the onion and pepper combination and sauté until transparent, then add the garlic.

While the vegetables are cooking, drain and reserve the clams, keeping the juice.

Add the clam juice, the tomatoes, and the wine to the pot.

Bring the mixture to a gentle boil and then reduce the heat to a simmer. Cook the soup, covered, for 10 minutes.

At this point add the shrimp and reserved clams. Simmer, uncovered, for 4 to 5 minutes.

Taste and adjust the seasonings. You can use a blended Italian seasoning instead of the basil and oregano.

PREPARATION TIME: *10 minutes*
TOTAL TIME: *20 to 25 minutes*

Improved Minestrone Soup

A GOOD bowl of minestrone served with a crusty French or a dark rye bread and a salad is my idea of the perfect cold-weather lunch. Problem is, the canned minestrone soups don't have the hearty flavor I like so much. How do you add that heartiness with a minimum of effort? Look to the freezer and the spice rack, gather a few ingredients, start these on the stove top, and *then* add the canned soup.

You'll need a little extra time to make the base to which you'll add the canned soup, but only a *little* extra time. In fact, once, when I learned that out-of-town guests were arriving (unexpectedly, naturally) at lunch-time, I pulled this soup off in 20 minutes flat. Everyone thought it was homemade and had taken hours.

The soup can be made the day before it is served, but don't over-cook it. Unlike many soups and stews, whose flavors blend through hours of cooking, this is one that blends perfectly well during the "resting" process.

Sage Advice

The wonderful thing about this recipe is that it is so flexible. If you don't have onion flavored beef broth, but you do have a can of French onion soup on hand, use that. You can use whatever small pasta you have in the pantry—little shells, elbow macaroni, small bow ties, even a few strands of angel hair pasta broken into small pieces if that's all you have. If you have Italian stewed tomatoes instead of the diced variety, use those. Or, if you're out of flavored Italian tomatoes, use a can of unflavored ones, but add a hefty amount of oregano, or an Italian spice blend, and even a little garlic. If you can't find cannellini, use white or red kidney beans.

SERVES 6 TO 8

1 (14-ounce) can onion-flavored beef broth

1 teaspoon olive oil

4 or 5 dried bay leaves

¼ teaspoon dried oregano

½ cup frozen Fordhook lima beans (they're the large variety)

½ cup small elbow or shell macaroni

1 (14-ounce) can cannellini (white kidney) beans

1 (14-ounce) can Italian-style diced tomatoes

½ cup frozen zucchini or yellow squash slices

1 (16-ounce) can ready-to-serve minestrone soup

Salt and freshly ground pepper, to taste

Grated Parmesan cheese, for serving

Cookware needed: large pot

In a large pot, combine the beef broth with the olive oil, bay leaves, and oregano and bring to a boil.

Add the lima beans and macaroni. Return the liquid to a boil while you open and rinse the beans.

Add the beans, tomatoes, and frozen squash slices and stir.

As soon as the soup begins to bubble, add the minestrone soup and reduce the heat to medium.

Cook for approximately 10 minutes to blend the flavors. Remove the bay leaves and add salt and pepper to taste.

Serve with grated Parmesan cheese passed in a bowl.

PREPARATION TIME: *10 minutes*
TOTAL TIME: *20 minutes*

Lentil Soup

MY GREEK FRIENDS tell me that lentil soup is from Greece. My German friends tell me their grandmothers made it in Germany. Actually, lentils have been found in Egyptian tombs that date from 2000 B.C., and they are as much a staple in Eastern European countries as they are in South America and the western reaches of the United States. It matters not where the lentils or the recipe originated. What matters is that this recipe is full of vitamins and fiber, is delicious, and can be made in less than half an hour.

SERVES 6 TO 8

1 cup diced potatoes from a 20-ounce package or 3 medium potatoes, diced

1 (8-ounce) package already diced ham bits, or frankfurters, finely chopped

2 (19-ounce) cans ready-to-serve lentil soup

¼ cup frozen, diced onion

8 to 10 grinds black pepper

½ teaspoon dried oregano

½ teaspoon dried thyme

2 or 3 dried bay leaves

Salt, to taste

Croutons

Cookware needed: small pot, large pot

In a small pot, cover the potatoes with water and boil the potatoes until tender, about 10 minutes. Meanwhile, chop the frankfurters, if using them, or open the package of ham, and empty the cans of lentil soup into a large pot. Drain the potatoes and add them to the soup along with the meat, onion, herbs, and spices. Simmer about 20 minutes.

Serve with a round of warm bread on the side or croutons as a garnish.

PREPARATION TIME: *15 to 25 minutes*
TOTAL TIME: *approximately 40 minutes*

The
Finishing Touch

A thin slice of lemon, with all the seeds removed, is a nice garnish if you're serving this soup for a special occasion.

Tell Me It's
Homemade Clam Chowder

The
Finishing Touch

Like so many delicious but cream-based soups, clam chowder needs a bright finishing touch. The usual choices are parsley and chives. But with colorful cherry and grape tomatoes now available year-round, try adding a very thin slice of one of these along with a small parsley leaf. Then surround the garnish with a couple of grindings of fresh pepper.

TALK ABOUT NERVE! That's what one notable food guru (who chooses to remain anonymous) had when she served clam chowder to a family that's in the seafood restaurant business. In her defense, she didn't know that when she planned the menu. "I never would have been so brazen, or so foolish," she now laughingly admits.

Fortunately the story, or should I say the meal, had a happy ending—so happy that her guests begged for her homemade clam chowder recipe. When she hesitated, they backed off, knowing that special recipes are often well-guarded secrets.

Little did they know that she was serving them canned clam chowder...with an extra touch she had learned from another friend who worked for a clam chowder specialty house in Maine!

Proof once again that you can have the best restaurant food right in your own home—straight out of the can.

SERVES 4 TO 5

2 (15-ounce) cans Snow's Clam Chowder

1 (6-ounce) can minced clams with juice

½ cup cream

Fresh ground pepper, to taste

Cookware needed: large saucepan

Blend and heat all the ingredients.

PREPARATION TIME: *10 minutes*
TOTAL TIME: *15 minutes (until well heated)*

Tomato Soup Collage

Think soup and tomatoes come to mind. As well they should. Tomato soups are always crowd pleasers, in addition to which they are colorful and start the meal off on a cheerful note. Here are three varieties of tomato soup that can be formal or casual, depending on how you serve them.

Too-Easy Spicy Tomato Soup

WHO'D EVER THINK of serving a favorite cocktail as soup? They did it in the 1970s, but Bloody Mary Soup seems to have been forgotten in recent years. Back then, the cook chopped and sautéed onions and celery, which were then added to tomatoes. The mixture was then pureed and strained. No wonder it passed out of fashion!

These days, try serving your favorite bottled or canned Bloody Mary mix as a soup—either chilled or heated. Whether or not you add the vodka is your choice.

The
Finishing Touch
This cocktail/soup makes a great first course when served in mugs with a leafy stalk of celery for garnish. If you're serving it in traditional soup bowls, a couple of pretty green leaves, be they cilantro, parsley, or celery, add a dressy touch.

Zesty Tomato Starter

TOMATO SOUP has a real affinity for beef bouillon. Years ago, everyone served that simple combination as an appetizer, and it's as good today as ever, especially if you dress it up a little. Do this by adding a couple of large fistsfuls of frozen, diced onions and green peppers and an ample sprinkling of dried basil to the soup while it's heating. The flavors punch up the taste, and the diced onion and pepper give the soup that "homemade" look.

Garnish it with a teaspoon of sour cream, straight out of the squeezable bottle, and chives.

SERVES 6

1 (10-ounce) can tomato soup

2 (10-ounce) cans beef bouillon, or broth

½ cup frozen, diced combo of onion and green pepper

1 heaping teaspoon dried basil

¼ teaspoon sugar

Sour cream, for garnish

Cookware needed: large pot

Sage Advice

If you are not going to add the sour-cream garnish, stir in a tablespoon of butter while the soup is cooking for added richness of flavor.

Combine all the ingredients except the sour cream in a large pot. Stir, and bring the soup to a gentle bubble over medium-high heat. Immediately turn down the heat and allow the soup to simmer for 10 to 15 minutes.

PREPARATION TIME: *5 minutes*
TOTAL TIME: *15 to 20 minutes*

Love Apple Fromage Soup

WHEN my friend Jean Carol Vernon isn't entertaining audiences with her beautiful voice, presiding over a civic club meeting, or traveling with her grandchildren, she is preparing lunch for her church or theater or club friends. This delicious starter always helps to start things off on the right foot. It's simple to cube a block of Velveeta cheese, but you can use the already cubed variety to save even more time.

**SERVES 4 TO 8,
DEPENDING ON SIZE OF CUP OR BOWL**

1 (10 ¾-ounce) can tomato soup

1 soup can whole milk, not skim or low fat

4 (1-ounce) cubes Mild Mexican Kraft Velveeta or another mildly spicy cheese

Cookware needed: microwave-safe mixing bowl

Combine the soup and milk in a microwave-safe mixing bowl. Add the cheese pieces and set the microwave to 4 minutes on 50% power. After 30 seconds, stir, and continue to stir the mixture every 30 seconds, until thoroughly blended and heated. (The time may vary according to individual microwaves.)

PREPARATION TIME: *5 to 10 minutes*
TOTAL TIME: *10 to 15 minutes*

*The
Finishing Touch*

Serve the soup in individual punch or demitasse cups, or in mugs (no spoon needed) or a bowl (spoon needed). Garnish each serving with a few seasoned croutons and serve the soup with cheese straws, or a slice of bruschetta (broiled bread with salsa and cheese) right on top.

*When the tomato was introduced to France,
the Parisians called it "pomme d'amour,"
and imbued it with aphrodisiac qualities, which
is why, in Elizabethan times, it was
known as the "love apple."*

Tomato and Chili Bean Soup

LIKE so many of the recipes in this book, this one grew out of "desperation." It started out with that panicked question, "What on earth can I *feed* them?" I'm sure you know the feeling well.

Even when I was writing this book and definitely had a well-stocked pantry, just such a panic set in. A business acquaintance, who lives some 30 miles away, ran by just a little after 12 o'clock noon one February day. At five minutes to two, I felt compelled to fix a bite of lunch. The day called for soup.

There was a problem with every idea I had in mind. Clam chowder—no clams. Brunswick stew—no more cans of Mrs. Fearnow's stew. Peanut butter? Two jars of extra crunchy, but no smooth.

I grabbed a can of Roasted Garlic Tomato soup, a new product I'd bought to try out, and some hot chili beans. It was that simple. In fact, deciding what to have took longer than mixing up the soup.

SERVES 4

1 (10-ounce) can Roasted Garlic Tomato soup

1 can water

1 (14-ounce) can hot chili beans (red kidney beans)

Cookware needed: pot

The Finishing Touch

Add some Parmesan cheese—a few hefty shakes, or a heaping tablespoon of the finely grated type is fine. Or, if you have it on hand, use some grated Cheddar cheese from the bag. And don't forget the tortilla chips, or, if you have time to make it, corn bread.

Combine the tomato soup and water and mix well.

Pour off and reserve the top juices from the can of chili beans.

Add the beans and the juices that naturally cling to them to the soup and stir.

Add half the reserved bean liquid. Cook for 3 to 4 minutes, until the flavors begin to blend.

Taste, and add additional reserved kidney bean liquid to your liking.

PREPARATION TIME: *5 minutes*
TOTAL TIME: *15 minutes*

Lady Wellington's Summertime Soup

MINA WOOD serves this soup in the summer, when she's having a lunchtime committee meeting as President of the Garden Club of Virginia. Try it, and everyone will think you slaved for hours. (It's the addition of the fresh tomatoes that does the trick.)

SERVES 8 TO 10

- 3 to 5 ripe, homegrown, medium-size tomatoes
- 1 (48-ounce) can V-8 juice
- 1 cup sour cream
- Dried basil, salt, and pepper, to taste
- **Cookware needed:** blender or food processor, large bowl

Coarsely chop the juicy, summertime tomatoes in a blender or food processor.

Combine the tomato pieces (removing the seeds that will have separated in the chopping process), the V-8 juice, and the sour cream in a large bowl.

Stir together and season to taste with the basil, salt, and pepper.

Chill for 2 to 3 hours before serving.

PREPARATION TIME: *10 minutes*
TOTAL TIME: *2 to 3 hours to chill*

The Finishing Touch

Garnish the soup with a sprinkling of chopped chives or a sprig of parsley.

Virginia Cream of Peanut Soup

CREAM of peanut soup is a legendary Virginia delicacy, served at many restaurants and inns, including those in Williamsburg. Recipes are found in countless Virginia cookbooks, but they all call for chopping and straining and all those steps that I'm trying to avoid these days.

Although you can buy canned peanut soup in some gourmet shops or departments, it's not on every grocery shelf. For those of you who can find it, skip the recipe below and go straight to *The Finishing Touch*.

For those less fortunate, here is a really simple recipe that requires only a little patient stirring and is guaranteed to delight your guests with its delicate flavor.

SERVES 6 TO 8

1 quart whole milk, not skim or low fat

2 tablespoons butter, softened (honey-flavored, if available)

1 tablespoon flour

1 cup creamy or smooth peanut butter, not crunchy

Salt, to taste

Cookware needed: large pot, small bowl

The Finishing Touch

Though optional, a little sherry enhances the soup's flavor. Whether you use dry or sweet sherry depends on your taste. Once the soup is ladled into soup bowls, top each serving with a small dollop of whipped cream.

Heat the milk over medium-low to medium heat. Do not allow it to boil.

Combine the butter and flour in a small bowl or measuring cup. Add a little of the hot milk and blend until smooth. Stir this paste, little by little, into the rest of the milk, blending it thoroughly.

Add the peanut butter by large spoonfuls, stirring each one into the milk until completely blended. Keep the soup hot, but do not allow it to boil. Add salt to taste.

PREPARATION TIME: *15 minutes*
TOTAL TIME: *25 minutes*

Chilled Soups

There are times, especially in the hot summer, when nothing is more refreshing than a chilled soup. Gazpacho has become a universal favorite, but for variety, why not try serving a fruit-based chilled soup?

I did, back in the 1980s, when I found a recipe for a fruit and Champagne soup in one of the women's magazines. It was incredibly easy to make and entailed little more than combining a bottle of Champagne with some fruity ingredients. Everyone wanted the recipe, and I shared it—obviously one time too many because, though I've searched high and low, I can't find it. (If you know it, please send it to me!)

Luckily, the following delicious chilled soups come close to that lost Champagne delight. They're light, delicious, and colorful.

Chilled Strawberry Soup Number 1

SERVES 6

2 cups Dole's orange-strawberry-banana juice

⅓ cup sifted powdered sugar

2 (10-ounce) packages frozen sliced strawberries, defrosted

½ cup Burgundy or other dry red wine (optional)

½ cup sour cream

Cookware needed: blender, pitcher

Combine the juice, powdered sugar, and strawberries in an electric blender and process until smooth. Add the Burgundy, if using it, and sour cream and process 2 more minutes.

Cover and chill for several hours.

PREPARATION TIME: *10 minutes*
TOTAL TIME: *only however much longer*
as it takes to defrost the strawberries

Sage Advice

Experienced cooks will tell you, "If you won't drink it, don't cook with it." They're referring to "cooking wine," of course, and who would drink that! Remember these words when you add the Burgundy or another dry red wine to this soup.

The Finishing Touch

If you refrigerate the soup in a pretty glass, or even plastic, pitcher, you can pour it straight into cups, mugs, or small bowls at the table. Top off each cup or mug of this chilled fruit soup with a slice of a strawberry or mint leaves.

Chilled Strawberry Soup Number 2

JUST in case you're looking for a lighter, and even easier soup, try this.

SERVES 6

2 (10-ounce) packages sliced frozen strawberries, slightly defrosted

1 cup ginger ale, or, why not... Champagne

Cookware needed: blender, large mixing bowl or pitcher

In an electric blender, reduce the slightly defrosted strawberries to a crushed, not pureed, consistency.

Combine the strawberries with the liquid, either in a large bowl or in a pitcher, and refrigerate.

See *The Finishing Touch* for Chilled Strawberry Soup Number 1 (page 81).

PREPARATION TIME: *5 minutes*
TOTAL TIME: *5 minutes*

Summer Peach and Apricot Delight

SERVES 6

2 (11 ½-ounce) cans apricot nectar

2 (6-ounce) jars pureed baby-food peaches

¾ cup orange juice

½ cup whipping cream

½ cup sour cream

1 (10-ounce) package frozen sliced strawberries, defrosted

Pinch cinnamon

Cookware needed: mixing bowl

Stir all the ingredients together in a bowl, and refrigerate.

PREPARATION TIME: *5 minutes*
TOTAL TIME: *5 minutes*

Anything-Goes Fruit Soup

BY NOW you see how easy it is to make chilled soup, and you've realized, Hey! there's no cooking involved. So tuck this generic recipe away and prepare it according to your taste and the ingredients you have on hand.

SERVES 4

1 medium banana

1 (8-ounce) can crushed pineapple, drained

1 cup of any of the numerous varieties of fruit blends available today, such as Welch's wild raspberry, Minute Maid tropical fruit punch, or Tropicana orange-tangerine blend

½ cup half-and-half

Cookware needed: large mixing bowl

In a large mixing bowl, mash the banana.

Add the drained crushed pineapple and stir.

Add the fruit blend and half-and-half, and mix well.

Refrigerate until thoroughly chilled.

PREPARATION TIME: *5 minutes*
TOTAL TIME: *as long as it takes to thoroughly chill, approximately 3 to 4 hours.*

The
Finishing Touch

Garnish with Cool Whip or whipped cream topped with a small piece of fruit—strawberry, cherry, kiwi, peach, mango, banana, whatever.

Gazpacho Plus

SPEAKING of gazpacho, it's the perfect starter for a relaxed buffet when you're serving the Mexican-Chicken Casserole (page 199), or almost any other entrée. Unlike the summertime chilled fruit soups, gazpacho is a soup for all seasons. To give the canned variety a homemade touch, try the following.

SERVES 4 TO 6

¼ cup frozen, diced combo of onion and green pepper

1 (5.5-ounce) can spicy V-8 juice

2 tablespoons wine vinegar

1 tablespoon lemon (or lime) juice

2 (15-ounce) cans gazpacho

Worcestershire sauce, to taste

Cookware needed: large mixing bowl

The Finishing Touch

The usual dollop of sour cream is fine, of course, but a thin slice of lemon, lime, or cucumber is equally attractive.

While the frozen onion and green pepper mix is defrosting on a paper towel, open the cans and combine all the other ingredients in a large mixing bowl.

Pat the onions and green peppers dry and add them to the bowl.

Stir, and refrigerate for 3 to 4 hours minimum.

PREPARATION TIME: *5 minutes*
TOTAL TIME: *as long as it takes to chill thoroughly*

Mock Vichyssoise

VICHYSSOISE is another one of those once-popular soups that seems to have faded into the past. When you look at the old recipes that call for a sieve and a blender, well, you know why.

But our mothers were pretty cunning, and sometime during the vichyssoise era, someone came up with this "mock" vichyssoise recipe that I found scribbled on a card in my mother's recipe box. It doesn't have the leek flavor of a true vichyssoise, but when garnished with chopped chives, it's close. Still, this soup is awfully good and easy, doesn't need any cooking, and requires only a mixing bowl to prepare. That's my kind of "cooking."

SERVES 8 TO 10

2 (10-ounce) cans chicken broth
2 (10-ounce) cans cream of
   potato soup
2 (8-ounce) cartons sour cream

2 teaspoons frozen, diced onion
Chopped chives, for garnish
Cookware needed: large mixing
   bowl

Thoroughly combine all the ingredients, except the chives, and chill for several hours. Serve garnished with the chopped chives.

PREPARATION TIME: *6 to 7 minutes*
TOTAL TIME: *6 to 7 hours to chill*

"A circle of chairs is never provocative of good talk unless there is a table in the middle. In France when conversation was even more of an art than it is now they never rose at the end of a meal fearing to break the flow of thought with the flow of [the] bowl."

—LOUISE HALE,
*WE DISCOVER THE
OLD DOMINION,* 1916

Easy Entrées

HOW MANY TIMES have you complimented a delicious entrée only to have the cook tell you, "It's so easy. There's nothing to it."

"But there *is* something to it," you've thought, all the time knowing that deep down you would be *afraid* to try it.

Or maybe you're the one who orders salmon every time you eat out. Only a professional chef can prepare it, you've reasoned. Certainly you couldn't.

Well, it's time to shed those fears.

I myself, never fixed a pork tenderloin until one day when I dropped by to visit with my friend Charlotte Pennell, who was putting one in the oven. We talked so long that the roast was finished before we were! Charlotte carved a slice for me on the spot. It melted in my mouth. When I realized how sinfully simple pork tenderloin is to prepare—and how many ways it can be fixed, it became a regular at my house.

And as far as salmon goes—when I was young, all the cookbooks gave instructions for poaching a *whole* salmon, not just a couple of fillets. Why, it would have taken the two of us a month to finish off an 8-pound fish, and I didn't know enough just to ask for a smaller piece!

The message here is: Be brave. Remember, this chapter is named *Easy Entrées*.

Don't be afraid to try the entrée recipes that require only baking or poaching, such as pork tenderloin or salmon. They are like Jan Karon's favorite roasted chicken recipe in the Foreword. These entrées will cook by themselves while you tend to the other items on the menu.

"You see, we can't always do things the same way.
…If a favorite recipe calls for celery or other
seasoning, and it isn't on hand, we have our own
dried and crushed celery leaves in jars, or we grate
orange rinds, etc. as needed. We may not have the
same things on hand the next time we make
something, so we improvise."

—LILIAN BRITT HEINSOHN, *SOUTHERN PLANTATION*, 1962

Champagne Chicken

WHAT would we do without chicken? Actually, a better question is, how do you give chicken a distinctive flavor?

Dress up that everyday bird in an easy and succulent sauce made of cream and Champagne. It's a dish suitable for the gods.

This is one of the few recipes in this book that requires a little more time to prepare. But it's easy, and because you won't find these flavors in any already prepared sauce, everyone will think that you've been slaving in the kitchen for hours, instead of spending just a few minutes "assembling" the dish. Plan to serve it over wild rice or noodles.

SERVES 6 TO 12, DEPENDING ON APPETITES AND THE ACCOMPANIMENTS

Sage Advice

Don't scrimp on the cream. This is a rich, flavorful sauce and one that blends beautifully with broccoli or asparagus when those vegetables are served as an accompaniment on the plate.

4 tablespoons butter

6 whole chicken breasts, fresh or frozen, but uncooked

3 cups dry (brut) Champagne

1 quart heavy cream

1 (4- or 6-ounce) can or jar sliced mushrooms, drained

1 cup frozen, diced onion

4 to 5 dried whole bay leaves

½ teaspoon dried thyme

1 teaspoon nutmeg

Cookware needed: skillet with a lid

Place 3 tablespoons of the butter, the chicken breasts, and 2 cups of the Champagne in a covered skillet. Cook over medium-low heat for 15 to 20 minutes.

Turn the chicken, baste well, and continue to cook it for another 15 to 20 minutes, or until it is golden brown.

Remove the chicken and wrap it in a piece of heavy aluminum foil to keep warm while you prepare the sauce.

Blend the cream into the liquid in the skillet.

Add the mushrooms, onions, bay leaves, and thyme. When the mixture begins to bubble ever so slightly, turn the heat to low and simmer the sauce for about 15 minutes, stirring occasionally.

At the end of this time, remove the bay leaves and add the remaining tablespoon of butter, the remaining cup of Champagne, and the nutmeg. Stir, and return the chicken breasts to the skillet to warm in this succulent sauce while you prepare the plates.

PREPARATION TIME: *15 minutes*
TOTAL TIME: *approximately 1 hour*

Chicken à la Simon and Garfunkel

MINISTERS' WIVES must have an endless supply of delicious, quick, easy-to-prepare recipes. Considering all the entertaining that they are called on to do and the frequency with which they have to take a dish to church functions—well, it's a necessity.

But where do *they* get them? And what if you *are* the minister—*and* a woman?

This is the case for Becky Powell, Assistant Minister of The First Presbyterian Church in Danville, Virginia. When in need, Becky called on her aunt, Bea Garrett, a caterer in Richmond, Virginia. Aunt Bea gave her this handy recipe, but doesn't have a clue where it got its name.

Do you? Read the ingredients: parsley, sage, rosemary, and thyme. It's the name of the old Simon and Garfunkel hit.

SERVES 4

½ stick margarine or butter

2 tablespoons chopped parsley

¼ teaspoon dried sage

¼ teaspoon dried rosemary

¼ teaspoon dried thyme

4 ready-to-serve grilled chicken breasts

1 cup dry white wine

4 slices mozzarella cheese

2 cups cooked instant rice (½ cup per person)

Cookware needed: saucepan, skillet with a lid

Melt the butter in a small saucepan.

Add the herbs and stir. (This step can also be done in a measuring cup in the microwave.)

Lay the chicken breasts in a skillet and pour the herb mixture over them.

Cover the skillet and simmer on low heat for 10 to 15 minutes.

Add the wine and cook another 10 or so minutes, until the flavors have blended.

Lay the slices of mozzarella cheese on top of the chicken.

Cover the skillet just long enough to melt the cheese, approximately 4 minutes.

Serve over white rice, pouring the remaining pan sauce over the chicken and prepared rice.

PREPARATION TIME: *10 minutes*
TOTAL TIME: *30 minutes*

Chicken Marsala

SO MUCH FOR THE OLD RULE: white wine with white meat, red wine with red meat. It is well known that tastes truly do complement one another, and it can be vitally important to blend the grape with the meal. Perhaps it is because I am hardly a wine expert that I, personally, belong to the school that says, eat what you like, drink what you like—and red wines are usually my choice.

This recipe is one instance where the flavor of a little red wine greatly enhances the mild taste of the chicken. And by using ready-to-serve flavored chicken strips, this entrée can be prepared in just a few minutes.

SERVES 4 TO 6

2 tablespoons olive oil

½ cup frozen, diced onion

1 clove garlic, or ½ teaspoon prepared garlic

1 (4-ounce) can sliced mushrooms

2 tablespoons flour

½ cup Marsala wine

1 ½ cups red table wine

2 (10-ounce) packages ready-to-serve (fully cooked, breaded) Italian, or herbed chicken breast strips

Cookware needed: skillet

The Finishing Touch

Good served either on top of, or next to, pecan rice. Be sure to spoon up liberal amounts of the tasty Marsala sauce over the chicken for color and flavor.

In a skillet large enough to hold all the ingredients, heat the olive oil and sauté the onion and garlic for approximately 3 minutes. Add the mushrooms and sauté another 2 minutes, tossing lightly.

Sprinkle the onion and mushrooms with the flour, blending well.

Gradually add the 2 wines, stir well, and simmer on low heat for 15 minutes.

Add the chicken strips and heat thoroughly on medium-low for approximately 10 minutes.

PREPARATION TIME: *Approximately 10 minutes*
TOTAL TIME: *30 minutes*

Easy Chicken Tetrazzini

IN MY storehouse of memories of culinary delights is the wonderful turkey tetrazzini that Virginia Vincent, one of Mother's lifelong friends, made. Whether we ate it at the Vincents' house, or she brought it as a casserole to our house for a potluck supper—any time, any place, it was one of my favorites.

And with good reason. When made the old-fashioned way, it took hours to prepare—beginning with roasting a turkey (usually around the holidays) so there'd be leftovers for the tetrazzini. By using ready-to-serve chicken and other modern convenience foods, tetrazzini is now an easy-to-prepare treat any time of the year.

SERVES 6 TO 8

¾ cup frozen, diced combo of onion and green pepper

¼ cup chopped celery (optional)

1 tablespoon butter

2 tablespoons diced pimiento

1 (10-ounce) can cream of mushroom soup

1 (10-ounce) package ready-to-serve unflavored chicken pieces

1 box chicken and noodle dinner

1 cup herbed stuffing (crumbled), not croutons

4 ounces Cheddar cheese, grated

Cookware needed: large skillet, baking dish or casserole

Sage Advice

The celery adds a lot of crunch and flavor to this dish, even though it takes a little extra time and effort to chop. Rather than leave it out, remember to pick some up from the salad bar at the grocery store. Or, substitute a can of chopped water chestnuts (drained) from your well-stocked pantry.

Sauté the onion, green pepper, and celery in the butter over medium heat until tender and transparent.

Add the diced pimiento, soup, chicken, and chicken and noodle dinner and stir to combine.

Turn the mixture into a greased 3-quart baking dish or casserole.

Combine the stuffing and cheese and sprinkle the mixture on top of the chicken.

Bake at 350 degrees for 30 minutes.

PREPARATION TIME: *10 to 12 minutes*
TOTAL TIME: *approximately 45 minutes*

Cranberry-Sauce Chicken

Sage Advice

If desired, assemble the recipe in advance and refrigerate until ready to cook later in the day.

"**YOU** absolutely have to put in the pretty chicken dish!" Judie Bennett exclaimed as we piled my suitcases into the back of her SUV in the parking lot of the Civic Center in Beaumont, Texas, where I'd just given a talk.

"Yes, yes!" echoed her good friend Susan Kent, who was along for the ride and the fun. "It's just beautiful."

"You mean 'lovely,'" Judie Bennett corrected her. "That's what Lady Jan would say. 'Lovely. It's lovely.'"

"Who's Lady Jan? What chicken dish? What makes it so pretty...I mean, lovely?" I asked my two new friends.

Seems Lady Jan is Susan's sister, who married a real-life English Lord. The chicken dish is this easy chicken, and it's the cranberries that make it so lovely and, I quickly add, delicious.

Put it on your must-try list. It will become an instant hit, especially when you learn that you can assemble it hours, or even a day ahead.

SERVES 6 TO 8

The
Finishing Touch

Surely you've come up with this one yourself by now. For a festive, trouble-free dinner, serve the chicken with rice and your favorite green vegetable accompaniment—perfect during the Thanksgiving or Christmas season.

8 boneless chicken breast halves, frozen or fresh

Garlic powder

1 (8-ounce) bottle Russian dressing

1 (2-ounce) envelope Lipton's dry onion soup mix

1 (16-ounce) can cranberry sauce, the whole berry variety

½ cup water

Cookware needed: baking dish or casserole, mixing bowl

Preheat the oven to 350 degrees.

Place the chicken breasts in a greased baking dish and sprinkle them lightly with garlic powder.

Combine the Russian dressing, dry onion soup mix, cranberry sauce, and water and pour the mixture over the chicken.

Bake for 1 hour, basting occasionally to ensure that the chicken absorbs the delicious cranberry flavor.

PREPARATION TIME: *10 minutes*
TOTAL TIME: *a little more than 1 hour*

Russian Apricot Chicken

THERE ARE LOTS of recipes that make you say to yourself when you read them, "Why didn't I think of that?"

This is not one of those. For who would ever dream of combining Russian dressing and apricot preserves? Well, someone did, and the result is mouth watering, and easy to make.

SERVES 6

6 to 8 fresh or frozen chicken breasts, thawed

1 (8-ounce) bottle Russian salad dressing

1 envelope dry onion soup mix

1 (10-ounce) jar apricot preserves

Cookware needed: covered baking dish or casserole

Preheat the oven to 350 degrees.

Place the chicken in a baking dish.

Combine the other ingredients, and pour the mixture over the chicken.

Cover and bake for 45 minutes. Uncover and cook for an additional 15 minutes, or until browned.

PREPARATION TIME: *5 to 10 minutes*
TOTAL TIME: *1 hour 10 minutes*

The
Finishing Touch

Of course, this is one of those chicken dishes that's just fine served over rice. But it is equally good with pecan rice (page 180) served on the side or a box of dressing "dressed up" with the addition of pecans or pine nuts to give it an extra crunch.

Suzy's Microwave BBQ Chicken

SUZY BARILE, a North Carolina writer friend of mine, cooks a mean barbeque chicken. The recipe is one that goes back a couple of generations in her family—well, sort of. When you read Suzy's story, you'll realize that every generation looks for shortcuts to help them pass treasured mealtime traditions down through the years.

Dear Emyl...One of my favorite meals when I was growing up was my mom's BBQ chicken served with white rice and corn on the cob. Looking back, it wasn't a difficult meal that she prepared, and her family history explains why: She grew up in Orlando, Florida, in the days when the city was considered a part of the "Old South." Her family had a full-time cook, Mamie.

Mamie prepared all the family's meals, even working Saturday morning to fix the roast or ham or whatever the family was having for Sunday dinner. I have no recollection as to whether my grandmother could cook. With someone else to prepare the family's meals, however, Mom didn't learn to cook until after she graduated from college and married.

By then it was the early 1950s, and "instant" rice and potato flakes, canned soups, and frozen vegetables were making their way onto supermarket shelves. As a novice cook, Mom must have been thrilled! It's for that reason that many of her recipes reflect the availability of those convenience foods. Perhaps those "instant" foods came in handiest after a long day spent meeting the needs of seven children.

I can certainly understand the allure. When my daughter, Jennifer, was in elementary school and I was a single mom working full time at a community newspaper, it was tough for me to get home in the evening, get her settled doing homework, and still have dinner prepared quickly enough to suit my seemingly starving child.

That's when I took my Mom's BBQ chicken recipe a step further, adapting it for cooking in a microwave oven. It doesn't quite have her special touch, but when served with the "juice" poured over white rice as she used to do, and corn or sweet peas added to the menu, my daughter is in heaven. To her, it's still Granny's BBQ chicken!

Mom used to brown a 2-pound cut-up, frying chicken in ¼ cup of shortening, add 1 can of tomato soup (canned tomatoes work, as well), ¼ cup of pickle relish, ¼ cup chopped onion, and 1 teaspoon Worcestershire sauce, then reduce heat to simmer, cover, and cook for 1 hour.

I do it this way:

SERVES 4 TO 6

1 cup ketchup

1 cup mustard

1 cup molasses

1 chicken, precut

Cookware needed: mixing bowl, microwave-safe baking dish or casserole

Combine the ketchup, mustard, and molasses in a bowl.

Place the precut chicken pieces (from a whole chicken) in a microwaveable dish.

Pour the sauce over the chicken.

Cover the dish with wax paper and cook in a microwave oven on high for 18 minutes, turning the dish every 6 minutes for even cooking.

PREPARATION TIME: *7 to 10 minutes*
TOTAL TIME: *approximately 30 minutes*

Sage Advice

To Suzy's instructions, I'll add that by using the precut whole chicken, you're carrying on the look and feel of the original, old-fashioned recipe. You'd lose that if you used all boneless breasts, something our moms and grannies didn't have at their disposal.

Pepper and Mushroom Chicken Delight

THIS CHICKEN entrée is one of those dishes that is sinfully easy to prepare. Further, you can serve it over rice or with a side of potatoes, pasta, or noodles as a starch. Add a simple green salad with a dressing of your choice, or, if you're tired of salad and your taste buds are craving peas, broccoli, or asparagus, fix those. With all these choices, there's no excuse to not have dinner taken care of.

SERVES 6 TO 8

½ to 1 teaspoon prepared garlic, or 2 or 3 garlic cloves, minced

1 cup frozen red pepper, onion, and mushroom combo (Bird's Eye makes this), or make the mixture from individual packages

¼ cup olive oil

2 (14-ounce) cans Italian-flavored tomatoes

8 already grilled chicken breasts

Salt, pepper, and dried oregano to taste

Cookware needed: skillet, with lid

Sauté the garlic, pepper, onion, and mushrooms in the olive oil until the vegetables are lightly browned.

Add the Italian-flavored tomatoes and simmer on medium-low heat to blend the flavors, approximately 5 minutes.

Add the already grilled chicken breasts and continue to simmer for 10 to 15 minutes. Adjust the seasoning with additional salt, pepper, and oregano, if desired.

PREPARATION TIME: *10 minutes*
TOTAL TIME: *25 minutes*

Timeless Chicken

THERE are times when even food writers need help, and this was one of them! I had agreed to introduce a speaker at a 4 PM event, and, without thinking, had invited several people to a sit-down dinner in his honor at 6 PM.

I wanted it to be a lovely occasion, but time was working against me. Why, I'd be lucky to get home and put on fresh lipstick before the guests arrived. This truly had to be a do-ahead event.

The more I looked through my supply of recently purchased cookbooks for a special entrée, the worse it got. All the recipes ended with "serve immediately." Then I remembered a company dish that once had been regular fare at my parties.

When I found the recipe, the page was splattered with food stains—proof of its success.

I made the recipe in 2000 the same way I had made it in 1962—down to the last ingredient. And my guests enjoyed it just as much as they had thirty-eight years earlier—down to the last morsel.

That's when I decided to name it Timeless Chicken.

SERVES 6 TO 8

1 (10-ounce) can cream of mushroom soup

1 (8-ounce) carton sour cream

8 to 10 chicken breast halves, frozen or fresh

8 to 10 thin slices of ham, prosciutto, or dried chipped beef

½ cup dry sherry

1 can mushrooms, drained

Paprika

Cookware needed: mixing bowl, rectangular baking dish or casserole

Preheat the oven to 350 degrees.

Combine the mushroom soup and sour cream. Spoon a small amount in the bottom of a baking dish and spread it out to cover.

Sprinkle the chicken breasts with a little paprika.

Wrap a piece of the ham, prosciutto, or chipped beef around each breast.

Place the wrapped breasts in the baking dish in a single layer.

Add the sherry and mushrooms to the remaining soup and sour cream mixture. Pour this over the chicken.

Bake 1 to 1 ½ hours until bubbly and crusty around the sides.

PREPARATION TIME: *10 minutes*
TOTAL TIME: *approximately 1 ½ hours*

Sage Advice

Use the saltiest ham you can for this dish. That's a Virginia, Smithfield, or Country ham, in my part of the world. What you don't want is a sweet, honey-baked ham. That's why the choices of prosciutto or chipped beef (right out of a jar) are offered as alternatives.

The Finishing Touch

Serve with a wild rice mix to dress the meal up a little more; otherwise, long-grain rice is just fine. But this is a "white" entrée, so be sure to serve it with a colorful accompaniment such as green beans garnished with red peppers, or well-seasoned zucchini, spinach, or asparagus garnished with pimiento or small tomatoes, sliced or quartered.

Baked Rainbow or Brook Trout

FRESH TROUT is the best reason I know of to go to the mountains. Years ago, that was the only time lots of people could get trout. Of course, these days we can pop into the local grocery store and pick up good trout, even if it's not fresh out of a brook.

Though I love simple, pan-cooked trout lightly seasoned with lemon, it can be hard to watch the skillet when you're chasing the kids, finishing up a phone call, or just tending to the rest of your dinner menu. Not having to stand by the stove makes this quick, oven-baked trout a handy, and good, fish entrée.

SERVES 6

Sage Advice
When I gave a friend this recipe, she asked why I didn't use the prepared Roasted Garlic Parmesan Cheese Sauce. It's because I think the garlic is a little heavy for the delicate flavor of trout.

¼ cup chopped parsley
¼ cup chopped chives
Salt and pepper, to taste
6 to 8 dressed trout
¼ cup Alfredo sauce of your liking

¼ cup grated Parmesan cheese, plus additional for cracker crumbs (optional)
½ cup fine cracker crumbs
Cookware needed: baking dish or casserole, mixing bowl

Preheat the oven to 375 degrees.

Sprinkle the parsley and chives over the bottom of a buttered shallow baking dish large enough to hold the fish in a single layer.

Salt and pepper the fish, and place them on the bed of parsley and chives.

Combine the sauce and ¼ cup of grated Parmesan cheese, and gently spread the mixture on the fish.

Sprinkle the cracker crumbs (to which you may add additional cheese, if desired) over the fish.

Bake the trout for 15 minutes, or until it is easily flaked with a fork.

PREPARATION TIME: *5 to 10 minutes*
TOTAL TIME: *25 minutes*

Crab Imperial

COOKS, especially those with sterling reputations, sometimes have to cross their fingers behind their backs when asked if a particularly delicious item is "homemade." Of course, polite guests really shouldn't ask.

Charlotte Pennell, whose culinary talents put most of us to shame, was caught in such a predicament when she served this adaptation of an old Charleston, South Carolina, recipe (or receipt, as they called recipes back in the eighteenth century). Seems that a particularly persistent guest kept raving about this Crab Imperial and insisting that Charlotte tell where she had bought the fresh crabmeat. Luckily, the store where she bought the canned crabmeat also had a fresh fish department.

This recipe is a sure winner for a special company dinner. Yes, crabmeat is expensive, but this is a special dish.

SERVES 6

4 (4-ounce) cans lump crabmeat
   (Orleans Lump)
½ teaspoon Worcestershire sauce
1 tablespoon horseradish
¼ teaspoon salt
¼ stick softened butter

1 beaten egg
½ cup mayonnaise
1 tablespoon sherry
4 ounces mild Cheddar cheese,
   grated
Cookware needed: mixing bowl,
   baking dish or casserole

Rinse the crabmeat under cold water and gently press it dry between paper towels or in a strainer.

In a mixing bowl, combine all the other ingredients except the cheese, then add the crabmeat.

Refrigerate the mixture for 30 to 60 minutes. During this time, preheat the oven to 300 degrees.

After it has chilled, divide the mixture among individual scallop shells or ramekins, or turn it into a baking dish or casserole.

Sprinkle the cheese on top and bake for 30 minutes.

Accept the compliments graciously.

The
Finishing Touch

The individual, inexpensive scallop shells available in kitchen stores add a special touch to Crab Imperial. And to dress up your dinner plates further, place the shell on a lettuce leaf just before serving. Boston or "living" lettuce is usually the right size and shape to curl up around the shell.

PREPARATION TIME: *15 minutes*
TOTAL TIME: *about 1 hour and 30 minutes*

Crabmeat in Shells

Sage Advice

Carolyn suggests that capers (2 to 3 heaping tablespoons) and frozen petite peas (½ to ⅔ cup) can be added, as well. If adding the peas, cook them in boiling water for only about 1 to 2 minutes before draining and combining with the crabmeat mixture.

YOU KNOW it's going to be a good recipe when a friend is so anxious to tell you about it that she calls you from her car phone! Grace Litzenberg did just that as she was leaving Greensboro, North Carolina, after having breakfast with her cousin, Carolyn Hill Hesselbach.

Carolyn has lived in the Grand Cayman Islands for some twenty-five-plus years, but as a constant reminder of her North Carolina roots, she prepares this delicious crabmeat entrée in serving shells from the North Carolina coast.

Put away your fears that the recipe will call for fresh crabmeat, because even though the Caymans are surrounded by water, fresh seafood, especially crab, can be as hard to come by there as it is here, so Carolyn uses canned crabmeat. But, she confessed, she does use fresh parsley, which she grows in her small garden. Luckily for us, fresh parsley is now available in the produce section of most grocery stores.

SERVES 6

The Finishing Touch

Don't forget to garnish with a pretty sprig of parsley and even a lemon curl or slice. This dish can be served in store-bought pastry puffs, if you don't have the shells or ramekins.

¼ cup diced celery

2 tablespoons butter

Several sprigs fresh parsley

2 (6-ounce) cans crabmeat drained

⅔ cup mayonnaise

Juice of half a lemon

Salt and pepper, to taste

½ to 1 cup Parmesan cheese, grated

Cookware needed: mixing bowl, individual serving shells

Preheat the oven to 350 degrees.

Sauté the celery in the butter, then add the parsley.

Remove from heat and combine with the crabmeat, the mayonnaise, the lemon juice, and salt and pepper, to taste.

Put into individual shells or ramekins and top with an ample amount of grated Parmesan cheese.

Bake for 15 minutes.

PREPARATION TIME: *15 minutes*
TOTAL TIME: *30 minutes*

Navy Wives Shrimp Curry

I'M TOLD that this shrimp dish got its name because Navy wives served it so frequently. The use of curry and fresh seafood certainly qualifies it as the sort of dish that these ladies would have concocted when living in a foreign port. Add to that the tradition of serving "toppings" along with the dish, and this is clearly a variation on the traditional East Indian curry.

It's a tasty dish and one that's easy to make, now that cream of shrimp soup is once again on the grocery store shelves. (For a few years, it was very hard to find.) If you can't find the shrimp, substitute canned lobster bisque. That seems to be in most stores.

To guarantee that you're getting the plumpest, most tender shrimp, consider purchasing ready-to-eat shrimp from the grocery store. Otherwise, rely on fully dressed, tails-off, frozen shrimp.

SERVES 6

¼ cup frozen, chopped onions

3 teaspoons (or more to taste) curry powder

1 tablespoon butter or olive oil

1 (10-ounce) can cream of shrimp soup

1 cup sour cream or half-and-half

8 ounces (or more) cooked shrimp

Cookware needed: skillet

If using frozen shrimp, allow them to defrost.

Sauté the onion and curry powder in the butter till the onion is tender.

Add the soup and stir, then the sour cream or half-and-half, and stir again.

Add the shrimp and cook just until they are heated thoroughly—3 to 5 minutes.

Serve the shrimp curry over hot rice (the instant variety, of course) with the following condiments, or others of your choice, set out in individual bowls, each with its own spoon:

- chopped tomato
- chopped green pepper
- chopped cucumbers
- chopped scallions
- raisins soaked in brandy
- chutney
- grated coconut
- chopped nuts

PREPARATION TIME: *15 minutes*
TOTAL TIME: *15 minutes plus, depending on your choice of condiments*

Sage Advice

Don't let the list of condiments frighten you off with visions of chopping and dicing. Much of this work has already been done for you. Think about it. Many of the items can be found in any well-stocked salad bar. You can open a can of chopped tomato and green pepper and drain off some of the extra liquid. Or you can quickly defrost frozen green peppers by spreading them out on a paper towel while you prepare the curried shrimp. Even coconut comes already grated these days, and there is a great variety of canned, chopped nuts.

The Finishing Touch

Tart, citrusy, fresh lime juice is the perfect finishing touch for this creamy curried seafood dish. Garnish individual plates with large lime wedges, or for a buffet, include a bowl of lime wedges with the condiments. And for the easiest centerpiece ever, fill a bowl with whole limes and lemons and stick in sprays of darker greenery gathered from shrubs.

Corned Beef

The
Finishing Touch

Say the words "corned beef" and everyone thinks St. Patrick's Day or New England boiled dinner (especially if your father was from Massachusetts, like mine). Either way, the traditional accompaniments are boiled white potatoes and cabbage, sliced into wedges. These are quickly prepared by dropping them into the pot with the corned beef about 30 minutes before the end of the cooking time. Add fresh chopped parsley for the luck of the Irish.

AT THE TOP of my list of easy-to-prepare, but usually-not-in-your-repertoire of quick entrées is corned beef.

I can't count how many times people have asked, "Hhmmmm, what are you cooking?" only to reply, "I've never tried that," when I've told them it was corned beef.

All it takes is water, beef, spices, and time. If you're a Crock-Pot cook, this is an ideal meat with which to vary your usual fare. And if you're one of those cooks who loves the smell of good food, but you don't like to spend a lot of time in the kitchen, corned beef is just the ticket.

Do try it. It is very good when served with an onion casserole (try the Vidalia Onion Casserole, page 166), a vegetable dish, and good bread—especially on a weekend, since there is usually some left over for another busy day.

SERVES 12 TO 16,
BUT YOU'LL WANT THE LEFTOVERS FOR SANDWICHES,
SO DON'T SKIMP WHEN YOU'RE COOKING.

2 onions, peeled and halved

2 to 3 celery stalks, or ½ cup diced celery from the salad bar

3 heaping tablespoons pickling spices (the spices from the package of corned beef, plus more from a jar of pickling spices)

4 quarts water

1 (4-pound) corned beef, with spices included in the packaging

Cookware needed: Crock-Pot or large (8-quart) covered pot

Put the onions, celery, and spices in the water; cover and bring to a boil.

Add the meat, cover and, when the water has returned to a boil, turn the heat down to low.

Simmer for approximately 4 hours, or until the center of the corned beef is easily pierced with a long, sharp fork. Check occasionally to see if more water is needed in the pot.

PREPARATION TIME: *15 minutes*
TOTAL TIME: *approximately 4 hours, 15 minutes*

Old-Fashioned Pot Roast

MY STEPDAUGHTER, ERIKA, can be hard to please at mealtime, but it's really not her fault. She inherited her picky eating habits from her father, my husband.

Trying to be a good stepmother, I always ask her what she'd like to eat when she's coming in from graduate school. Knowing that I'm not going to settle for the usual "pizza" request, she answers, "How about one of your good pot roasts?"

That's the same answer I get when I ask other young folks who are coming to dinner what they'd like to eat.

It makes sense. Few young folks will take the time to cook a roast. And if they did, chances are the leftovers would grow mold in their refrigerators. One day, though, things will be different.

So, for Erika, and others like her, here's how to cook your own pot roast and make it flavorful by using prepared seasoning mixes right off the grocery store shelf. You won't cook it today, and maybe not even this year or next. But you'll have it on record for when you do need it, because you won't find this recipe in today's nouvelle cuisine or gourmet cookbooks.

YIELDS 3-4 SERVINGS PER POUND

2 tablespoons olive oil
1 (3-to-5 pound) chuck roast
1 cup water
1 medium onion, halved or quartered
2 stalks celery, or an ample handful-size serving of pieces from the salad bar
5 or 6 dried bay leaves
1 envelope seasoning mix (see *Sage Advice*)
⅔ cup red wine

Cookware needed: covered skillet or heavy 4-quart pot

Heat the oil in a heavy skillet over medium-high heat.

Sear the roast quickly on all four sides, if you wish. (Some cooks insist on searing roasts before cooking them to hold in the juices; others don't.)

Add the water, onion, celery, and bay leaves. Cover and bring to a boil.

Thoroughly mix the envelope of seasoning with the red wine. Add the mixture to the pot.

Turn the heat to low and allow the roast to simmer for 2 ½ to 3 hours or longer, depending on how tender you want the meat to be.

PREPARATION TIME: *10 minutes*
TOTAL TIME: *approximately 3 hours*

Sage Advice

There is no end to the variety of seasoning mixes you can use to tenderize and flavor a basic pot roast. When making your selection, think about the flavor you want the roast to have. For example, you can use a fajita mix if you want a spicy roast, while a meat loaf-flavoring mix will give you more of a "roast" taste. Actually, two of my favorites are Knorr's Coq Au Vin sauce and Knorr's Peppercorn Gravy. The point is to urge you to try various mixes or try turning to your pantry shelf. A can of onion soup or cream of mushroom soup—even a bottle of ketchup or some barbeque sauce—will do. Brown sugar, vinegar, Worcestershire sauce, soy sauce, or teriyaki sauce are other possibilities. Before the days of mixes and soups, cooks prepared the roast with onions, wine, and, if available, celery and bay leaves. That combo works just as well today as it did a hundred years ago.

Chipped Beef Deluxe

THOUGH I find it hard to believe, I used to push the plate aside when Mother served chipped beef. It must have been the name, surely not the taste. These days, there are times when I absolutely crave a hearty serving of chipped beef with a fresh, juicy tomato on the side as the perfect complement.

Chipped beef is a cinch to fix, thanks to Stouffer's, and so good that I serve it to company—most of whom used to push their plates aside when their mothers served it, too. To dress up this old standby, try this recipe.

SERVES 6

2 boxes frozen, creamed chipped beef

¼ cup (or more) sliced Spanish olives with pimiento

½ teaspoon Angostura bitters

Pepper, to taste

Cookware needed: medium saucepan or microwave-safe bowl

The Finishing Touch

Older cookbooks always say "serve over toast points." But English muffins, waffles, noodles, or even rice work equally well.

Follow the package directions for cooking the creamed chipped beef on the stovetop.

When done, open the packages and pour the contents into a microwave-safe serving bowl.

Stir in the olives, bitters, and pepper, to taste.

Cover with plastic wrap, being sure to leave one corner open to vent, and microwave for 30 to 60 seconds. Or, if you prepared the frozen creamed chipped beef in a microwave oven, stir in the olives, bitters, and pepper, to taste, and microwave for 20 seconds.

PREPARATION TIME: *3 to 5 minutes*
TOTAL TIME: *15 minutes*

Easy Beef Stroganoff

FOOD is like fashion. What goes around comes around.

For years, no one even mentioned Beef Stroganoff. The rage was all Beef Wellington or London Broil or Beef Medallions.

Suddenly, Beef Stroganoff is beginning to make a comeback at dinner parties and even in some restaurants. It's about time.

This long-ago favorite is as good as ever, and much, much less time-consuming to make than it used to be. And for the generation that missed it— it's a brand-new taste!

SERVES 6

1 tablespoon butter

½ cup frozen, diced onion

1 (4-ounce) can sliced
   mushrooms, drained

½ teaspoon prepared garlic, or 1
   garlic clove, minced

2 (17-ounce) packages Hormel
   Always Tender Beef Tips

1 ½ cups sour cream

½ cup dry white wine

Cookware needed: skillet
   with lid

Melt the butter in a heavy skillet.

Add the onion, mushrooms, and garlic, and sauté gently over medium-high heat for 3 to 4 minutes.

Gradually add the beef tips, blending them with the vegetables.

When the mixture is beginning to bubble, lower the heat to a simmer, cover, and cook for about 6 to 7 minutes longer.

In a large measuring cup, combine the sour cream and white wine.

Add the wine mixture to the meat and simmer just until blended, about 5 to 6 minutes.

PREPARATION TIME: *5 minutes*
TOTAL TIME: *20 minutes*

The
Finishing Touch

The traditional way to serve Beef Stroganoff is over wide egg noodles, but rice does just as well. Be sure to add a colorful garnish. Sprinkle the serving platter with freshly snipped chives, dill or parsley, or, if you're preparing individual servings, arrange a few herb leaves and cherry tomatoes on the side of each plate before you dish up the Stroganoff.

Beef Tenderloin

FORGET "a rose is a rose is a rose." A tenderloin is a tenderloin is a tenderloin. Whether it's beef or pork, this cut of meat can't be beat for tenderness or ease of cooking. No wonder it's becoming a popular meat during the holidays for families where the tradition of eating a homecooked meal is important, but the cook is pressed for time.

In fact, one of the beauties of a tenderloin is that it can be served at a cocktail party, dinner party, or holiday event. It's good any time.

But if the tenderloin falls short, it's in the flavor category. Without a little help from spices or seasoning, the meat can be bland. That's where marinades get to show off.

There are countless delicious ready-to-use marinades, but when you consider how simple it is to stir together a few ingredients for a more distinctive taste, you may want to go that route.

The number of servings will vary greatly, depending on how thin the meat is sliced and how large a tenderloin you cook. A general rule of thumb is to allow ⅛ to ¼ pound per person. Thus, a 3-pound tenderloin will yield from 9 to 12 servings.

1 (2-to-3 pound) beef tenderloin
For marinade:
1 cup bourbon
½ cup soy sauce

½ cup brown sugar

Cookware needed: rectangular baking dish or casserole, mixing bowl

Place the tenderloin in a baking dish.

Thoroughly combine the bourbon, soy sauce, and brown sugar and pour the mixture over the tenderloin.

Cover the dish with aluminum foil and marinate the meat at room temperature for 3 to 4 hours, or in the refrigerator overnight. Turn the meat occasionally, so the full tenderloin will be immersed in the marinade. (If the meat was refrigerated after marinating, allow it to sit, uncovered at room temperature to take the chill off, or for about 1 hour, before cooking it.)

Preheat the oven to 425 degrees.

Baste the meat well before cooking and bake it, uncovered, in the marinade for 35 to 45 minutes.

For a larger tenderloin, weighing 4 to 6 pounds, increase the cooking time to 50 to 60 minutes.

(These cooking times are for a rare tenderloin. Of course, the time can be extended for a more well-done meat, but almost everyone agrees that tenderloin tastes best when it is pink, not brown, in the middle.)

Remove the pan from the oven, baste the tenderloin with the marinade and juices one last time, and allow it to rest for at least 10 to 15 minutes before carving. Or, allow it to cool, then refrigerate it for 2 to 3 hours before carving, and serve it chilled. Chilled, sliced beef tenderloin is an elegant addition to any cocktail party.

PREPARATION TIME: *10 minutes*
TOTAL TIME: *from 45 to 60 plus minutes,*
depending on cooking time

The
Finishing Touch

Garnish your serving platter with parsley, fresh herbs, cherry or grape tomatoes—even lemon slices—whatever you have on hand to add color and a little pizzazz to this delicacy.

City-Style, Country-Style Steak

IT'S THE OLD SAYING that necessity is the mother of invention.

When Gene Brown couldn't find a recipe for Country-Style Steak, that old, delicious and reliable standby in many a Southern household, he decided it was time to share his. But not before jazzing it up a little.

Now, thanks to Gene, we Southerners will no longer be forced to go to our favorite "down home" diner or restaurant to order this favorite. And, if you're from another region of the county, Gene's addition of red wine takes the "country" out of the name and makes it acceptable anywhere! That's why we've renamed it City-Style, Country-Style Steak.

SERVES 4

2 tablespoons vegetable oil

4 pieces cube steak

Flour for dredging

Salt and freshly ground pepper, to taste

¼ to ½ cup dry red wine, or Madeira (optional)

1 (14-ounce) can beef broth

Cookware needed: large skillet with lid

While the oil is heating over medium to medium-high heat, dredge the steaks in flour, salt, and pepper. (I put a liberal amount of these 3 ingredients in a large plastic bag for this process. It keeps the flour from getting all over the countertop and floor.)

Shake the excess flour off each steak while holding over the plastic bag, then brown them on both sides in the oil. Remove steaks to a plate.

Splash in the wine and, using a wooden spoon, scrape the brown bits off the bottom of the pan, blending them into the wine.

Add the can of beef broth and, when the liquid returns to a gentle boil, put the steaks back in the skillet, cover, turn the heat to low, and allow them to simmer for an hour, or until very tender.

When the meat is done, if the liquid is a little too "runny," remove the skillet cover, put the meat on a plate and cover with aluminum foil to keep warm. Turn up the heat to medium and let the liquid cook down to the desired consistency.

Return the meat to the pan for just a couple of minutes to reheat, and then serve.

PREPARATION TIME: *15 minutes*

TOTAL TIME: *1 hour and 15 minutes, or until the meat is tender, which may vary according to the meat itself*

That Other White Meat

There's not much you can do to mess up pork (or ham). It lends itself equally well to tomato or cream sauces, fruits or vegetables, potatoes or rice.

Many pork recipes can be cooked either in a skillet on the stove top, or in a baking dish in the oven. Further, once you've assembled any one of these dishes, you can leave it alone to do its own thing—short of letting it burn. I guess I think of pork chops the same way I think of cream cheese. Whatever you do to it, chances are it will turn out just fine.

On top of those advantages, ham has long been a ready-to-serve favorite. Canned deviled ham, ham products like Spam, and even fully cooked canned hams have been around since the first part of the twentieth century. The recent addition of fully cooked ribs, already diced ham cubes, and even roast pork make the cook's job even simpler. In many instances, you can pull one of these products out of the refrigerator or freezer, combine it with whatever else you have on hand, and put together a delicious entrée.

To get you started, here are some of my own and other cooks' favorites that use either ready-to-serve or fresh pork.

Sage Advice

Pork or ham? Most people call any cured or smoked pork "ham." But the reference books inform us that only the pig's hind leg is technically a ham. That still leaves a lot of delicious pork—the roasts, ribs, chops, tenderloins, and even bacon—to enjoy.

Pork Tenderloin with Sauerkraut

MY SON, Langdon, is a great cook. But his preference, as is true for lots of thirty-something guys, is for the grill. I, on the other hand, am more of a kitchen cook.

There's another difference in our culinary preferences. He loves sauerkraut, as does his sister. I'm not really sure where they cultivated that taste, since I never fixed sauerkraut for the family when they were growing up.

But when he fixes pork tenderloin with sauerkraut and easy dumplings, I know why they like it so much, and wish I had known about this recipe earlier.

SERVES 6 TO 8

The **Finishing Touch**

Serve with baked apples or a spiced apple-sauce for a really easy **From Storebought to Homemade** *meal!*

1 (32-ounce) package sauerkraut, drained, with liquid reserved

1 (4-to-5-pound) pork tenderloin, sliced and tied

½ cup distilled white vinegar

For dumplings:

1 package frozen dumplings

2 quarts water

Cookware needed: skillet with lid, medium saucepan

Buy an already-sliced and tied pork tenderloin, or have the butcher slice and tie it for you (½-inch thick slices).

Spread ½ the drained sauerkraut in the bottom of a heavy skillet or a large saucepan.

Lay the tenderloin on this layer; then cover it with the remaining sauerkraut.

Add the sauerkraut liquid and the vinegar to the pan.

Cover, and bring to a boil; then simmer on medium-low heat for about 20 minutes or until done.

To prepare the dumplings, bring 2 quarts of water to a rolling boil. Drop the dumplings into the boiling water. They will rise to the top as they are done.

Remove the dumplings from the water with a slotted spoon and drop them into the pan with the tenderloin and sauerkraut. Cover the pan and simmer for 10 to 12 minutes.

PREPARATION TIME: *15 minutes*

TOTAL TIME: *40 to 45 minutes*

Apple-Kraut Pork Chops

FOR a slight variation on the basic Pork Tenderloin with Sauerkraut recipe, try this quick and easy dish.

SERVES 6 TO 8

1 (32-ounce) package sauerkraut, drained

1 (25-ounce) jar applesauce

6 to 8 pork medallions or chops

Cookware needed: baking dish or casserole

Line the bottom of a baking dish, large enough to hold the pork in a single layer, with all the sauerkraut.

Spoon the applesauce over the kraut and lay the pork on top.

Cover the pan and cook at 350 degrees for 1 hour, or until the chops are white in the center.

PREPARATION TIME: *5 minutes*
TOTAL TIME: *approximately 1 hour*

Sage Advice

For whatever reason, some people just don't like meat served on the bone. That pretty much eliminates pork chops and T-bone steaks. I, personally, love the bones and can be found sucking every last morsel of meat and juice off mine. But for those who do not share my enthusiasm, trimmed pork medallions are a perfectly good substitute to use in all these pork chop recipes.

Sweet and Sour Pork, American Style

LOOKING for a way to jazz up pork chops? It's hard to imagine anything easier than this way of cooking the "other white meat." You can select whatever type of chop you prefer—center cut, thin, thick—or even pork medallions. Further, this quick dish can be prepared on the stovetop (or, if you wish, in the oven). Of course, the cooking time will vary according to the cut of meat and the method you use to cook it, but the taste will always be pleasing.

SERVES 6 TO 8

2 tablespoons canola or peanut oil

½ cup frozen, diced onion

6 to 8 pork chops of your choice

½ of an 11-ounce jar sweet and sour sauce

Cookware needed: skillet with lid, or baking dish or casserole

The
Finishing Touch

Take a hint from our Asian friends and serve these with egg rolls, fried rice, glazed carrots, green pepper strips, and pineapple.

Heat the oil in a skillet large enough to hold the chops in a single layer. Add the onion and sauté for 3 to 4 minutes.

Add the chops to the skillet and brown them on both sides.

Pour the sweet and sour sauce over the chops, cover the pan, and simmer for approximately 30 minutes, or until done (when the chops are white in the center). (If you wish to bake the chops in the oven, do so covered at 350 degrees for approximately 1 hour, or until done.)

PREPARATION TIME: *10 minutes*
TOTAL TIME: *40 to 45 minutes, or 70 minutes if baked*

Pork and Cherry Supreme

MY FATHER was partial to anything with cherries. Every Christmas he received a box of chocolate-covered cherries from anyone who couldn't think of anything else to give him. Cherry preserves were his favorite. (Blueberry preserves were a close second.)

This preference even extended to furniture. He much preferred "cherry wood" to walnut or even mahogany, and he always attributed this love for the tree and its fruit to his New England childhood.

In his later years, when Mother could no longer do the cooking, I'd ask him if there was something he'd particularly like me to prepare, and he'd often answer, "pork chops." After a moment's pause, he'd add, "You know, the ones with the cherries."

To prepare this dish you have to make the sauce, but that takes only a minute, and it cooks while you're browning the pork, so it's next to no effort.

SERVES 4 TO 6

2 tablespoons canola oil

6 to 8 pork chops or tenderloin medallions

½ cup orange juice

1 teaspoon lemon juice

¼ teaspoon allspice

½ teaspoon cinnamon

¼ cup brown sugar

1 teaspoon butter

⅔ cup cherry preserves

Cookware needed: skillet with lid, medium saucepan

Heat the oil in a skillet large enough to hold the pork chops in a single layer and brown the chops on both sides.

Combine the juices, spices, brown sugar, butter, and cherry preserves in a sauce pan and cook over medium-low heat until the ingredients have blended, or for about 5 to 7 minutes. (Do not boil.)

Pour the sauce over the browned pork chops, cover, and cook on low or medium-low heat for approximately 30 minutes, or until done.

PREPARATION TIME: *10 to 15 minutes*
TOTAL TIME: *approximately 45 minutes*

The
Finishing Touch

Just like the Cranberry-Sauce Chicken on page 92, this is a pretty (or lovely, if you prefer) entrée to serve at holiday time as a nice change from the usual turkey or baked ham.

Everybody's Mother's Pork Chop Casserole

WHEN I was growing up, this pork-chop-and-creamed soup–based casserole was such a standby that it actually became known as "everybody's mother's pork chop casserole." But like so many of our mother's recipes that were quick and easy, it seems to have been forgotten or lost in our attempts to serve fancier fare.

It is still just as good as it was 50 years ago, and, take it from this grandmother, it's a real favorite with the up-and-coming kiddie generation. They'll even eat their green beans if you smother them in some of the "sauce" from the casserole (though you might have to pick out some of the larger bits of mushrooms for the very pickiest eaters!).

SERVES 6 TO 8

The
Finishing Touch

Serve this over rice, with something spicy, like a pickled peach or cinnamon-flavored apples, whose zingy flavor will really pick up the mellower pork and rice tastes.

1 (10-ounce) can cream of mushroom soup

Salt and pepper, to taste

6 to 8 pork chops or tenderloin medallions

Cookware needed: baking dish or casserole

Preheat the oven to 350 degrees.

Spoon enough of the mushroom soup into the bottom of a baking dish to cover it.

Salt and pepper the pork chops and place them on top of the soup.

Spoon the remaining soup over the pork and cover the pan with aluminum foil.

Bake for 45 minutes to 1 hour. Halfway through baking, either baste or turn over the pork.

PREPARATION TIME: *5 minutes*
TOTAL TIME: *approximately 1 hour*

Spanish Pork Chops

IF YOUR MOTHER, or your friend's mother, served the pork chops baked in mushroom soup, you can bet she also served "Spanish" pork chops. The green peppers, onions, and tomatoes gave the dish an "exotic" flavor back in those days when people didn't jet about the way they do today.

Mother, who loved peppercorns, always tossed a handful of them into her version of Spanish pork chops. I discovered my friends' mothers didn't do this when they whispered to me, "What are these black bullets?" or, heaven forbid, they unexpectedly bit down on one.

These days, rather than chopping and dicing the onions and adding the peppercorns, I smother the pork chops with Rotel Tomatoes and Green Chilies and add some diced celery for the extra crunch I've always liked. The dish would be equally tasty if you used Italian-flavored tomatoes, I'm sure.

In other words, once you have the pork chops, use whatever variety of canned tomatoes you find on your pantry shelf.

SERVES 6 TO 8

1 (14-ounce) can onion-flavored beef broth

6 to 8 pork chops of your choice

¼ cup chopped celery

1 (10-ounce) can Rotel Tomatoes and Green Chilies

Cookware needed: baking dish or casserole

Preheat the oven to 350 degrees.

Pour a little of the onion-flavored beef broth into the bottom of a baking dish.

Add the pork chops to the pan and sprinkle the celery over them.

Spread the tomatoes and chilies and the remaining beef broth on top of the chops.

Cover and bake for approximately 1 hour.

PREPARATION TIME: *10 minutes*
TOTAL TIME: *approximately 1 hour and 15 minutes*

Sage Advice

If you wish, you can cook this in a covered skillet on top of the stove. That usually cuts down on the cooking time by 15 to 20 minutes, or even more. Either way, serve the pork over rice to keep the broth from going to waste.

Quick as a Wink Roast Pork

Remember when pork was served with gravy and noodles? Or with dressing? I do, but I'm not sure my own children do. They always preferred roast beef to pork roast, so that's what we had.

But now the very convenient Hormel Pork Roast Au Jus makes it possible to return this old-fashioned favorite that skipped a generation to the family dinner table. Of course, you don't have to gussy it up at all, but I'm one of those cooks who can never leave anything alone—even a can of soup. So here are two ways to turn this storebought entrée into a homemade dinner.

Roast Pork with Noodles

SERVES 4 TO 6

The Finishing Touch

Serve the pork over hot buttered noodles and garnish it with fresh parsley.

2 (1-pound) packages Hormel Pork Roast Au Jus

¼ cup dry white wine

½ cup mushrooms, fresh or canned, drained

¼ cup sliced green olives

Cookware needed: skillet

Pour the au jus sauce from the roast pork pouches into a skillet.

Stir in the white wine, mushrooms, and green olives. Bring the liquid to a gentle simmer and add the pork. Continue to simmer for 5 to 7 minutes.

PREPARATION TIME: *10 minutes*
TOTAL TIME: *20 minutes (includes cooking noodles)*

Sunday Dinner Pork

SERVES 4 TO 6

2 (1-pound) packages Hormel
Pork Roast Au Jus

½ cup sour cream

1 teaspoon white vinegar or
white wine

3 to 4 dried bay leaves

Fresh ground pepper, to taste

Cookware needed: skillet with lid

Pour the au jus sauce from the roast pork pouches into a skillet.

Stir in the sour cream and vinegar or wine. Add the bay leaves and bring the liquid to a gentle simmer.

Cook for approximately 5 minutes, then add the pork and cover it well with the sauce.

Cover the skillet and continue to simmer the pork for 5 to 7 minutes.

Remove the bay leaves, add a few turns of freshly ground pepper, and serve.

PREPARATION TIME: *10 to 15 minutes*
TOTAL TIME: *15 minutes*

The
Finishing Touch

Serve this with stovetop dressing or pecan rice (page 180), mango soufflé (page 146), and string beans for a delicious, different, colorful, and satisfying meal.

Garlic-Roasted Pork Tenderloin

THE ALREADY MARINATED pork tenderloins found in the meat section of the grocery store are real time savers. You don't have to take the time or trouble to marinate them, and they cook quickly, making it possible to serve a scrumptious appetizer or a company-quality meal on just a couple of hours' notice.

But if you have a couple of days' warning, buy a plain tenderloin and try this marinade. I think it's wonderful.

SERVES 8 TO 10

1 teaspoon salt

1 teaspoon pepper

1 teaspoon dried oregano

1 teaspoon dried thyme

4 to 5 cloves garlic, crushed, or 2 to 2 ½ teaspoons prepared garlic

1 (5- to-6-pound) pork tenderloin (not seasoned or marinated)

2 tablespoons distilled white vinegar

Cookware needed: rectangular baking dish or casserole

The **Finishing Touch**

Garnish the platter with orange, mango, lemon, and apple slices.

Two days before cooking, combine the salt, pepper, dried oregano, dried thyme, and garlic.

Put the meat in a baking dish and cut ½- to ¾-inch-deep slits every 2 to 3 inches down the length of the tenderloin.

With your hands, thoroughly rub the seasoning mixture over all sides of the tenderloin, pushing some of it down into the slits.

Pour the vinegar along the length of the tenderloin.

Cover the pan tightly with plastic wrap and refrigerate it for 2 days, turning the meat halfway through the time.

When you're ready to cook, preheat the oven to 350 degrees.

Remove the plastic wrap, turn the tenderloin, and cover it tightly with aluminum foil.

Puncture the foil in a few places to let the steam escape.

Bake for 2 hours.

Remove the pan from the oven and allow the tenderloin to sit, uncovered, for 10 to 15 minutes before slicing and serving.

PREPARATION TIME: *10 to 15 minutes*
TOTAL TIME: *2 days, plus 2 hours and 10 minutes*

Wild Rice and Sausage

VERSATILITY, that's what I like in a recipe. I've pointed out that experienced cooks have a repertoire of dishes they cook over and over again.

Wild rice and sausage fits the bill perfectly. It is equally at home on the breakfast table or a dinner buffet.

Though it calls for browning the sausage and cooking the rice instead of just "assembling" already prepared foods, the compliments you'll receive for this traditional Deep South dish will make it well worth the effort. It certainly isn't hard to make. It just takes a little time. Try using this as your "signature" piece on a menu with other, more quickly prepared, dishes.

SERVES 6 TO 8

1 (6-ounce) box wild rice, instant or regular

1 pound bulk pork sausage, not links or patties

¼ cup frozen, diced onions

1 (10-ounce) can cream of mushroom soup

1 teaspoon dried thyme

1 (4-ounce) jar pimientos

Cookware needed: saucepan, skillet, mixing bowl, baking dish or casserole

Sage Advice

Use either mild or hot bulk sausage, according to your preference. And, in case you're out of cream of mushroom soup, cream of chicken soup will work perfectly well.

Preheat the oven to 350 degrees.

Prepare the rice according to the package directions.

While the rice is cooking, brown the sausage in a skillet, stirring and breaking it up with a spoon. Add the diced onion at the end of the cooking so they are gently sautéed. Drain the sausage and onion and transfer the mixture to a bowl.

Add the rice, soup, dried thyme, and pimientos, and combine.

Pour the mixture into a greased baking dish.

Bake for approximately 25 to 30 minutes, or until bubbly.

PREPARATION TIME: *20 minutes*
TOTAL TIME: *50 to 60 minutes*

Veal Scaloppini Picatta

AT THE TOP of my top-ten favorite foods list (if David Letterman were ever to ask me) is Veal Picatta. But when I made it, though good, I just couldn't get it lemony and flavorful enough for my taste.

Then one day I thought, what if I were to add some dried lemon seasoning mix right out of the envelope? But how could I get this flavor into the veal itself, and not just make the sauce lemon flavored?

When I began cooking in the early 1960s, veal cutlets were so thick they had to be pounded between pieces of wax paper to thin them and make them tender. Although we now can buy veal scallops that are already paper thin, I decided to use the same technique to coat the veal with the seasoning.

I spread a layer of the lemon seasoning on a sheet of plastic wrap, placed the veal on this, and sprinkled more seasoning on top. After covering the veal with another sheet of plastic wrap, I gently pounded the meat just enough so some of the lemon seasoning was absorbed. It worked. Suddenly my veal picatta tasted like the dish I'd had in restaurants, especially when I used the rest of the dried lemon mix to make the sauce.

But there was yet another problem. Since the entrée was prepared in a skillet on top of the stove, sometimes the slices tended to dry out while I dished up the rest of the meal. Or, if I served up the veal first, the thin slices got cold.

This recipe both gives veal picatta the rich lemon flavor I love and also eliminates those last-minute worries. Though this is a two-step recipe, I find the results well worth the small amount of extra work.

SERVES 2 TO 3

The Veal:

1 envelope dried lemon
    seasoning mix (Knorr,
    Sun Bird, and McCormick
    make varieties)

6 veal scallops, thinly sliced

1 tablespoon butter

1 tablespoon olive oil

1 tablespoon (or more)
    lemon juice

Zest of one lemon (optional)

Salt and pepper, to taste
    (see *Sage Advice*)

The Sauce:

Remaining lemon seasoning mix

Water

1 cup chicken broth, easily made
    from instant bouillon crystals,
    or the canned variety

1 tablespoon (or more)
    lemon juice

White wine (optional)

Salt and pepper, to taste
    (see *Sage Advice*)

Cookware needed: skillet,
    rectangular baking dish
    or casserole, mixing bowl

Preheat the oven to 350 degrees.

Spread a couple of tablespoons of lemon seasoning on a piece of wax paper or plastic wrap.

Place two veal slices on top of the seasoning. Sprinkle the veal with a couple of more tablespoons of the lemon seasoning. Cover it with another sheet of wrap, and pound it gently. (The bowl of a serving spoon, the back of a spatula, or the handle of a chopping knife all work perfectly well.) Repeat this process until all the slices are coated.

Brown the veal in the butter and olive oil over medium to medium-high heat for just a minute or two on each side, or until lightly browned. You will probably have room in your skillet to cook only 3 or 4 slices at a time. When all the veal is cooked, turn the heat down to low.

As the slices are done, lay them in a baking or casserole dish lightly greased or sprayed with nonstick cooking oil.

To make the sauce: In a small mixing bowl combine the remaining lemon seasoning with just enough water to moisten it to a pastelike consistency.

Stir in the chicken broth and lemon juice. Add a little wine if you wish, and salt and pepper to taste.

Add this mixture to the skillet with the warm pan juices from cooking the veal and blend quickly, until the liquid begins to bubble gently.

Pour the sauce over the veal slices, scraping the bottom of the skillet well to get all the delicious brown bits.

Cover the pan with foil, and bake for 15 minutes, so the juices and veal blend well. If it is necessary to hold the veal longer, simply turn off the oven.

Sage Advice

*If you prefer, use a
lemon-pepper seasoning
in place of the usual
pepper to add even
more lemon flavor.*

PREPARATION TIME: *15 minutes*
TOTAL TIME: *30 minutes*

Elegant Veal Scalloppini Picatta

SERVES 2 TO 3

6 slices prosciutto, sliced thin

6 slices Monterey Jack cheese

½ cup heavy cream

Cookware needed: skillet, rectangular baking dish or casserole, mixing bowl

Prepare the Veal Scaloppini Picatta recipe on page 121 through cooking the veal in the skillet, and preheat the oven to 375 degrees.

When you place the veal slices in the baking dish, cover each one with a slice of prosciutto and a slice of cheese.

When preparing the sauce, add the heavy cream and stir. Pour over the veal.

Bake for 15 or 20 minutes, until the cheese has melted. Do not cover the baking dish unless you need to hold it longer, in which case, cover the pan and turn off the oven.

PREPARATION TIME: *20 minutes*

TOTAL TIME: *35 to 40 minutes*

Lamb, No Longer Just for Spring

"I LOVE LAMB, but what can you do with it?" I was asked once. It's a good question because lamb usually is served either as chops with mint jelly or, in the spring, as a "leg of lamb."

And, unlike chicken and pork which we like to "dress up" because we serve it so often, lamb is thought of as being a delicacy, an expensive meat that is saved for special occasions.

Further, lamb really does have a distinctive taste, and if you like it, that's what you want—lamb that tastes like lamb.

But no longer is lamb as expensive as it once was, and, as America's taste buds have become more adventuresome, curried lamb and barbequed lamb are being served more frequently.

So if you're looking for a different dish that's very good, try one of the following quickly prepared lamb recipes. You may be surprised at how well received they will be by your family and guests.

Sage Advice

To my way of thinking, lamb is best when it is cooked medium well to well done. There are some people, though, who like rare lamb. So, if you're preparing any of these lamb chop entrées for a small party, you might ask your guests how they like their lamb cooked.

Lamb Chops in Sherry Marinade

IT ONLY TAKES a matter of minutes to mix together this marinade, even if you take the time to press a couple of garlic cloves. Just be sure to bring the chops back to room temperature before grilling. The chops can either be grilled or prepared on the stovetop.

SERVES 4 TO 6

1 teaspoon dry mustard

1 teaspoon salt

½ teaspoon pepper

½ cup dry sherry

¼ teaspoon prepared minced garlic, or ½ teaspoon minced pressed garlic

8 lamb chops

Cookware needed: broiler pan or skillet

Sage Advice

If preparing for real lamb lovers, increase the amount of marinade made and number of lamb chops accordingly.

Combine the mustard, salt, pepper, sherry, and garlic.

Pour the mixture over the lamb chops. Cover them and refrigerate for about 3 hours, turning occasionally.

Forty minutes before broiling time, remove the chops from the refrigerator.

Broil the chops for 4 to 5 minutes on each side, basting with the marinade, or prepare on the stovetop in a heavy skillet (with a tablespoon of oil added) over medium-high heat, using the marinade for basting.

PREPARATION TIME: *5 to 10 minutes, including turning time*
TOTAL TIME: *approximately 20 minutes (plus 3 hours to marinate)*

Barbequed Lamb Chops

PREPARING barbequed lamb chops is as simple as spreading a little of your favorite light barbeque sauce on both sides of the chops, letting them rest for about 30 to 40 minutes, and then either grilling or cooking them on the stovetop as described in the previous recipe.

The
Finishing Touch

To add a finishing touch to barbequed lamb chops, garnish them with very thin lemon slices.

"Thoughtful seasoning may make a good dish into a memorable one. Experiment with various condiment and seasonings, but use them subtly so that the effect is elusive rather than overpowering."

—*THE BOSTON COOKING-SCHOOL COOK BOOK*
BY FANNIE MERRITT FARMER, 1943

Curried Lamb

IF YOU LOVE LAMB STEWS OR CURRIES, and I do, then you've been overjoyed to find that packages of cubed lamb are now available in the meat department of your grocery store. No longer do you have to mess with cutting the meat off the shoulder (a very fatty cut of meat) or the leg. The work has been done for you. All you have to do is make a little curry paste and check on the cooking process every so often.

SERVES 8

½ cup frozen, diced onion

2 tablespoons butter

2 pounds diced lamb

2 tablespoons curry powder

1 teaspoon brown sugar

2 tablespoons distilled white or apple-cider vinegar

¼ cup milk

1 (14-ounce) can chicken broth

Cookware needed: mixing bowl, skillet with lid, baking dish or casserole (optional)

Sauté the onion in the butter.

Add the diced lamb and brown.

Blend together the curry powder, the brown sugar, and the vinegar in a mixing bowl.

Add the mixture to the meat and stir well.

Combine the milk and the chicken broth in the mixing bowl and then pour half into the meat mixture, stirring again to blend all together. Reserve the other half to be added midway through the cooking process.

At this point you can cover the skillet and cook the lamb on the stovetop, simmering for 30 to 40 minutes, or preheat the oven to 325 degrees, put the curried lamb into a baking dish, cover well with aluminum foil, and bake for 1 hour and 15 minutes.

Midway though the cooking time, or when you think it is needed, add the reserved milk and chicken broth mixture and stir well.

PREPARATION TIME: *20 minutes*
TOTAL TIME: *approximately 1 to 2 hours, depending on cooking method*

Mint Jelly Lamb Chops

WHEN I WAS A LITTLE GIRL, I always looked forward to the obligatory Easter leg of lamb—not for the lamb, but for the delicious mint jelly that was served along with it. Several years later, I was delighted when lamb chops smothered in mint jelly were the entrée at a fancy dinner party.

Licking my chops (no pun intended), I begged for the recipe. My gracious hostess produced it on a trusty index card, which I slipped into my pocket and immediately added to my recipe box when I got home. But index cards can be misplaced.

Once when I thought I had lost it, but then found it in some unlikely place, I copied the recipe down in one of my favorite cookbooks so I wouldn't have to panic in the future. But then I couldn't remember which cookbook. Now that it's in this book, I'll know where to find it.

SERVES 4 TO 8

1 (10-ounce) jar mint jelly
4 to 8 lamb chops

Garlic salt
Cookware needed: saucepan,
broiler pan

Melt 4 or 5 tablespoons of the mint jelly in a saucepan over very low heat, or in the microwave.

Meanwhile, sprinkle the lamb chops with a generous amount of garlic salt and broil them for 4 to 5 minutes on one side.

Turn and broil them for 4 minutes on the other side.

Remove the broiler pan, spoon the melted mint jelly over the lamb chops, and return the pan to the oven and broil the chops for an additional 2 to 3 minutes.

If desired, put some more of the mint jelly on the hot chops. Otherwise, offer the remaining jelly in a bowl at the table.

PREPARATION TIME: *5 minutes*
TOTAL TIME: *20 minutes*

Sage Advice
To my way of thinking, lamb is best when it is cooked medium well to well done. There are people, though, who like rare lamb. So, if you're preparing any of these lamp chop entrées for a small party, you might ask your guests how they like their lamb cooked.

The Finishing Touch
You've figured this one out already, I'm sure. Garnish the mint jelly-glazed lamb chops with a sprig or two of fresh mint, and even a thin lemon slice to add color.

Salads, Vegetables, Potatoes, and Rice

Salads

SEVERAL years ago I read a survey that asked working women what single invention had made their lives easier. Hands down the answer was the microwave. A few years later, I read another such survey, but this time the answer was the food processor.

Today, if someone were to ask me the question, I'd say prewashed, ready-to-serve salads. Even with the help of the handy salad spinner, I have always found it takes a lot of doing to rinse and spin and then layer lettuce leaves between paper towels to soak up that last bit of unwanted moisture.

Thanks to the new cello bags of salad greens—from iceberg lettuce to mesclun—that eliminate those time-consuming steps, today's cooks can create more imaginative salads. Try some of these suggestions, most of which begin with a cello bag of healthy greens.

Lettuce, Orange, and Almond Salad

REMEMBER this deliciously light recipe when the best navel oranges begin arriving in the stores from Florida or California (if you don't live in one of those beautiful states).

Not only is this orange and almond salad a change from the usual, but it goes equally well with chicken, pork, or beef.

SERVES 6 TO 8

1 (3-ounce) package slivered almonds

2 or 3 oranges, navel (seedless) if possible, or 1 (15-ounce) can mandarin oranges

3 tablespoons olive oil

Salt and pepper, to taste

2 tablespoons lemon juice

2 packages shredded lettuce

Crumbled feta cheese, to taste

Cookware needed: mixing/salad bowl

Preheat the oven to 325 degrees.

Roast the almonds for approximately 10 minutes, and cool.

Peel and segment oranges, if using fresh, catching the juices in a bowl. Or, pour the juice from the mandarin segments into a bowl.

Add the olive oil, salt, pepper, and lemon juice to the orange juice.

Place the shredded lettuce in a serving bowl.

Add the olive oil mixture and toss well.

Place the oranges and crumbled feta cheese on top, and garnish with the almonds.

PREPARATION TIME: *10 minutes*
TOTAL TIME: *25 minutes*

Greek Salad

WHEN trying to think of a salad to jazz up an All-in-One-Meal, don't forget this one. It doesn't come in a cello bag because of the ripe olives and pepperoncini (which are, along with the feta cheese, what give Greek Salad its distinctive taste). But it's very easy to assemble once you have the ingredients, so give it a try.

SERVES 4 TO 6

For the salad:

1 small bag lettuce or mixed greens/mesclun

1 small red onion, sliced in rings (this is one time where fresh, not frozen, is necessary)

½ fresh green pepper, diced

10 pitted ripe olives

3 to 5 mild pepperoncini, sliced

1 (4-ounce) package crumbled feta cheese, either plain or one of the herb-flavored varieties

For the dressing:

⅓ cup olive oil

2 tablespoons red wine vinegar

½ teaspoon prepared minced garlic

1 teaspoon fresh oregano, chopped (or ½ teaspoon dried)

Salt and pepper, to taste

Cookware needed: 2 bowls

Combine all the salad ingredients in a bowl.

To make the dressing, whisk together all the ingredients.

Pour the dressing over the salad and toss to coat all the ingredients.

PREPARATION TIME: *10 to 15 minutes*
TOTAL TIME: *10 to 15 minutes*

Bag It!

THERE'S YET another way you can make this simple, but so wonderful modern invention work for you. Instead of dumping the salad out into a bowl and then dousing it with dressing, open the bag carefully so you don't split it down the seam. Then add the allotted amount of dressing to the lettuce in the bag and gently shake.

This trick saves you the chore of washing an extra bowl if you are using individual salad plates or bowls, plus the additional aggravation of strewing lettuce leaves all over the countertop or table while you attempt to distribute the dressing evenly—an almost impossible task in itself.

Pickled Cole Slaw

WORRIED about too much mayonnaise in your diet, or just looking for the freshest, coolest slaw you've ever eaten? This cole slaw has something else going for it too, in addition to not using mayonnaise.

It has a long refrigerator life, and because it's vinegar-based you don't have to worry about it going bad if you take it on a picnic on a hot day.

In fact, I got the recipe from my former husband's aunt's cook, Bird, back in the 1960s. They lived in South Carolina, where it really did get hot in that big, 1850s un-air-conditioned house! Bird, who made the slaw from scratch starting with a head of cabbage from her garden, called it "pickled" cole slaw because of the vinegar—a name that has stuck with me all these years.

Many are the times when I've taken the fifteen minutes required to mix up this slaw the night before (it needs some chilling time for the flavors to blend), and served it the next day along with storebought barbeque (make mine Eastern North Carolina pork barbeque, please) and fried chicken, plus some *From Storebought to Homemade* A Side of Beans (page 281) and Jalapeño Corn Bread (page 230). Then I've sat back and accepted the compliments.

SERVES 6

1 (14-ounce) package slaw (cabbage-based)

½ cup frozen and defrosted, diced green pepper

½ cup frozen and defrosted, diced red pepper (optional)

½ cup diced celery

½ cup distilled white vinegar

2 tablespoons sugar

1 tablespoon celery seed

Salt and pepper, to taste

Cookware needed: mixing bowl or saucepan

Combine the already shredded slaw, peppers, and diced celery (remember the salad-bar trick).

Either in a saucepan on the stovetop or in a bowl in the microwave, heat the vinegar, sugar, celery seed, and salt and pepper over medium-high for 2 to 3 minutes, until the sugar has dissolved. Stir with a wooden spoon, and do not let the mixture burn.

Pour the warm liquid over the slaw, and refrigerate the salad for several hours. Then enjoy the best cole slaw you ever tasted.

PREPARATION TIME: *10 to 15 minutes*
TOTAL TIME: *at least 6 hours to chill*

Frozen Slaw

A **VARIATION** on Bird's Pickled Cole Slaw, this Frozen Slaw would be suitable for an indoor buffet, but would hardly work for a picnic. Still, it is novel enough to deserve sharing.

SERVES 6

For the dressing:
2 cups sugar
1 cup distilled white vinegar

½ cup water
1 teaspoon celery seed
Cookware needed: mixing bowl, cake pan

Combine the slaw mixture, green pepper, and celery in a large mixing bowl, as for the earlier recipe. Stir in 1½ tablespoons of salt. Cover the bowl and let the slaw stand for 2 hours, then drain it thoroughly. Transfer the slaw into a metal cake pan. (The metal conducts the cold more quickly.)

Combine all the ingredients in a saucepan and prepare as for the Pickled Slaw.

When the sugar has thoroughly dissolved, pour the dressing over the cabbage mixture, cover, and freeze for several hours. Then slice and serve.

PREPARATION TIME: *15 minutes*
TOTAL TIME: *several hours for chilling and freezing*

Confetti Beans with Jalapeño

LOOKING for a pretty salad to serve with a steak or chops or even fried chicken? Try this mixture made by opening cans and bags—the amounts of all the contents of which you can adjust to your own likes and tastes.

SERVES 10 TO 12

Sage Advice
You may use either white or yellow corn, or a mixture of the two.

2 (15-ounce) cans black beans, drained and rinsed

1 (15 ½-ounce) can garbanzo beans, drained and rinsed

1 (10-ounce) bag frozen corn kernels

1 (10-ounce) bag frozen, mixed bell peppers (red, green, and yellow)

3 stalks celery, finely chopped (or about 1 cup if you're buying it from a salad bar)

½ cup diced onions (the frozen variety is fine)

¼ cup diced jalapeño peppers from a can (or to your taste)

1 cup Italian-style salad dressing of your choice (not creamy)

Cookware needed: large mixing bowl

While you are draining the canned beans and preparing the celery, allow the frozen ingredients to thaw on paper towels to absorb the extra moisture.

Then, combine all the vegetable ingredients in a large mixing bowl.

Add the Italian dressing and toss well.

Chill 6 hours before serving.

PREPARATION TIME: *10 minutes*
TOTAL TIME: *10 minutes plus the additional chilling time*

Artichoke, Rice, and Pepper Salad

IF YOU'RE looking for a really unusual salad to pick up an ordinary meal, try this. The multicolored peppers make it as colorful as the Confetti Beans salad, and the curry adds the same element of surprise here that the jalapeños do in that one.

Sage Advice
This salad will hold well in the refrigerator for a day or so.

SERVES 6

1 (6-ounce) package Chicken Vermicelli Rice Mix or another flavored rice

2 (6-ounce) jars marinated artichoke hearts

¼ cup mayonnaise

½ to ¾ teaspoons curry powder

¼ cup frozen, diced onions

¼ cup pimiento-stuffed olives, drained and sliced

¼ cup frozen, diced peppers (red, green, and yellow combination) or strips of peppers if you prefer to use them as a garnish

Cookware needed: saucepan, small bowl, mixing bowl

Cook the rice according to package directions, and while it is cooling, prepare the other ingredients.

Drain the artichokes, reserving the liquid from 1 jar, and slice them into halves or quarters.

Combine the artichoke liquid, mayonnaise, and curry powder.

Combine the rice, artichokes, onion, diced peppers (if using in the salad), and olives in a mixing bowl, toss with the curry mixture, and chill. If diced peppers are omitted, garnish with sliced peppers on top of the salad if it is served in a bowl, or over the individual portions.

PREPARATION TIME: *15 minutes*
TOTAL TIME: *15 minutes, plus the additional time to cook the rice and chill the salad*

Shrimp-Filled Avocado Salad

THIS RICH and delicious salad can be used as an elegant first course for a seated dinner, the main course for a ladies' luncheon, or the perfect accompaniment for a holiday meal when you want something a little different and showy to celebrate the festivity of the season.

It takes literally no time to prepare, but it can't be tossed together in one bowl—unless, that is, you dice the avocado, chop the shrimp, mix in the dressing, sprinkle it extra-well with lemon, and then serve it on a bed of shredded lettuce.

The
Finishing Touch

If you love lemon as much as I do, garnish each portion with a slice or even a wedge of lemon that can be squeezed over the salad just before digging in.

SERVES 6

½ cup zesty Italian-style dressing of your choice

⅓ cup mayonnaise

⅛ teaspoon pepper (preferably white, if on hand)

Juice of ½ lemon plus 1 tablespoon

3 pounds medium (not large) cooked shrimp, purchased from the fish section of the grocery store, or bought frozen and thoroughly thawed

3 ripe avocados

Cookware needed: medium mixing bowl

In a medium bowl, combine the dressing, mayonnaise, pepper, and 1 tablespoon lemon juice. Add the shrimp and toss lightly.

Refrigerate overnight.

Just before serving, peel, halve, and pit the avocados.

Place each avocado half on a plate, cavity-side-up, and take a moment to squeeze a few drops of juice from the ½ lemon over each (this keeps the color fresh).

Fill the avocado halves to overflowing with the shrimp mixture.

PREPARATION TIME: *15 to 20 minutes*
TOTAL TIME: *20 minutes, plus overnight refrigeration time*

Grapefruit, Avocado, and Shrimp Salad

IF YOU ARE planning an extra-fancy dinner party where you might be serving beef or chicken, try this super-easy salad that is absolutely delicious, different, and instantly prepared. In fact, the hardest thing about this recipe is deciding which dressing you want to use on it.

SERVES 8 AS A FIRST COURSE OR
4 AS A MAIN COURSE

1 cup shrimp, frozen and ready to serve, or from the seafood counter

1 jar grapefruit sections, drained

1 medium avocado, cubed

¼ cup dressing of your choice (see instructions)

1 head "living" (or hydroponic), or Boston lettuce

Cookware needed: mixing bowl

Sage Advice
You can substitute lobster pieces or even the now-popular imitation lobster for the shrimp.

Thaw shrimp, if using frozen, pat them dry, and combine them with the grapefruit sections and cubed avocado.

Decide which dressing you wish to use. A vinaigrette, poppy, light French, or another lightly flavored dressing (not spicy) would be the right choice. Measure the dressing (you do not want to drown this salad in dressing or overpower the light, distinctive flavors of the shrimp, avocado, and grapefruit), add it to the other ingredients, and toss gently.

Cover and refrigerate the salad for 30 to 45 minutes, then spoon it onto the pretty lettuce leaves.

PREPARATION TIME: *10 minutes*
TOTAL TIME: *50 to 60 minutes*

Stalking the Ripe Avocado

"**JUST THINKING** about shrimp and avocados makes my mouth water," I said to Charlotte Sizer, my trusty assistant. "Trouble is, lots of people don't know how to tell a raw avocado from a ripe one," I added.

"Like the man who stole our avocados," Charlotte laughed, remembering those days when, as a little girl, she lived in Miami, that semitropical region where people gather bright green key limes, sweet coconuts, juicy mangos, and, yes, ripe avocados from trees growing right in their own yards.

It seems that there was a particularly large and beautiful avocado tree in Charlotte's family's backyard, which yielded plentiful fruit. Called "alligator pears," those avocados were bumpy and, when ripe, very dark green (almost black), shiny, and soft to the touch.

"There were alleys behind

Avocado and Tomato Salad

TOMATO, mozzarella, and basil salad has become a popular standard. As well it should be. It's delicious. But there's an alternative salad that is just as simple to assemble and will be a change—avocado and tomato salad.

Sage Advice
For the dressing, I recommend a balsamic vinaigrette or one of the fancier tomato vinaigrettes. Catalina is another possibility, but it should be used sparingly so the distinctive avocado taste is not overwhelmed.

SERVES 6 TO 8

1 to 2 ripe avocados

Juice of ½ lemon

3 to 4 tomatoes

Lettuce leaves (a mixture of romaine and endive, or bagged lettuce)

Light dressing (see *Sage Advice*)

Cookware needed: individual plates

Peel the avocado and cut into slices. Sprinkle these with lemon juice to keep them green.

Cut the tomatoes into slices or wedges.

Arrange the avocados and tomatoes on the lettuce and drizzle the salad with a light dressing. If using endive, alternate the leaves with the tomatoes and avocado.

PREPARATION TIME: *10 minutes*
TOTAL TIME: *10 minutes*

the houses in Miami Shores," Charlotte continued, "and one evening, just before dark, I walked into the kitchen, looked out the back window, and saw a pickup truck parked in the corner of the garden under the avocado tree.

"A man was very carefully, so he wouldn't bruise the fruit, picking the bright green avocados off the tree," she explained.

"Rather than calling the police, my mother and I watched him, grateful that we would not have to gather all of the avocados when they ripened, turned black, and fell to the ground—all the while laughing at the surprise the man would get when he discovered that, as beautiful as the green avocados looked, the fruit he was stealing was still raw, gritty,

and unsuitable for eating."

So how *do* you tell a good avocado? Simple.

You go to the grocery story and look for an avocado that is soft to the touch and appears to be on the verge of rotting—dark green to black.

Or you just get the avocado with the little white sticker on it that says "RIPE!"

English Pea and Potato Salad

I STILL remember how delicious this fresh, light, mayonnaise-free potato salad tasted when I had it in England some twenty years ago. There was no way to get the recipe for it, so I picked through my serving—potatoes, celery, peas, and then all those little specks that had to be herbs. It was held together with a wonderful light dressing, something as simple as oil and vinegar.

As soon as I recovered from the inevitable jet lag, I was in the kitchen trying to re-create this English delicacy. Several days had passed since that memorable meal, so my taste buds and memories weren't exactly crystal clear. But this Americanization of the ingredients comes close, and it always receives lots of attention when I serve it, especially in the summer.

Sage Advice

Whole olives or a relish make a nice complement to this salad.

SERVES 8 OR MORE

10 to 12 small new potatoes, unpeeled

1 (8-ounce) bottle Italian-style dressing, regular or zesty, but not creamy

1 (10-ounce) package frozen petite peas

1 cup celery, diced

Salt and pepper, to taste

Cookware needed: saucepan, microwave-safe bowl

The
Finishing Touch

Particularly good to serve at a buffet along with mayonnaise-based salads—a nice alternative to pasta salad.

Wash the potatoes, cutting away any bad spots. Dice, put them in a saucepan, and cover them with cold, lightly salted water.

Boil until just soft, or for about 10 minutes.

While the potatoes boil, open the peas into a microwave-safe bowl, add just enough water to barely cover them, and microwave on high for 2 to 3 minutes, or just long enough to thoroughly defrost them.

When the potatoes are done, drain and return them to the saucepan. Then drown, while still warm, with the dressing. Drain the peas and add them to the saucepan followed by the diced celery; toss all the ingredients together, and season to taste.

Transfer all to a serving bowl, and chill before serving.

PREPARATION TIME: *20 minutes*
TOTAL TIME: *2 hours to chill well*

Ham It Up Salad

THIS hearty salad is a great side dish for those times when you're throwing together a simple soup for a trouble-free, but delicious meal. The smoked sausage links make this more substantial than the usual lettuce and tomato salad. The hard-boiled eggs are a plus if you have the time to prepare them, although it is just fine without them.

SERVES 6

6 Roma tomatoes, cut into eighths

2 packages lettuce—Italian, Romaine, or European mix

12 to 18 pitted ripe olives

1 bunch green onions, sliced

1 heaping teaspoon diced pimiento

½ cup vinaigrette or Italian-style dressing (regular, not creamy)

Salt and pepper, to taste

6 to 8 cooked smoked sausage links, sliced or 1 (8-ounce) package of small diced ham bits

4 hard-boiled eggs, quartered (optional)

Cookware needed: mixing/salad bowl

Place lettuce pieces in a salad bowl.

Distribute the tomatoes over the lettuce. Scatter the olives, green onions, and pimiento over all.

Pour the dressing over the salad.

Add a little salt and pepper if you wish.

Garnish the salad with the sausage and eggs, if you are using them.

PREPARATION TIME: *10 minutes*
TOTAL TIME: *10 minutes, or longer if eggs are included*

Sage Advice

You can add to, or subtract from, the number of olives and sausages or ham given in the recipe, according to your preference. Also, so you can plan on how much salad you wish to prepare, this recipe will make 6 ample servings—sometimes more. Experience has taught me that some people like lots of salad, and some, given the choice, take only a couple of lettuce leaves—and then only to be polite.

" *It's difficult to think anything but pleasant thoughts while eating a home-grown tomato.*"

—LEWIS GRIZZARD,
SOUTHERN HUMORIST

Shrimp and Snow Pea Salad

THE RED BELL PEPPER and pink shrimp give this salad a cheerful look. It makes it a great accompaniment for any monochromatic chicken entrée—such as the Champagne Chicken (page 88) or Timeless Chicken (page 97). Feel free to add just a few water chestnuts if you like, and, whatever you do, be sure not to overcook the snow peas.

SERVES 4 TO 6

Sage Advice

Sugar brings soy sauce to life. The addition of just a teaspoon gives the dressing in this recipe an extra-tasty zing.

1 (10-ounce) box frozen snow peas, cooked according to package directions, and cooled

1 tablespoon soy sauce

2 tablespoons lemon juice

1 teaspoon sugar (optional)

3 tablespoons peanut oil

1 small red bell pepper, diced

8 ounces frozen, cooked, and cleaned shrimp, salad size or larger, thoroughly defrosted

1 (4-ounce) can sliced mushrooms, drained

Cookware needed: saucepan, mixing bowl

The Finishing Touch

For serving, mound the salad onto a leaf of Boston lettuce, and sprinkle it with toasted sesame seeds.

Place the snow peas into boiling salted water. Cook for 3 minutes after water returns to a boil. Drain and refresh in cold water. Cool to room temperature.

Combine the soy sauce, lemon juice, sugar if you're using it, and oil in a mixing bowl.

Add the bell pepper, shrimp, mushrooms, and snow peas, and toss to coat all the ingredients with the dressing.

PREPARATION TIME: *10 minutes*
TOTAL TIME: *30 minutes*

Too, Too Tabouli Salad

I WAS introduced to tabouli, or tabuleh, or tabooleh, at a wedding reception. I didn't have a clue what I was eating, but I was hooked. That was long before the convenient boxed varieties became available on our neighborhood grocery shelves. Nevertheless, I was determined to make it, and so I did—spending much time soaking, chopping, and dicing.

Nowadays, I grab a box, follow the directions, and then add a few extra touches left over from those long ago "from-scratch" days. They do involve some chopping and take a little longer, but this is one time I never complain.

If you haven't dared try this Middle Eastern salad, please do. You're missing a delicious and healthy dish if you don't. Even picky eaters go back for extra helpings, once they've tried it.

SERVES 6 TO 10

1 (5.25-ounce) box tabouli

½ cup frozen, diced green pepper, defrosted

1 small cucumber

1 to 2 scallions

5 to 6 mint leaves (optional)

Several sprigs of parsley

1 lemon

Cookware needed: mixing bowl, food processor

Prepare the tabouli according to package directions. Set it aside in the refrigerator.

While the tabouli is chilling, cut the cucumber in half lengthwise and remove and discard the seeds.

Cut the cucumber halves into several chunks. Do the same with the scallions.

Chop both in a food processor to small pieces, about the size of the diced pepper. Transfer these, and the diced pepper, to a small bowl.

Wash and pat dry the parsley, then give it a couple of swirls in the food processor, being careful not to puree it. Add it to the pepper, cucumber, and scallions.

Hand chop the mint leaves. Although these are optional, and they definitely add to the effort, the additional flavor is worth it. Add the mint to the pepper, cucumber, scallions, and parsley.

Squeeze the juice of one lemon over the vegetables, being careful that no seeds slip by. Stir, and then add all to the tabouli.

Chill for at least 1 hour before serving.

The
Finishing Touch

For individual servings, spoon an ample helping into a curled lettuce leaf and garnish the dish with a few small cherry (or grape) tomatoes—sliced, halved, or whole. Or serve the salad in a large bowl without the lettuce leaves, but decorated at the center with thin lemon slices and a sprig of mint leaves or parsley.

PREPARATION TIME: *about 20 minutes*
TOTAL TIME: *1 hour and 20 minutes*

Jelled Salads

Although I'm a great fan of today's salads in a bag, they can get monotonous when served week in and week out. When our mothers wanted an easy way to add interest, color, and variety to family meals, they turned to Jell-O—lime, lemon, Bing cherry, even blueberry Jell-O (which seems to have disappeared from the grocery shelves).

To make a jelled salad, you still have to boil the water, or warm the juice drained from the can of fruit to add to the gelatin, and it takes some time for the gelatin to jell. But these salads can always be made ahead of time and pulled out of the fridge at the last minute for lunch or supper.

Here, to add variety to your meals, are some salads that are quickly assembled and awfully good. In fact, because they aren't served as frequently these days as the stand-by green salad, jelled salads are often considered special. And there's more. Sugar free Jello-O works equally well in these recipes.

Apricot Salad

The Finishing Touch

Sprinkle the salad with chopped nuts, if desired, just before the gelatin has set, to give it a little extra crunch. Serve cold salads—especially jelled salads—on chilled plates, if possible, but never on plates that have gotten warm or hot by being placed on the stove.

THIS TIME, baby food comes to the rescue of the modern cook! A jar of already prepared apricots saves you from having to get out the blender or sieve to prepare the fruit yourself. Another reason to put this recipe on your to-make list is that it can be mixed together all at once, which isn't true of all jelled recipes.

SERVES 8 OR MORE

⅔ cup water

⅔ cup sugar

2 (3-ounce) packages peach or apricot Jell-O

1 (8-ounce) package cream cheese, softened

1 (15-ounce) can crushed

pineapple, drained

1 (4-ounce) jar apricot baby food

1 (12-ounce) container Cool Whip, softened, at room temperature

Cookware needed: saucepan, bowl, mold or muffin tins

Combine the water, sugar, and Jell-O in a saucepan, and bring the liquid to a boil. Remove from the heat and stir in the cream cheese, blending until smooth.

Combine the pineapple, baby food, and Cool Whip, and add to Jell-O mixture.

Pour into a lightly oiled mold or individual muffin tins, and refrigerate until set.

PREPARATION TIME: *10 minutes*
TOTAL TIME: *4 hours to chill thoroughly*

Avocado Aspic

LOOKING for a salad that's a little different? Why not try an avocado aspic?

Mother used to use unflavored gelatin and add lemon juice when she made it, but it's much easier just to use lemon Jell-O instead. This unbelievably easy-to-make salad adds a nice touch to a meal and makes it seem special. Ladies particularly seem to enjoy it.

SERVES 4 TO 6

1 (3-ounce) package lemon Jell-O
1 ripe avocado

2 tablespoons mayonnaise
Cookware needed: square baking dish or casserole, mixing bowl

Prepare the Jell-O according to package directions. Transfer it to a square baking dish, and place it in the refrigerator to cool.

Mash the avocado and stir in the mayonnaise to make a smooth paste.

When the Jell-O is partially set, or after about 30 minutes, fold in the avocado mixture and return the mixture to the refrigerator until completely set.

Cut into squares to serve.

PREPARATION TIME: *10 minutes*
TOTAL TIME: *about 3 hours to chill*

The
Finishing Touch

Serve on lettuce leaves with a dollop of mayonnaise on the side, topped with a thin slice of lemon, and, if you wish, a slice of avocado.

" When the salad is served as a separate course, pass with it crackers which have been spread with butter or some tasty cheese, and crisped in the oven. If the buttered crackers are used, serve cream cheese with them."

—*THE BUTTERICK COOK BOOK*, EDITED BY HELENA JUDSON, 1911

Cream Cheese Salad

OF ALL the gelatin recipes, this is my favorite. It's so simple that I used to help Mother prepare it when I was just a little girl in the 1940s. I don't know how, but I had forgotten it until I began looking through her old cookbooks, when I began working on this book.

At the end of the recipe, Mother had written in her well-schooled hand, "Consider the season in selecting flavor for Jell-O and mold used." I'm sure she did, but I only remember it as being green.

And in those days before central air-conditioning, when ladies wore flowered dresses with slips beneath them and glowed, rather than perspired, the pastel-green color and frothy consistency of this salad epitomized summertime to me. It still does, even when I serve it at Christmas. After all, green is a year-round color.

SERVES 6 TO 8

1 (3-ounce) package lime (or other flavor) Jell-O

2 cups hot water

1 (8-ounce) package cream cheese

½ cup chopped pecans

Cookware needed: mixing bowl, mold

The
Finishing Touch

Add a few drops of food coloring to deepen the green and serve on Saint Patrick's Day! Add a dollop of whipped cream or Cool Whip, and this can become a dessert salad.

Dissolve the Jell-O in 1 cup of the hot water and the cream cheese in the second cup. Stir both until smooth.

Combine the Jello-O and cream cheese, and refrigerate approximately 30 to 45 minutes, until the mixture begins to set. Then add the chopped pecans.

Pour the "salad" into an oiled mold, and chill until set.

PREPARATION TIME: *10 minutes*
TOTAL TIME: *3 hours or until set*

Lime Yogurt Salad

THE DIFFICULT thing with multilayered jelled salads is getting the timing right. To make some recipes, it takes a battery of alarm clocks to remind you when it's time to add the ingredients or assemble the layers.

In this recipe, both layers reach the right consistency at about the same time. So, though you have to be available when the layers are ready, the job is much easier.

SERVES 8

1 (15-ounce) can sliced pears
2 (3-ounce) packages lime Jell-O
2 cups boiling water

1 (8-ounce) container vanilla-flavored yogurt
Cookware needed: saucepan, 2 mixing bowls, 8-inch square pan or salad mold

Drain the pears, reserving ½ cup of the syrup.

Dissolve the Jell-O in the boiling water, and stir well.

Measure 1 cup of the Jell-O mixture into a mixing bowl. Whisk in the yogurt and pour this mixture into a square baking pan or a lightly oiled mold.

Refrigerate until set but not firm, approximately 45 minutes, or about 10 minutes longer for a deeper mold.

Meanwhile, add the measured syrup to the remaining Jell-O, and chill until the yogurt mixture is ready.

Arrange the pear slices on the yogurt layer, and gently spoon all of the clear lime Jell-O on top. Repeat, *gently*. The Jell-O will very easily tear a hole in the delicate yogurt layer if it is added too hastily.

Return the salad to the refrigerator, and chill until firm, about 3 hours.

Cut the salad into squares, and serve it on individual plates, with or without a lettuce leaf underneath. If using a mold, dip it briefly in warm water, set a serving plate on top of the mold, and flip plate and mold over to release the salad. Place the whole salad on the table or buffet with a pretty serving spoon.

PREPARATION TIME: *15 minutes*
TOTAL TIME: *4 hours*

Sage Advice

Just as the temperatures of ovens vary, so do the temperatures of refrigerators. Further, different parts of a refrigerator can be cooler or warmer than others. This means that the cooling process for any jelled dessert can vary, and the "chilling" times given in recipes must be taken as approximate.

The Finishing Touch

This is another one of those salads that works equally well as a fruit salad or a light dessert. If using it as a salad, serve it on lettuce and accompany it with a little mayonnaise or even yogurt. But if serving it as a dessert, add extra sweetness by topping it with whipped cream or ice cream and a slice or two of lime, or an extra slice or two of pear.

Mango Soufflé

LIGHT, frothy salads are perfect for the summertime. That's a given. But often they are a welcome contrast to a heavy entrée like roast beef or even a cream-based chicken casserole, whatever the time of year.

The perfect solution—mango soufflé.

I was introduced to this Americanized tropical treat in Beaumont, Texas, where it is a real favorite. So much so that I heard about it several times before I actually tasted it!

First, I was told that my hostess would have a light snack, "and mango soufflé" waiting for me when I arrived at her home around 9 PM. When I made an interim stop before getting there, I was reminded that "Martha has some mango soufflé waiting for you."

When I did arrive at her home, Martha Hicks graciously reminded me that she had a light snack waiting, "and mango soufflé." By then my mouth was watering.

Although calling this trouble-free Jell-O salad a soufflé may be a slight exaggeration, its taste will never disappoint.

On the other hand, since a little whipped cream (or Cool Whip) served with this accompaniment immediately transforms it into a dessert, maybe calling it a soufflé is appropriate after all.

The
Finishing Touch

This pretty, apricot-colored salad is particularly lovely when served on a ruffled, red-tipped lettuce leaf. Garnish it with a slice of fresh mango, if available, or a few mandarin orange segments, whether serving it as a salad or a dessert.

SERVES 12

1 (8-ounce) package cream cheese

2 (15-ounce) cans mango

3 (3-ounce) boxes lemon Jell-O

3 cups boiling water

Cookware needed: food processor, mixing bowl

Combine the cream cheese and mango in a food processor (or blender) until perfectly smooth.

Dissolve the Jell-O in the boiling water.

Combine the mango and Jell-O mixtures and refrigerate in an oiled mold until set, approximately 3 to 4 hours.

PREPARATION TIME: *10 minutes*
TOTAL TIME: *3 to 4 hours to chill*

Orange-Pineapple Mold

THE BLENDER does all the work of preparing this simple, but very refreshing and attractive salad. Further, there's no reason to buy a whole package of carrots, then peel and chop them. Buy already sliced carrots in a cello package, or buy just the amount you need from a salad bar.

SERVES 6 TO 8

1 cup hot water

1 (3-ounce) package orange-pineapple flavored Jell-O

1 (20-ounce) can crushed pineapple, drained, juice reserved

½ cup sliced carrots

Cookware needed: blender, 1½-quart mold or ring mold

Place the hot water and Jell-O in a blender. Cover and blend for 25 seconds.

Add the reserved pineapple juice to the Jell-O in the blender. Slowly add the carrots to the mixture and blend until they are finely chopped. Turn blender off and fold in the crushed pineapple.

Pour the mixture into a lightly oiled 1½-quart (ring) mold, or into 6 to 8 individual molds.

Chill until firm, approximately 4 hours.

PREPARATION TIME: *5 minutes*
TOTAL TIME: *approximately 4 hours*

The
Finishing Touch

This is a particularly good salad to have for a luncheon when chicken salad is on the menu. Mound the chicken salad in the middle of the ring mold for a very pretty presentation.

Tangy Tomato Aspic

THERE'S an unspoken rule in the South when it comes to luncheon menus: You can't serve chicken salad without an accompaniment of tomato aspic.

When growing up, I never particularly liked tomato aspic. I preferred a few sliced tomatoes, or a jelled fruit salad. But then Tangy Tomato Aspic appeared on the scene. It's the V-8 juice combined with the lemon-flavored Jell-O that make this such a tangy and refreshing treat. Try it, with or without chicken salad.

SERVES 12

1 envelope unflavored gelatin

¼ cup cold water

6 cups V-8 juice (use the spicy variety if you want real zing)

3 (3-ounce) packages lemon Jell-O

Cookware needed: mixing bowl, saucepan, 9 x 13-inch baking dish

The
Finishing Touch

For even more flavor and a little crunch, try stirring in one (or more) of these additional ingredients about 30 minutes after the aspic has begun to set: diced green pepper, sliced Spanish olives (with, or without, the pimiento), diced celery, diced or grated onion, grated carrot.

In a small bowl, sprinkle the gelatin over the cold water to soften it.

Heat 2 ½ cups of the V-8 juice in a saucepan and stir in the lemon Jell-O until it has dissolved.

Add the unflavored gelatin and stir well.

Add the remaining juice and mix thoroughly.

Pour the mixture into a 9 x 13-inch baking dish, and refrigerate until set, approximately 3 hours.

PREPARATION TIME: *15 minutes*
TOTAL TIME: *3 hours and 15 minutes*

Vegetables and Fruits

Some memories never fade. Like the time my daughter, Joslin, called me for an old family recipe. (Well actually, you'll probably identify this as one of *your* old family recipes, too.)

Seems that she and her husband, Mike, were having friends for dinner, and she wanted to prepare her grandmother's asparagus casserole. "You know, the one we loved so much at Thanksgiving and Christmas. When you find it, give me a call, and I'll write it down," she said.

"I don't need to look it up, and you're not even going to need a pencil and paper for this one, honey," I replied, smiling to myself, remembering when my mother had told me the same thing.

"Just drain three cans of asparagus and mix them with one can of cream of mushroom soup. Toss in lots of slivered almonds. Put it in a baking dish. Top with extra-sharp Cheddar. Bake at 350 for 25 to 30 minutes, and you've got it."

"But it's so good," Joli (as I call her) exclaimed. "I thought it *had* to be complicated."

It's not. And neither are any of the other vegetable dishes included in this section.

While there seems to be an endless supply of quickly made entrée and dessert recipes available in cookbooks, there doesn't seem to be as large a selection of different, really imaginative, vegetable recipes to choose from.

Don't get me wrong. Your grocer's freezer section is filled with vegetables, but they're usually just that...the vegetable in its most basic form—peas, corn, okra, broccoli, carrots, or a mixture.

By occasionally dressing up those vegetables, your family (especially the kids, if they are young) will enjoy them more.

That's what this chapter does. It takes the basic vegetable (whether frozen, canned, or fresh) and combines it with other ingredients to make it special and provide more mealtime variety, the same way our mothers and grandmothers did—quickly and effortlessly.

The results are often so good that they will surprise you.

Artichoke and Spinach Casserole

I'VE MENTIONED in the first chapter that I always stock up on artichokes when Joli is coming home. That's so I can make an Artichoke and Spinach Casserole. She's so crazy about it that, when she was pregnant, this was one of her cravings. Some people include a stick of butter with the ingredients, but frankly, we find it is just as good without it.

SERVES 8 TO 10

3 (10-ounce) packages frozen, chopped spinach

1 tablespoon lemon juice

1 (8-ounce) package cream cheese, softened

1 (14-ounce) can artichoke hearts

1 stick butter (optional)

Cookware needed: saucepan, baking dish or casserole

Preheat the oven to 350 degrees.

In a saucepan, warm the frozen, chopped spinach over low heat just enough to thoroughly defrost it, or defrost in the microwave.

Drain the spinach very well, squeezing it if necessary, and put it into a baking dish.

Squeeze the lemon juice over the spinach, add the cream cheese, and blend well with a fork.

Stir in the artichoke hearts and bake for 30 to 35 minutes.

PREPARATION TIME: *20 minutes*
TOTAL TIME: *approximately 1 hour*

Pureed Artichokes

THIS DELICIOUS and surprising vegetable is an excellent accompaniment to beef tenderloin or a simple chicken dish. You can make it in the blender or food processor without using any additional bowls, and then heat it according to your own schedule—in a saucepan, in a baking dish, or even in the microwave. Furthermore, the dish works equally well for a seated dinner or a buffet.

" It's a little known fact that in 1949, Marilyn Monroe, then just a budding starlet, was crowned Artichoke Queen in Castroville, California."

SERVES 4

∎∎∎∎∎∎∎∎

2 (7-ounce) cans artichoke bottoms, drained

½ cup whipping cream

1 stick butter, cut in pieces

1 teaspoon salt

½ teaspoon freshly ground pepper

Cookware needed: food processor or blender, baking dish or casserole, saucepan, or microwave-safe bowl

Put the drained artichoke bottoms in a food processor or blender and chop.

Add the remaining ingredients and puree until smooth (this will take only a minute or two), scraping down the sides of the container.

Heat thoroughly (about 20 minutes in the oven at 350 degrees, 10 minutes in a saucepan over low heat, or 2 to 3 minutes in the microwave) and serve.

∎∎∎∎∎∎∎∎∎

PREPARATION TIME: *5 minutes*

TOTAL TIME: *approximately 20 minutes*

Asparagus Casserole

IN THE INTRODUCTION to this section, I recounted telling Joli how to make that perennial favorite, Asparagus Casserole. But here it is in "proper" recipe form so you can easily find it for the holidays—or for just any day.

SERVES 6 TO 8

2 to 3 (15-ounce) cans asparagus tips or spears

1 (10-ounce) can cream of mushroom soup

½ cup slivered almonds

1 cup Cheddar cheese, grated

Cookware needed: baking dish or casserole

Preheat the oven to 350 degrees.

Drain the asparagus and put it in a baking dish, add the cream of mushroom soup and almonds, and blend.

Sprinkle the Cheddar cheese on top.

Bake for approximately 30 minutes, or until the cheese has melted and the casserole is bubbling.

PREPARATION TIME: *5 minutes*
TOTAL TIME: *35 minutes*

Thank goodness my children ate their vegetables!

OTHER MOTHERS weren't so lucky, and I still remember watching one good friend, with green beans on a fork, chasing her daughter around the house, all the while begging her to please eat just one green bean for Mr. Green Jeans, a popular TV character.

I usually served our family vegetables tossed in a little butter and salt and pepper in the saucepan while they were cooking.

At mealtime, we may have had barbequed chicken or pork chops prepared with cream of mushroom soup, but the vegetables were served au naturel.

But that doesn't mean I never whipped up a Vidalia Onion Casserole or Tomato Puddin'. I did and I do. But only when serving a simple steak, chops, or fish.

In fact, in my storehouse of memorable meals is a menu from one "fancy" dinner party that totally failed because the hostess served nothing but casseroles. The meat was in a casserole, the potatoes were in a casserole, the green beans were in a casserole, and the broccoli was in a casserole. My entire plate was a puddle of cream-colored, cream-based food that all tasted alike.

So, when planning your meals, remember that simply served vegetables are sometimes the best choice. If you want to dress them up just a little, sprinkle them with toasted sesame seeds or French Fried Onion Bits, or stir in a few toasted almond slivers (almondine), or even crunchy pine nuts.

Broccoli, Dressed-Up with Fried Bread Crumbs

JUST LIKE quiche did a few years ago, broccoli is taking it on the chin these days. I wonder if former President Bush would have been so critical of this nutritious vegetable if he'd been served Broccoli, Dressed-Up with Fried Bread Crumbs.

SERVES 4 TO 8, DEPENDING ON THE AMOUNT OF BROCCOLI USED

1 to 2 (14-ounce) bags frozen broccoli florets (or pieces with stems), thawed

6 tablespoons butter

6 tablespoons dry bread crumbs

1 hard-boiled egg, chopped (optional)

Salt and pepper, to taste

Juice of 1 lemon

Cookware needed: skillet, aluminum pan or heat-resistant bowl

Melt 4 tablespoons of the butter in a skillet, and fry the bread crumbs, stirring until lightly browned.

Transfer the bread crumbs to an aluminum pan (or heat-resistant bowl) and set it on the back of the stove to keep warm. Add the chopped egg (if including) and salt and pepper to taste.

Put the remaining 2 tablespoons of butter in the skillet, add the broccoli, sprinkle it with the lemon juice, and cook until heated through.

Arrange the broccoli on a serving platter and garnish it with the buttery bread crumbs.

PREPARATION TIME: *15 minutes*
TOTAL TIME: *15 minutes*

The
Finishing Touch

Create a sweeter dish by eliminating the bread crumbs and adding ¾ cup raisins (golden or brown) to the broccoli while it is heating. Then garnish the dish with 2 ounces of slivered, toasted almonds.

Broccoli au Gratin

TRY serving the prevous broccoli recipe "au gratin" by putting the vegetable and the bread-crumb mixture in a baking dish after it has heated through, and covering it completely with additional dry bread crumbs, dots of butter, and grated cheese.

Run this under a preheated broiler, 5 inches below the heat for less than 5 minutes, until a glazed, golden crust has formed. Beware of stepping away from the kitchen when you have food under a broiler—it browns very quickly.

Sage Advice

The finished product will be more moist, or "fondant" in texture if you select an American or Cheddar cheese, and drier if you use Parmesan or Romano.

SERVES 8

PREPARATION TIME: *15 minutes*
TOTAL TIME: *20 minutes*

Dressed-Up Broccoli Casserole

YOU CAN create a creamy version of the Broccoli, Dressed-Up with Fried Bread Crumbs (page 153) by adding 1 (10-ounce) can of a cream-based soup [(broccoli, celery, chicken), diluted with enough milk or cream to make it pourable (about ½ cup)], to the broccoli and bread crumbs, and pouring the mixture into a buttered baking dish.

Sprinkle the top with crushed Cornflakes or Ritz crackers and grated cheese and run it under the broiler until golden.

SERVES 8

PREPARATION TIME: *15 minutes*
TOTAL TIME: *20 minutes*

California Casserole

FOR A SLIGHT variation on the Dressed-Up Broccoli Casserole (on the previous page), use the frozen California blend of vegetables. This adds a few more vitamins, and the carrots give it the color your plate may be lacking.

SERVES 6

1 (16-ounce) bag frozen blend of broccoli, carrots, and cauliflower, thawed

1 (5-ounce) can sliced water chestnuts

1 (10-ounce) can cream-based soup (broccoli, celery, chicken)

1 soup can milk or cream

1 (3-ounce) package Parmesan cheese, grated

Cookware needed: baking dish or casserole

Preheat the oven to 325 degrees.

Combine the vegetables with the water chestnuts, and pour the mixture into a greased baking dish.

Combine the soup and milk or cream, and pour this mixture over the vegetables.

Top with Parmesan cheese, and bake for 35 minutes, or until bubbly.

PREPARATION TIME: *10 minutes*
TOTAL TIME: *approximately 45 minutes*

Carrot Surprise

WHAT'S IN A CAKE? Eggs, sugar, flour, vanilla. We know how good that is. Add the natural sweetness of baby carrots and you have an especially tasty combination. One that even the picky vegetable eaters will eat and then ask, What *is* this? That's why my friend Elizabeth Clement calls this recipe her Carrot Surprise.

SERVES 4

" I think people get more tired of vegetables fixed the same way than of anything else about a meal.
I am always on the lookout for new and interesting ways to vary the cooking of vegetables to eliminate this monotony."

—VIRGINIA MCDONALD,
HOW I COOK IT, 1949

1 (1-pound) bag baby carrots
1 stick butter, melted
3 eggs
½ cup sugar

3 tablespoons flour
1 teaspoon baking powder
1½ teaspoons vanilla extract
Cookware needed: blender, baking dish or casserole

Preheat the oven to 350 degrees.

Boil the carrots in water until tender, about 15 minutes. Drain.

Transfer the carrots to a blender, add the butter, and blend for 1 minute.

Add the remaining ingredients, and blend well.

Pour the carrot mixture into a greased baking dish, and bake for 45 minutes.

PREPARATION TIME: *15 minutes*
TOTAL TIME: *60 minutes*

Glazed Carrots

SOME recipes (like tuna casserole) have been around so long that I assume everyone knows them. Not so, as I've discovered while writing this book.

Take glazed carrots, for example. Just the other day, while I was visiting with my daughter and some of her friends, the age-old question, "How *do* you get the kids to eat their veggies?" came up.

Invariably, the recipes started flying—including a couple for glazed carrots. When the pens and scraps of paper came out, I knew what the kids in that neighborhood were going to be eating that night! And I realized that some of the moms were going to be fixing glazed carrots for the first time.

Hopefully, the parents were going to be eating them too. They're tasty and good for you, and a cinch to make in no time at all.

SERVES 4

3 tablespoons butter
2 tablespoons brown sugar
1 can Le Seur baby carrots

Cookware needed: saucepan or microwave-safe bowl

Combine the butter and brown sugar in a saucepan, for stovetop cooking, or a microwave safe bowl. Heat over medium-low or in the microwave just long enough to melt and blend the ingredients.

Add the baby carrots, and stir gently. Heat until warm.

PREPARATION TIME: *3 minutes*
TOTAL TIME: *10 minutes*

Glazed Carrots with Onions

FOR MORE adult palates, try this variation.

SERVES 8

3 tablespoons butter

2 tablespoons peanut oil

1 (2-pound) bag baby carrots

½ cup frozen, chopped onion

2 teaspoons fresh thyme

2 tablespoons brown sugar

1 tablespoon water

Salt and pepper, to taste

Cookware needed: skillet with a lid

Heat the butter and oil in a skillet with a lid.

Add the carrots, onion, thyme, brown sugar, and water.

Season with salt and pepper to taste and mix well.

Simmer, covered, for 15 minutes, stirring from time to time.

Remove the cover and cook another 5 minutes on high heat until the liquid is reduced to a syrupy glaze.

PREPARATION TIME: *3 to 5 minutes*
TOTAL TIME: *approximately 25 minutes*

The
Finishing Touch

Garnish the finished dish with chopped parsley, if you wish.

The Great Celery Mystery

FOR THE LIFE OF ME, I can't figure it out, and neither can some of my chef friends.

We can buy frozen seasoning blends and soup starters that have celery in them.

Why, then, can't we buy packages of frozen, diced celery? A tremendous number of recipes, whether they are meat or vegetable casseroles, mixed vegetable dishes prepared on the stovetop in a skillet, or salads, call for diced celery. Frozen, diced onions and peppers (the red, green, and yellow, sweet or bell varieties) are available, *why* not celery?

Celery Casserole

FEW PEOPLE cook a celery casserole, and I know why. It takes too much time to cut, chop, and dice the main ingredients. Sometimes, when I've been really pushed for time but I wanted to serve this vegetable accompaniment, I've raided the chopped-celery bin at the salad bar. (One time, a fellow customer actually asked me what I was going to do with it! I was tempted to say something about rabbits, but I didn't.)

This is actually a very good casserole, and one that I hope will become more popular. I had it the first time at Geri Winstead's house around 1970, and I've never forgotten it.

SERVES 6

3 cups diced celery

¼ cup slivered almonds

1 (5-ounce) can sliced water chestnuts

1 (10-ounce) can cream of chicken soup or 1 (10-ounce) can cream of celery soup (for a vegetarian version)

¾ cup half-and-half

1 (4-ounce) can sliced mushrooms, drained

Salt and pepper, to taste

Dash Worcestershire sauce

½ cup Parmesan cheese, grated

½ cup Ritz cracker crumbs

Cookware needed: small saucepan, 1 ½-quart baking dish or casserole

Preheat the oven to 350 degrees.

Boil the celery until almost tender, approximately 5 minutes. Drain well and put it in the bottom of a baking dish.

Add almonds and water chestnuts to the celery.

Empty the soup into a saucepan, and slowly stir in the half-and-half. Add the mushrooms, salt, pepper, and Worcestershire sauce, and heat over low heat until bubbly.

Pour the soup mixture over the celery, then sprinkle all with the Parmesan and cracker crumbs.

Bake until hot and bubbly, about 25 to 30 minutes.

PREPARATION TIME: *15 minutes, or less if you buy the celery already diced*
TOTAL TIME: *approximately 45 minutes*

Scalloped Corn

Sage Advice

Canned corn isn't all the same. Large-kernel yellow corn has the strongest flavor. White corn is more tender and milder. Shoepeg is sweeter yet. Which one you choose for this dish really depends on your family's taste buds.

WHEN THE SNOW is knee-deep up New Hampshire way and writer Bea Cole is trying to make a newspaper deadline—she also takes care of her three active daughters—she often relies on this trusty, sure-to-please, dinner standby.

SERVES 4 TO 6

1 (15-ounce) can corn kernels
1 cup Cornflakes
¾ cup milk

1 tablespoon butter
Cookware needed: baking dish or casserole, with lid

Preheat the oven to 350 degrees.

Combine the corn, Cornflakes, and milk in a greased baking dish.

Dot the top with the butter.

Cover and bake for 30 minutes, or until milk is absorbed. Stir occasionally.

Serve hot.

PREPARATION TIME: *5 minutes*
TOTAL TIME: *35 minutes*

"It is not elegant to gnaw Indian corn.

The kernels should be scored with a knife,

scraped off into the plate, and then eaten with a

fork. Ladies should be particulary careful how

they manage to ticklish a dainty,

lest the exhibition rub off a little desirable

romance."

—CHARLES DAY, *HINTS ON ETIQUETTE*, 1844

Eggplant Soufflé

THERE'S nothing prettier than unblemished, deep purple eggplants piled high in a basket at the farmer's market. At the height of the summer, eggplant is like squash—so plentiful, it goes begging. That's when I buy twice as much eggplant as we can possibly eat, even if I served it for breakfast—not an appetizing thought.

Then I move on to the baskets of zucchini and crookneck squash and buy double portions of those.

When I get my bounty home, I first arrange a big bowl of the vegetables for the dining room table. What's left over goes into the kitchen.

Though I love fried eggplant, I've usually overstayed at the market, chatting with friends, exchanging recipes, and just enjoying the day. Now I don't have the time or the inclination to stand over a hot skillet and turn each carefully battered eggplant slice at that split second when it reaches golden brown.

It's much easier just to boil some water, get a bag of grated cheese from the refrigerator, take down the canister of storebought bread crumbs, and whip up an eggplant soufflé. It will be ready by the time I've sliced some homegrown tomatoes and put out the baked beans, slaw, and chicken I grabbed from the Colonel on the way home from the market.

SERVES 6 TO 8

2 medium eggplants
½ plus ⅛ teaspoon salt
2 tablespoons butter
2 eggs, lightly beaten
⅓ cup milk

⅛ teaspoon pepper
1 cup Cheddar cheese, grated
1 cup bread crumbs
Paprika
Cookware needed: saucepan, baking dish or casserole

Peel and cube the eggplant.

Place the eggplant in a saucepan and cover it with water to which ½ teaspoon salt has been added. Cook until soft, or about 10 minutes.

Drain the water, and mash the eggplant.

Add the butter, eggs, milk, the remaining salt, and the pepper, and blend well.

Preheat the oven to 350 degrees.

Put a layer of the eggplant mixture in a well-greased baking dish.

Spread a layer of cheese and then a layer of bread crumbs on top.

Repeat these layers, ending with the bread crumbs. Sprinkle the top with paprika.

Bake for 30 to 40 minutes or until set.

PREPARATION TIME: *20 minutes*
TOTAL TIME: *approximately 60 minutes*

ETZ Casserole

(Eggplant, Tomato, Zucchini Casserole)

OK. You bought the eggplant and zucchini at the market, not the grocery store. And the fresh tomatoes may have come from a neighbor's yard, or even your own yard. Not *every* single recipe in this book is made from *all* storebought canned or frozen ingredients. But the cheese and bread crumbs are definitely from the store.

And so, just in case you've gone overboard on the tomatoes, too, here is a quick and sure way to use all three of your fresh ingredients from the market, or from the fresh produce department of the grocery store.

Sage Advice

Our mothers always added "just a pinch" of sugar to any dish with tomatoes in it. Today, most canned tomatoes are already well flavored. But when preparing a casserole or skillet recipe that calls for **fresh toma-toes***, a pinch of sugar (¼ to ½ teaspoon) helps cut the natural acidity of the tomatoes.*

SERVES 6 TO 8

3 tablespoons olive oil

½ cup frozen, diced combo of onion and green pepper, or some of each

1 clove garlic, minced, or ½ teaspoon prepared garlic

1 medium eggplant, cubed

2 or 3 medium zucchini, sliced

3 or 4 medium tomatoes, peeled and cut into small chunks

½ cup stuffed Spanish olive pieces (not whole)

¼ teaspoon sugar (see *Sage Advice*)

Salt and pepper, to taste

¾ cup unflavored and dry bread crumbs

¾ cup Parmesan cheese, grated

Cookware needed: covered skillet, baking dish or casserole

In a skillet with a lid, heat the olive oil, and sauté the onion, green pepper, and garlic for 2 to 3 minutes.

Add the eggplant and the zucchini, and cook over medium heat until the veg-etables are soft, approximately 10 to 15 minutes.

Preheat the oven to 325 degrees.

Add the tomatoes, the olive pieces, and salt and pepper to taste. Cover the skil-let and cook the mixture another 10 minutes.

Pour the mixture into a lightly greased baking dish, and top the vegetables with bread crumbs and Parmesan cheese.

Bake for 30 to 40 minutes.

PREPARATION TIME: *15 to 20 minutes*
TOTAL TIME: *approximately 1 hour*

Green Bean Bundles

REMEMBER Goldy Bear's caterer's advice to always use the French name for food? This green bean dish comes to you from the ladies of Beaumont, Texas, who sometimes call it "Paquets de Haricots Verts."

It matters not what you call it, or actually whether you use green beans or flat, Italian pole beans. This a delicious and ingenious way to serve green beans for a large buffet.

SERVES 9 TO 12

15 to 16 strips bacon

1 box plain wooden toothpicks (use as many as you need)

3 (15-ounce) cans whole green beans, or Italian pole beans, drained

1 cup brown sugar

1 cup butter, melted

½ teaspoon garlic salt

Soy sauce, to taste

Cookware needed: mixing bowl, 9 x 13-inch baking dish or casserole

Cut the bacon strips in half lengthwise.

Wrap 9 or 10 green beans in a "bundle" (or stack them if using the pole beans) using the bacon strips to "tie" them, and secure the bundles with toothpicks.

Place the bundles in a baking dish.

Combine the brown sugar, butter, garlic salt, and a splash of soy sauce, and pour the mixture over the bundles.

Refrigerate overnight.

Preheat the oven to 350 degrees.

Bake the beans uncovered for 30 minutes.

PREPARATION TIME: *15 minutes*
TOTAL TIME: *45 minutes*

Sage Advice

Experiment. Be creative. Have fun. That's just as much a part of cooking as the eating to my way of thinking. And that's just what I did when trying to dress up a simple chicken and rice main course for dinner. I really didn't have time to "bundle" the beans in the bacon. Furthermore, I only had turkey bacon on hand. Add to that, Bob is borderline diabetic (inherited, so I avoid dishes requiring lots of sugar). I simply put the contents of 1 (15-ounce) can of whole green beans, drained, between 6 turkey bacon strips in a small round baking dish (3 strips on top; 3 strips on bottom). Instead of preparing the ample amount of brown sugar and butter marinade called for in the recipe, I made a much smaller amount by using a heaping tablespoon of Dia-betiSweet™ and an equal amount of Land O Lakes honey butter, plus some soy sauce and garlic salt. It was simple, easy, took no time, and was delicious. Just the right accompaniment.

Green Bean Casserole

IF YOU'RE flipping through this book looking for new and different recipes, you should keep turning the pages because this green bean casserole has been a standard on almost every American dinner table for decades.

Whenever the Jenkins family held a large get-together or gathered for a holiday meal, Shipley Jenkins, my sister-in-law, offered to bring the green bean casserole. In fact, it got to the point where we'd just call Shipley and say, "Be sure to bring the green bean casserole," because that was what she was going to do anyway.

Since my kids loved Aunt Shipley and her green bean casserole, I was always delighted to know they'd have a favorite vegetable dish for these occasions, no matter what else happened to show up on the table.

The version given below is the simplest of all green bean casserole recipes, but read on to the variations for some additional ideas about how to prepare it.

SERVES 4 TO 6

1 (16-ounce) bag frozen French-style green beans

1 (10-ounce) can cream of mushroom soup

1 (2.8-ounce) can French Fried Onion Bits (a fat-free variety is now available)

Cookware needed: baking dish or casserole

Preheat the oven to 350 degrees.

Allow the string beans to defrost slightly, then combine them with the mushroom soup in a baking dish.

Lavishly sprinkle the top with as many of the onion toppers as you wish (or the ones you have left after nibbling on them while preparing the rest of the casserole).

Bake for 30 minutes or until bubbly.

PREPARATION TIME: *5 minutes*
TOTAL TIME: *35 minutes*

Cheerful Green Beans

ONE HOSTESS who served this colorful and quite delicious green bean dish called it her "Christmas" green beans. But it's too good to have just once a year, so I prefer to call it "Cheerful" green beans.

Incidentally, asparagus or broccoli may be used in place of the green beans if you like.

SERVES 4 TO 6

½ cup frozen red bell pepper strips, or 1 medium fresh pepper, cut in strips

2 tablespoons olive oil

1 teaspoon prepared garlic, or 2 cloves, finely minced

¼ cup balsamic vinegar

Salt and pepper, to taste

1 (16-ounce) bag frozen string beans, thawed (I prefer the very small, whole variety)

Cookware needed: skillet

In a skillet, sauté the pepper strips in the olive oil.

Stir in the garlic, vinegar, salt, and pepper, and add the green beans.

Cook for 3 to 4 minutes, stirring occasionally, or until the beans are thoroughly warmed.

PREPARATION TIME: *approximately 10 minutes, depending on vegetables used*
TOTAL TIME: *approximately 15 minutes, depending on vegetables used (see Sage Advice)*

Sage Advice

If you use the very small and tender string beans, you really don't have to thaw them, although you may if you prefer. If using another variety of frozen beans, you may wish to blanch them, or cook them according to package directions before combining them with the other ingredients.

The Finishing Touch

A little freshly grated Parmesan cheese on the top is a nice finishing touch.

Vidalia Onion Casserole

GOOD RECIPES travel fast.

I first tasted Vidalia Onion Casserole in Jackson, Mississippi, while touring with my book, *Southern Christmas.* When I begged for the recipe, my hostess, Martha McIntosh, gave me a copy of the newly published Jackson Junior League cookbook, *Come On In!*

The casserole (and the cookbook) became an instant hit in our home, especially with my daughter, Joslin. After graduating from college, when she moved to Richmond, Virginia, and began cooking and entertaining on her own, Joli copied the recipe down on an index card and kept it close at hand.

Like her mother and grandmother before her, Joslin soon began assembling her own collection of cookbooks. One of the first ones she bought was *Virginia Fare*, published by the Junior League of Richmond. You can imagine her delight when she found it included another, ever so slightly different recipe for Vidalia Onion Casserole.

That's the other thing about recipes. Often you can skimp on the milk and go heavy on the eggs, or substitute chicken broth for beef bouillon. You can even use Parmesan or Cheddar cheese. But there are certain main ingredients that should not be changed.

Such was the case with the two Vidalia onion casseroles. Although the secondary ingredients varied, both recipes contained the two magic components that give this casserole its soul—Vidalia onions and buttery crackers.

You can choose from several different brands of cracker (as long as they're buttery). But please. *Only* if Vidalia onions are not in season should you ever consider using a substitute. And then, be sure to use sweet yellow onions. Too pungent an onion taste doesn't work in this recipe.

If you haven't had this casserole, you're in for quite a treat, and I'll wager it will become a favorite in your house as well. Pass it on.

SERVES 8 (WELL, MAYBE ONLY 6—IT'S THAT GOOD!)

2 sticks butter

3 to 4 large Vidalia onions, sliced in rings

40 to 50 buttery crackers, crushed (one package of a 2-pack, 16-ounce box of Ritz or Town House crackers will yield the right amount)

1 (8-ounce) package Cheddar cheese, grated

3 large eggs, beaten

¾ cup milk

⅛ teaspoon paprika

Salt and pepper, to taste

Cookware needed: mixing bowl, baking dish or casserole

Sage Advice

There's no short cut around sautéing the onion. But using an already grated Cheddar cheese (I prefer the sharp variety) and crushing the crackers in their wrapping helps to speed the preparation time along.

Melt one stick of butter in a large skillet.

Sauté the onion rings in the butter until translucent.

Melt the second stick of butter in a microwave-safe mixing bowl, and add the crushed crackers, reserving at least ¼ to use on top of the casserole.

Preheat the oven to 350 degrees.

Grease a baking dish and cover the bottom with some of the buttered crumbs. Place a layer of sautéed onion over the crumbs, followed by some of the cheese. Repeat these layers, ending with the cheese.

Combine the beaten eggs, milk, and paprika, and add a little salt and pepper. Pour the milk mixture over the onions, bread crumbs, and cheese.

Top the casserole with the reserved, unbuttered crumbs.

Bake for 35 to 45 minutes, or until bubbly and golden brown.

PREPARATION TIME: *20 minutes*
TOTAL TIME: *approximately 1 hour*

Peas in a Boat

COLOR, nutrition, style, taste—this vegetable selection has it all. Plus, it's unusual; you won't see it served every day.

Thanks to the availability of canned peas (Le Seur, please), your trusty blender, and already flavored bread crumbs, most of the work required to make this attractive choice has been done for you. It's a wonderful accompaniment to a rotisserie chicken (straight from the store, of course), and a quickly assembled Pecan Rice casserole. It gives the whole meal a "homemade" look and quality.

SERVES 6

6 yellow (crookneck) squash, small and well shaped

1 (6-ounce) can Le Seur baby peas, drained

1 tablespoon butter

Salt and pepper, to taste

1 teaspoon sugar

2 to 3 tablespoons heavy cream

2 heaping tablespoons flavored bread crumbs

2 teaspoons Parmesan or Cheddar cheese, grated

Cookware needed: saucepan, blender, baking dish or casserole

Boil the whole squash until tender, no more than 5 minutes.

Drain, and cut the vegetables in half lengthwise. Scoop out the seeds to make a boat-shaped cavity. (Leave some of the meat on the squash peel, so that you don't scrape down to the outer skin.)

Preheat the oven to 350 degrees.

Combine the peas, butter, salt, pepper, sugar, and cream in a blender and puree until soft but not runny. (Begin with just 2 tablespoons of the cream, and add more only if needed.)

Fill the squash cavities with the pea mixture, and place them in a greased baking dish.

Combine the bread crumbs and cheese, and sprinkle over the squash.

Bake for 12 to 15 minutes.

PREPARATION TIME: *15 to 20 minutes*
TOTAL TIME: *30 to 40 minutes*

Peas in Tomatoes

LOOKING for an even more colorful way to dish up that year-round favorite, green peas? Try serving them in a hollowed-out tomato shell.

Do not purée the peas; simply season them with a little butter, salt, and pepper. It's that simple. But in this instance, frozen petite peas are a better choice than the canned variety.

SERVES 6

6 firm tomatoes

1 (10-ounce) package frozen petite peas

Salt and pepper, to taste

1 to 2 tablespoons butter

Cookware needed: microwave-safe bowl, baking dish or casserole

Preheat the oven to 350 degrees.

Slice the top off each tomato and scoop out the seeds and just enough of the pulp to make room for an ample quantity of the peas.

Put the unfilled tomatoes in a greased baking pan and bake for 12 to 15 minutes.

While the tomatoes are baking, barely cover the petite peas with water and microwave on high for 2 to 4 minutes—just long enough to thaw and warm them.

Season the peas with salt and pepper and add the butter, just as you would if you were going to serve them as is.

Fill the tomatoes with the peas and garnish with a sprig of fresh parsley.

PREPARATION TIME: *15 minutes*
TOTAL TIME: *30 minutes*

Sage Advice

For another variation, slice an acorn squash in half, and scoop out the seeds. Fill a baking pan with enough water to cover the bottom, and turn the squash flesh (flat) side down in the pan. Bake at 325 degrees for about 40 minutes, or until soft. (Or you can microwave them for 10 to 15 minutes.) Turn the squash over, fill with the peas, and season with salt, pepper, and freshly ground nutmeg.

Portobello Deluxe

MARY MURPHY loves to cook. But she seldom does. "Just don't have the time," she says.

I know why she doesn't have the time. When she's not running the family gas station, she's seeing about family members, or she's looking after an orphaned dog or injured bird someone has dropped by the station, or—most likely—she's reading a book. Mary's the most voracious reader I've ever known. But she does find time to fix this easy portobello mushroom dish.

When I asked Mary if she serves this as an entrée, a salad, or an appetizer, she replied, "It's a meal. The mushroom is filling, the cheese is the protein, and the tomato is the vegetable."

Truth is, you can serve this versatile item any number of ways. The availability of both whole and sliced, ready-to-serve portobellos helps too. And if onions are to your liking, try adding a slice or two before finishing the dish with the cheese topping.

Incidentally, if you've been timid about trying portobello mushrooms at home because they seem to be one of those exotic restaurant foods, this recipe will convince you otherwise.

Sage Advice

If the mushrooms and tomatoes are particularly plump and thick, prepare the recipe through the Italian spice stage, and then cook the vegetables under the broiler for 5 to 10 minutes. Then add the grated cheese and continue to broil until the cheese has melted to your liking.

PREPARE 2 HALVES OR 1 WHOLE MUSHROOM PER PERSON

Portobello mushrooms either whole, or halved

Olive oil or cooking spray

Fresh tomatoes (1 slice per mushroom)

Italian spices, to taste

Grated cheese (mozzarella, Cheddar, Monterey Jack, your choice)

Cookware needed: cookie sheet or shallow baking dish or casserole

Brush a little olive oil on each mushroom bottom, or over the slices, or spray with cooking spray.

Slice the tomatoes to conform to the shape of the mushrooms and place them on top.

Sprinkle the tomatoes with a generous helping of Italian spices.

Top with an ample layer of cheese.

Broil for 5 to 10 minutes, or until the cheese is bubbly and melted.

PREPARATION TIME: *10 minutes*
TOTAL TIME: *15 to 20 minutes*

Spinach, Cream Cheese, and Tomato Casserole

IF YOU LIKE spinach and cream cheese, but are not wild about the Artichoke and Spinach Casserole, here's a dish you may like that substitutes tomatoes for artichokes.

SERVES 8 TO 10

3 (10-ounce) packages frozen, chopped spinach

1 tablespoon lemon juice

1 (8-ounce) package cream cheese

3 to 4 large, perfectly ripe tomatoes, sliced thick

1 cup Parmesan cheese, buttered bread crumbs, or a combination of the two

Cookware needed: saucepan, baking dish or casserole

Preheat the oven to 350 degrees.

In a saucepan, warm the frozen, chopped spinach over low heat just long enough to thoroughly defrost it, or defrost in the microwave.

Drain the spinach very well, squeezing it if necessary, and put it into a baking dish. Squeeze the lemon juice over the spinach, add the cream cheese, and blend well with a fork. Top the spinach mixture with the tomato slices.

Sprinkle with the Parmesan cheese and/or bread crumbs, and bake for 30 to 35 minutes.

PREPARATION TIME: *20 minutes*
TOTAL TIME: *approximately 1 hour*

Very Good Winter Squash

DON'T let the cream, Madeira, and pecans in this recipe mislead you. This squash dish isn't just for company, at least not at our house. You'll find me serving it for dinner even when there are only the two of us.

I like winter squash seasoned with only a little butter and salt and pepper. But when I fix it that way, Bob always leaves his untouched. I wasn't about to give up this nutritious and colorful (how often have I used those words to describe some of my favorites?) vegetable. Time to get out the seasonings.

I think you'll like the results. Bob does. His exact words were, "Say, this stuff is good."

SERVES 6 TO 8

The
Finishing Touch

If you wish, you can combine ¼ cup of bread crumbs with 2 tablespoons of melted butter and sprinkle this mixture on top of the squash before baking. Another option is to top it with miniature marshmallows.

2 (12-ounce) packages frozen winter squash, defrosted

2 tablespoons butter, melted

1 ½ cups heavy cream

1 teaspoon cinnamon

¼ to ⅓ cup Madeira or cream sherry

¼ teaspoon salt

Freshly ground pepper, to taste

½ cup chopped pecans

Cookware needed: mixing bowl, baking dish or casserole

Preheat the oven to 350 degrees.

Put the defrosted squash in a well-greased baking pan or baking dish.

Add the melted butter, cream, cinnamon, Madeira or sherry, salt, and pepper, and mix well.

Fold in the pecans.

Bake uncovered for 30 minutes or until bubbling.

PREPARATION TIME: *5 minutes*
TOTAL TIME: *35 to 45 minutes*

Tomato Puddin'

I ALWAYS called the delicious combination of canned tomatoes and stale, crumbled bread, brought to life with a little butter and spices, "stewed tomatoes." But my dear friend Carolista Baum had a much better name for this old-timey dish.

"Tomato Puddin' " she called it, always dropping the final "g" in her soft, Eastern North Carolina accent. Though she prepared it no differently from anyone else, hers was always the best. I'm sure it's because it was "puddin.'"

SERVES 4 TO 6

¼ cup butter, melted

1 (28-ounce) can tomatoes, diced

3 or 4 slices stale bread, broken into quarter-size pieces

½ cup brown sugar

Salt and pepper, to taste

Cookware needed: mixing bowl, baking dish or casserole

Preheat the oven to 350 degrees.

Combine the butter, tomatoes, bread, sugar, and salt and pepper, to taste.

Pour the mixture into a greased baking dish, and bake for 40 to 45 minutes, or until set.

PREPARATION TIME: *10 minutes*
TOTAL TIME: *50 to 60 minutes*

Sage Advice

This is a great way to use up stale bread, especially if you have the tail end of a French or Italian loaf going to waste. The drier the bread, the better the puddin'. And don't even think about using fresh tomatoes. The flavor and texture of the canned ones, combined with the stale bread, butter, and sugar are what make this recipe good.

Gingered Vegetables

AH YOUTH! Many, many years ago, because I was young and didn't know any better, I brazenly asked the waiter at a fancy New York restaurant for a recipe. He told me that the chef wouldn't comply, but I begged so hard that the poor waiter finally must have approached the chef just to get an answer that would shut me up.

You can imagine my fellow diners' amazement when the chef actually appeared at our table.

"Now, which one of you Southerners wants to see me?" he asked in his own Southern drawl.

Obviously, the waiter had said something about the lady with the Southern accent, and *that* had prompted the chef (maybe a little homesick?) to venture into the dining room.

It turns out the chef was from Wilmington, North Carolina, and he gladly shared the ginger sauce recipe I was coveting. His "secret" recipe was so good, I wrote it down in the front cover of four or five different cookbooks so I wouldn't lose it!

When you glance at the recipe, please don't let the long list of sauce ingredients give you pause. You can measure them out in a couple of minutes.

Once that is done, you simply pour the sauce over your favorite blend of frozen vegetables, and you have a spectacular dish—one that will delight a serious vegetarian.

SERVES 12

For the sauce:

4 tablespoons butter

4 tablespoons Chinese oyster sauce

¼ cup sherry vinegar or 4 tablespoons lemon juice

2 tablespoons soy sauce

2 tablespoons freshly grated ginger

1 teaspoon each of the following dried herbs:

Parsley

Chervil

Coriander

Thyme

Oregano

For the vegetables:

1 (2-pound) package frozen vegetable blend that includes snow peas, mushrooms, broccoli, peppers, onions and other Oriental-style vegetables. You may want to mix and match the smaller boxes to make your own combination.

(Other good vegetables include baby corn, carrots, cauliflower. You want to avoid peas, beans, and potatoes.)

Cookware needed: skillet

To make the sauce, melt the butter in a skillet over medium-low heat, and then stir in the liquid ingredients, ginger, and herbs.

Add the vegetables, cover, and cook over medium heat until the vegetables are cooked to your taste—but not so long that they lose their crunch and crispness—for about 8 to 10 minutes.

PREPARATION TIME: *10 minutes*
TOTAL TIME: *approximately 20 minutes*

Curried Fruit

There's a wonderful and true saying: Scratch a cook and you'll get a recipe.

That happened one day when my assistant, good friend, and fabulous cook, Charlotte Sizer, and I began comparing notes on one of our favorite easy-to-make dishes, Curried Fruit. While the ingredients were just about the same, we prepared the dish quite differently. I just mix everything together, but Charlotte uses what I call the "sprinkle and spread" technique.

Following are two variations of the same recipe. You can decide which one you prefer. Charlotte's may be better suited to a party where the food is plated before serving, while mine works well when guests serve themselves.

Whichever way you prepare it, be sure to try this tasty fruit dish. It's colorful, filled with vitamins, combines many different textures, and makes a wonderful accompaniment to either meats or casseroles—and it's a change from the usual vegetables.

Emyl's Mix and Serve Curried Fruit

SERVES 8 OR MORE

1 (15-once) can sliced peaches

1 (15-ounce) can sliced pears

1 (11-ounce) can mandarin oranges

1 (8 ½-ounce) can apricot halves

1 (16 ½-ounce) can dark cherries (or Queen Anne, or maraschino)

1 (15-ounce) can diced pineapple

½ cup light or dark raisins, or a combination of the two for a variety in taste and color

Cookware needed: large saucepan

Reserve the peach and pear juices in a mixing bowl. Drain the remaining fruit, and pour the fruit (at random) into a large, heavy saucepan or pot.

To the reserved juice, add:

½ cup brown sugar

1 tablespoon cinnamon

¼ teaspoon nutmeg (about 5 turns of a nutmeg grinder)

2 tablespoons curry powder

2 tablespoons butter

The
Finishing Touch

This colorful fruit accompaniment looks pretty when served in a heat-tolerant crystal bowl.

Whisk to blend and pour the juice mixture over the fruit. Simmer about 25 minutes, stirring occasionally.

PREPARATION TIME: *5 minutes*
TOTAL TIME: *30 minutes*

Charlotte's Spread and Sprinkle Baked Fruit

SERVES 8

Cookware needed: Bake this version in a shallow, glass oven-to-table baking dish or casserole.

Use the same canned fruits as in the previous recipe, except omit the mandarin oranges and substitute pineapple rings (8 to 10 per 15-ounce can) for the diced pineapple, and halved peaches and pears for the sliced ones. Plan on enough to prepare at least one fruit ring (beginning with a pineapple ring) per person.

Preheat the oven to 325 degrees.

Begin by spreading the pineapple rings in a single layer on the bottom of a lightly greased baking dish. Arrange either a halved peach or a pear in the center of each ring, pouring in enough of the canned juices to reach a level of approximately ¼ inch.

Build the dish prettily, placing a cherry in the center of each fruit half. Fill in the bare spots in the baking dish with the raisins and apricots.

Sprinkle the brown sugar, cinnamon, nutmeg, and curry (optional) over the fruit and dot with the butter.

Bake for 35 to 40 minutes. Baste with the pan juices twice during cooking.

PREPARATION TIME: *10 minutes*
TOTAL TIME: *50 minutes*

"The pleasure of preparing and eating good food can only be enhanced by the pleasure of sharing it with friends."

—RUTH MELLINKOFF, *THE UNCOMMON COOK BOOK*, 1968

Sage Advice

If you prefer, flavor your baked fruit with sherry rather than curry. Pour ¼ cup over the fruit before sprinkling it with the spices, or soak 10 prunes in enough sherry to cover for 20 minutes, then add them to the baking dish before baking—delicious!

When buying raisins for baking, not just snacking, the cylindrical container with a plastic top does the best job of keeping the fruit moist and fresh. Light/golden raisins are sweeter and lighter tasting.

Potatoes, Pasta, and Rice

Potatoes were the standard fare in our home when I was growing up. Baked potatoes, new potatoes, sweet potatoes, boiled potatoes, fried potatoes, smashed potatoes, scalloped potatoes. Then I married.

My husband's family roots sprang from South Carolina, and they ate rice. White rice. Plain white rice.

Over the years, I grew to love rice just as much as potatoes, especially once I learned what you could do to plain white rice to vary it a little.

Today's boxed rices provide a lot of variety, but here are a few additional recipes that are quick, easy, and will give more of that "homemade" feeling at meal time.

"Skill in cooking is as readily shown in a baked potato or a johnny-cake, as in a canvas-back duck."

—*THE STAR COOK BOOK,*
BY MRS. GRACE
TOWNSEND, 1895

Bouillon Rice

WHEN MY GOOD FRIEND and Southern writer, Sharyn McCrumb, isn't meeting publishing deadlines or traveling to Europe to lecture on her Ballad series of books, she's busy with her three children. And whenever one of the kids has to take a "covered dish" somewhere, off they go to the kitchen to make Bouillon Rice.

SERVES 4 TO 6

1 stick butter

½ cup frozen, diced onion

1 (10-ounce) can beef broth

1 (10-ounce) can beef consommé

2 cups uncooked rice

Cookware needed: skillet, covered baking dish or casserole

Preheat the oven to 350 degrees.

Sauté the onion (or microwave it) in the butter, until lightly browned.

Transfer the onion and butter to a baking dish and add the beef broth and consommé.

Add the rice, cover (using aluminum foil if you do not have a fitted lid), and bake for 1 hour.

PREPARATION TIME: *7 to 8 minutes*

TOTAL TIME: *approximately 1 hour and 10 minutes*

Pecan Rice

IF YOU'RE as wild about pecans as I am, you're always looking for ways to slip their sweet, crunchy taste and texture into your meal time. Bouillon rice becomes a rice and pecan casserole with these simple additions.

1 ½ cups chopped pecans
¾ teaspoon dried thyme
2 tablespoons dried parsley

To this you can also add:
1 heaping teaspoon prepared garlic
1 (4-ounce) can sliced mushrooms, drained

Prepare Bouillon Rice as described in the previous recipe. When putting the rice in the casserole, also add the ingredients above.

PREPARATION TIME: *varies according to selected ingredients*
TOTAL TIME: *a little more than 1 hour*

Creamy Rice

REMEMBER RICE AND GRAVY? That one-time favorite seems to have all but disappeared from today's tables. But here's a rice dish that makes its own delicious "gravy" or sauce. You wouldn't want to serve it with a meat or vegetable casserole made with a cream soup, but it is awfully good with grilled meats and a salad.

If the recipe looks familiar, that's because it's another a variation on Bouillon Rice (page 179).

SERVES 4 TO 6

½ cup frozen, diced onion

1 stick butter

1 (10-ounce) can cream of
mushroom soup

1 soup can water

1 (10-ounce) can beef consommé

2 cups uncooked rice

Cookware needed: skillet, baking
dish or casserole, with a lid

Preheat the oven to 350 degrees.

Sauté the onion (or microwave it) in the butter until brown.

Transfer the onion and butter to a baking dish.

Add the mushroom soup mixed with the water and the consommé.

Add the uncooked rice and stir to blend. Cover the baking dish and bake for 1 hour.

PREPARATION TIME: *7 to 8 minutes*
TOTAL TIME: *approximately 1 hour and 10 minutes*

Easy Oven Rice

LIKE SHARYN MCCRUMB'S Bouillon Rice, the good thing about Joan Sprinkle's Easy Oven Rice is that it cooks in the oven—so that once you've assembled the ingredients you are free to do other things. Even though I'm a great fan of instant rice, you have to be close by to keep the rice from sticking or, as I've been known to do, burning up the pan!

SERVES 4

1 (10-ounce) can French onion soup, undiluted

½ stick margarine, melted

1 (4-ounce) can sliced mushrooms, drained, liquid reserved

1 (8-ounce) can sliced water chestnuts, drained, liquid reserved

1 ⅓ cups liquid (made from the liquids of the mushrooms and water chestnuts, plus added water)

1 cup uncooked long grain rice

Cookware needed: baking dish or casserole

Preheat the oven to 350 degrees.

Combine the soup and margarine and stir well.

Combine all of the ingredients and pour the mixture into a lightly greased 10 x 6 x 2-inch baking dish.

Cover and bake for 1 hour and 10 minutes.

PREPARATION TIME: *10 minutes*
TOTAL TIME: *1 hour and 20 minutes*

Apple Rice

RICE AND PORK CHOPS go together as, well, apples and pork chops. So why not make it easy on yourself and prepare this quick and unusual apple rice. It works very well for brunch too, if you're serving sausage links.

SERVES 8

¼ cup frozen, diced onion

½ cup diced celery

2 tablespoons butter

2 cups uncooked rice

1 cup apple juice

1 cup water

1 teaspoon onion salt

½ teaspoon cinnamon

1 medium apple, cored and finely chopped

Cookware needed: skillet, saucepan and baking dish or casserole

In the skillet, sauté the onion and celery in the butter, until lightly browned.

While the vegetables are cooking, prepare the rice according to package directions, but use 1 cup of apple juice and 1 cup of water, and onion salt rather than regular salt. Add the cinnamon and the apple to the rice mixture and cook.

When the rice is ready, stir in the sautéed celery and onion.

PREPARATION TIME: *10 minutes*
TOTAL TIME: *35 minutes*

FOR ANOTHER sweet rice that goes with simple pork dishes try this variation.

SERVES 8

1 to 2 teaspoons cinnamon

1 cup raisins (golden or brown)

1 (2-ounce) package slivered almonds, toasted is best or 1 (5-ounce) can sliced water chestnuts, drained

To either the basic Bouillon Rice recipe (page 179) or to 4 cups of instant rice (cooked), add the above ingredients.

Stir well and serve.

PREPARATION TIME: *10 minutes*
TOTAL TIME: *20 minutes if using instant rice*
1 hour and 10 minutes if using Bouillon Rice

Sage Advice

If you are going to serve this immediately, pour the cooked rice into a warmed baking dish (just rinsing the dish in hot water will heat it). But if it will be a while before you serve it, pour the rice into a baking dish, cover it with aluminum foil and let it rest in a warm oven, making sure it doesn't get too dry by covering with aluminum foil.

The Finishing Touch

Add a few chopped pecans, and you have an even fancier dish— almost good enough to call a rice pudding and serve for dessert, except for the onions!

No-Fail Potatoes

IT'S EASY to tell when my across-the-street neighbors are at home. There's a steady stream of cars in front of the house. Bobbye Raye Womack is having a baby shower, or a wedding party, or a gathering for out-of-towners who've come for a funeral, or a just-for-fun brunch, or a spur-of-the-moment afternoon tea party. Any occasion or no occasion at all, is her reason to have friends drop in, and there's always a fabulous spread.

This tasty and trouble-free potato dish is a standby she's been using for thirty-plus years. And, she says, when her guests wander back to the kitchen, it's because they want to lick the bowl.

SERVES 6

Sage Advice

Like all experienced cooks, Bobbye Raye gives directions for this recipe in a rather off-hand way. "Well, sometimes I use 4 eggs. And sometimes I'll use a big container of sour cream and a small container of cottage cheese. Sometimes I put cheese in it. Sometimes I cook it plain. Sometimes I put cheese on top. It always tastes good." Take her sage advice and try your own variations on this basic no-fail recipe.

2 cups instant mashed potato flakes

1 (8-ounce) container sour cream

1 (8-ounce) container cottage cheese

2 eggs, well beaten

Salt, pepper, and anything else you want to add, to taste (Suggestions are Cheddar, Parmesan, or other cheese; bacon bits; chives)

Cookware needed: mixing bowl and baking dish or casserole

Preheat the oven to 350 degrees.

Combine the potato flakes, sour cream, cottage cheese, and eggs.

Add salt and pepper to taste, along with any other additions you choose, and pour the mixture into a well-greased baking dish. Bake for 45 minutes.

PREPARATION TIME: *5 to 10 minutes*
TOTAL TIME: *approximately 1 hour*

Party Potatoes

THIS RECIPE is one you might want to use should you have cream cheese but no cottage cheese on hand. Otherwise, Party Potatoes and No-Fail Potatoes are very similar.

SERVES 8

4 cups hot, mashed potatoes, either prepared from a box or ready-to-serve from the refrigerated or hot deli section of the grocery store

⅓ cup butter

1 (8-ounce) package cream cheese, softened

¼ cup sour cream

Salt and pepper, to taste

Paprika, to taste

Cookware needed: 2 mixing bowls, baking dish or casserole

Stir the butter into the hot potatoes.

Whip the cream cheese with the sour cream until smooth and fluffy.

Preheat the oven to 325 degrees.

Stir the cheese mixture into the potatoes. Add salt and pepper, to taste.

Spoon the potatoes into a buttered baking dish, sprinkle with the paprika, and bake for 30 minutes.

PREPARATION TIME: *5 to 10 minutes*
TOTAL TIME: *approximately 1 hour*

Potato Mushroom Casserole

READY-TO-COOK frozen French fries were one of the first "quick" foods I remember using. No longer was it necessary to scrub and slice the spuds. Soon thereafter, stuffed, twice-baked, hash-brown, and fancy crinkled, and shoestring potatoes were available in the freezer section.

This casserole, which once required the obligatory scrubbing and slicing, can now be made in a snap, thanks to yet another, new potato product—frozen, herbed potato wedges.

SERVES 6 TO 8

1 (2-pound) package frozen, herbed potato wedges

1 (8-ounce) can sliced mushrooms, drained

1 cup Swiss cheese, grated

1 cup whipping cream

Cookware needed: rectangular baking dish or casserole

Preheat the oven to 375 degrees.

Layer the potato wedges and mushrooms in a rectangular baking dish.

Combine the cheese and whipping cream and pour the mixture over the potatoes and mushrooms.

Bake for about 30 minutes or until bubbly.

PREPARATION TIME: *10 minutes*
TOTAL TIME: *40 minutes*

Mama Mia Potatoes

USE ITALIAN CHEESES and herbs to give mashed potatoes a bit of pizzazz and make them exceptionally flavorful.

SERVES 8

4 cups hot, mashed potatoes, either prepared from a box or ready-to-serve from the refrigerated or hot deli section of the supermarket

Butter, salt and pepper, to taste

½ cup Parmesan cheese, grated

8 ounces mozzarella cheese, sliced

½ to 1 cup Italian-style bread crumbs

Cookware needed: mixing bowls, baking dish or casserole

Preheat the oven to 350 degrees.

Flavor the potatoes with butter, salt, and pepper, to taste.

Spread half the potatoes in a baking dish and sprinkle them with half the Parmesan cheese.

Layer the mozzarella cheese slices over the Parmesan, saving a few slices for the top.

Spread the remaining potatoes over the cheese layer, add more Parmesan and end with the remaining mozzarella slices.

Sprinkle the flavored bread crumbs on top and bake for about 15 minutes, or until the mozzarella cheese has melted.

PREPARATION TIME: *10 minutes*
TOTAL TIME: *approximately 30 minutes*

Sherried Sweet Potatoes

SPEAKING OF the new products that are showing up on grocery shelves these days, I distinctly remember watching one Thanksgiving-eve shopper down on her hands and knees reaching to the back of the bottom shelf, hoping to retrieve a can or two of orange-pineapple sweet potatoes.

No reason for me to follow suit. She got the last ones. I waited until after Thanksgiving, then helped myself to a couple of cans from the newly stocked shelves. They sure do make this next casserole easy to assemble!

SERVES 10

3 (15-ounce) cans orange-pineapple sweet potatoes

6 tablespoons butter, either melted or cut into small pieces

¼ cup chopped walnuts

½ cup raisins

⅓ cup dry sherry

Cookware needed: baking dish or casserole

Sage Advice

If you wish, you can add orange juice to taste to the can juices, or even a little orange zest. If you can't find the orange-pineapple variety of sweet potatoes, use candied yams and add a cup of orange juice to the can juices.

Preheat the oven to 325 degrees.

Scoop the sweet potatoes out of the cans one by one and transfer them to a baking dish, slicing them as you go. (This technique keeps you from having to dirty another bowl.)

Combine the juices from the potato cans into one can, add the butter, walnuts, raisins, and sherry, and pour the mixture over the potatoes.

Bake for about 30 minutes, basting occasionally, until the potatoes are well glazed.

PREPARATION TIME: *10 minutes*
TOTAL TIME: *40 minutes*

Dressed-Up Noodles

TIRED OF serving rice or potatoes with beef or pork? How about dressing up some egg noodles? That's what Mother used to do. These days Italian pastas seem to dominate the family dinner plate. That's what makes this dish a pleasant change.

SERVES 4

1 (8-ounce) box egg noodles
½ stick butter, cut up
Lots of freshly ground pepper
Salt, to taste

¼ to ½ cup finely chopped parsley
Cookware needed: large saucepan

Prepare the egg noodles according to package directions.

To the cooked and drained noodles, add all the remaining ingredients. Stir gently to combine without breaking up the noodles.

PREPARATION TIME: *5 minutes*
TOTAL TIME: *10 to 15 minutes,*
depending on your desired tenderness
for the noodles

You-Take-the-Credit Caramelized Onion and Blue Cheese Rissoni

WHEN FRIENDS of mine told friends of theirs about *From Storebought to Homemade* wonderful recipes began flooding in from folks I'd never even met. Caramelized Onion and Blue Cheese Rissoni is one of those.

I read through it (my mouth began watering) and got to the end. There, quite unexpectedly, a note was tacked on: "If there are any mistakes, they are Eric's fault. Otherwise, the credit is all mine! Linda." I didn't have a clue who Eric or Linda were!

That's the wonderful thing about great food. We love to share it, and when it's really good, to take all the credit.

There were no mistakes, so Linda is clear to take all the credit. Now it's your turn to take credit for this unusual, and unusually good, recipe.

SERVES 8

1 (1-pound) package rissoni, or other short soup pasta

1 tablespoon butter

3 tablespoons olive oil

4 onions, sliced

1 (6-ounce) package blue cheese

3 ½ ounces mascarpone

2 cups packaged shredded English spinach leaves, or baby spinach leaves

Salt and pepper, to taste

Cookware needed: large pot, large skillet, mixing bowl

Cook the rissoni in rapidly boiling salted water until al dente, about 5 minutes.

While the pasta is cooking, heat the butter and olive oil in a large heavy-bottomed skillet. Add the sliced onion and cook over low heat for about 20 to 30 minutes, until golden brown and caramelized. Remove the onion from the pan with a slotted spoon and drain it on paper towels.

Drain the rissoni well and return it to the pot.

Combine the blue cheese, mascarpone, and onion in a bowl and then add the mixture to the rissoni.

Add the spinach and toss thoroughly. Season to taste with salt and freshly ground black pepper before serving.

PREPARATION TIME: *20 minutes*
TOTAL TIME: *35 minutes*

Grits, No Longer Just for Southerners

Never, in all my memories, can I recall seeing my Massachusetts-born-and-bred father eat grits. Other than creamed onions, grits were the only dish I think he ever refused.

Of course, my Southern mother loved grits and served them often. But she never dressed them up the way we do these days. A little butter and salt and pepper were the only flavorings she added to that most Southern of dishes.

These days everyone loves grits, but that's because they've changed the flavor by adding lots of cheese to them. If Daddy had ever eaten cheese grits, I think he would have liked them. I prefer cheese grits too—I guess it's my "Yankee" half coming through.

Try these two "dressed-up" cheesy grits recipes. They are delicious served as a side dish in place of potatoes, pasta, or rice, with beef, pork, chicken, and even grilled fish. You'll be pleasantly surprised at how good they are. Even my young grandson, Benjamin, whose father is from Pennsylvania, smacks his lips and asks for more when I fix them for him.

Cheese Garlic Grits

SERVES 6

2 cups quick grits, cooked according to package directions, piping hot

½ to ¾ cup prepared Cheddar cheese sauce

2 to 3 tablespoons garlic salt

¼ to ½ cup cream

½ stick butter

Salt and pepper, to taste

Cookware needed: pot

Add the cheese sauce, garlic salt, cream (more or less, depending on how creamy you like your grits), and butter to the piping hot grits. Mix thoroughly and season with salt and pepper.

PREPARATION TIME: *5 to 10 minutes*

TOTAL TIME: *approximately 20 minutes*

Sage Advice

By using garlic salt and cheese sauce, you can make this delicious accompaniment more or less garlicky or cheesy as you prefer. An alternative way to make Garlic Cheese Grits is to use a garlic cheese roll, which can be found in the cheese section of your grocery store. Use it in place of the cheese sauce and garlic sauce.

The Finishing Touch

If you wish to serve this recipe as a casserole, the addition of 2 well-beaten eggs makes the mixture richer and more "solid." Add the eggs to the mixture at the end, then simply pour the grits into a well-greased baking dish or casserole and bake at 350 degrees for 30 to 40 minutes. You can also top the grits with French Fried Onion bits before baking—to add that finishing touch.

Swiss Grits

SERVES 6

2 cups quick grits, cooked
according to package
directions, piping hot

½ to ¾ cup Swiss cheese, grated

⅓ to ½ cup Parmesan cheese,
grated

1 teaspoon salt

⅛ teaspoon pepper

½ stick butter

Cookware needed: saucepan,
baking dish or casserole

Preheat the oven to 350 degrees.

To the piping hot grits, add the two cheeses, salt, pepper, and butter and mix
thoroughly. Adjust the flavoring to your taste.

Pour the grits into a well-greased baking dish, and bake at for 45 to 60 minutes.

PREPARATION TIME: *5 to 10 minutes*
TOTAL TIME: *60 minutes*

All-in-One Meals

"**WHAT'S** the absolute *easiest* meal-in-one dish you're putting in your book," a young bride asked me. "Easiest, *and* best," she quickly added, no doubt thinking about her new groom.

I couldn't answer. Easiest *and* best? I pondered.

The Brunswick Stew recipe is a long-standing favorite. But then, the Mexican Chicken Casserole is newer, and equally mouthwatering to my way of thinking.

Quickly Assembled Chicken requires only 4 ingredients, plus some peppercorns. And when you sprinkle condiments over Navy Wives Shrimp Curry you're topping a scrumptious dish with its own salad! (Salads are often served with one-dish meals.) Thinking it over, even some of the selections that need extra cooking time are extremely easy to assemble.

And speaking of assembly....There's always the matter of pots and pans when you step into the kitchen. But if you can mix an All-in-One-Meal in its own baking dish, or prepare it in a skillet on top of the stove, you've saved time and effort.

But back to the question at hand.

Easiest? Best? Easiest and best? When *you* decide, let me know!

Meanwhile, to put the whole matter into perspective, and to give credence to how storebought ingredients have changed our cooking habits, read about Country Captain Chicken, and smile!

Have You Had All Your Vitamins Today?

GREEN salads have become so much a part of almost every meal that even old-fashioned tomato-based beef stews with carrots, celery, and potatoes are served with a salad on the side.

There's absolutely nothing wrong with this—especially since the cello-bagged salads have taken all the work out of the process. These packaged salads are so easy, in fact, that they give you more options when preparing an All-in-One Meal. No longer must you be sure that your dinner includes the vegetables necessary to provide your family members with their full share of vitamins.

So fix the Chinese Tuna Casserole for a family meal and don't worry if the kids pick the celery pieces out of it—as long as they eat the Romaine lettuce and shredded carrots on their salad plates.

Country Captain Chicken

THERE are many reasons why chicken is so popular, not least of which is its versatility. The new, already cooked, ready-to-serve chicken products are the answer to many a hurried cook's prayers. They've made it a cinch to prepare everything from Queenly Chicken Salad (page 294) to Chicken Stew (page 205). How easy?

Just for fun, I recently pulled out the recipe for Country Captain Chicken that I used for years to make one of my favorite do-ahead company dishes and compared it with the recipe I've developed by using every convenience food available to me. Read them both and you'll become a convert.

The ingredients are basically the same. But numerous steps have been eliminated and you've cut thirty minutes off the preparation time and an hour off the cooking time.

What remains the same is a delicious dish that can be prepared ahead of time and never fails to delight.

Country Captain Chicken the "old way"

SERVES 8

1 fresh fryer chicken

1 cup flour

1 teaspoon salt

½ teaspoon pepper

1 teaspoon dried thyme

½ teaspoon dried savory

½ teaspoon dried basil

¼ cup butter

½ cup diced onions

½ cup diced green pepper

1 to 2 cloves garlic, minced

1 ½ to 2 teaspoons curry powder

2 cups stewed tomatoes

3 tablespoons currants

6 cups cooked rice

¼ cup slivered almonds, toasted

Cookware needed: a deep, 10-inch skillet, with a lid, a baking dish or casserole, plus a 2-quart saucepan for the rice

Cut up the fryer.

Combine the flour, salt and pepper, ½ teaspoon thyme, the savory, and the basil. Coat each piece of chicken well with this mixture.

Brown the chicken pieces in the butter. Remove, drain, and place the chicken in a baking dish.

To the pan drippings in the skillet, add the onion, green pepper, garlic, curry powder, and remaining thyme and cook, stirring gently, until golden. Add the stewed tomatoes, stir, and simmer for 45 minutes.

Preheat the oven to 350 degrees.

Pour this mixture over the chicken and bake uncovered for 30 minutes.

Add the currants during the last 5 minutes of cooking.

Serve over the rice, garnished with the toasted slivered almonds.

PREPARATION TIME: *40 minutes*
TOTAL TIME: 1 ½ *hours*

Country Captain Chicken the "new way"

I CAN'T believe I ever cut up a fryer chicken, but I did. That step alone took a good 10 to 15 minutes and created quite a mess. Later, I simply bought the cut-up chicken, which saved time and made less mess.

These days I use breaded or already flavored chicken strips and make the dish in no time.

Try this *From Storebought to Homemade* version of the same recipe. The total time it takes is less than the basic preparation time of the old way. I think you'll agree, we've come a long way, baby!

SERVES 8

1 tablespoon olive oil

1 to 2 tablespoons prepared garlic

½ cup combo of frozen, diced onion and green pepper

3 (15-ounce) cans Italian-style stewed tomatoes

1 ½ to 2 teaspoons curry powder

½ teaspoon dried thyme

2 (10-ounce) packages fully cooked breaded or herbed chicken strips

3 tablespoons currants

4 cups instant rice, cooked

¼ cup slivered almonds, toasted

Cookware needed: a deep, 10-inch skillet, with a lid, plus a 2-quart saucepan for the rice

Heat olive oil over medium-high heat in a deep, 10-inch skillet, with a lid.

Add garlic and green pepper and cook approximately 3 minutes to allow the flavors to blend.

To this, add the tomatoes, curry powder, and dried thyme.

Cover and simmer on low heat for 20 minutes.

Add the fully cooked chicken and currants and cook another 10 to 15 minutes.

During these last 10 minutes, prepare the instant rice according to package directions.

Serve the chicken over the rice, garnished with the almonds.

PREPARATION TIME: *10 minutes*
TOTAL TIME: *35 to 45 minutes*

Mexican Chicken Casserole

MEXICAN Chicken Casserole is a "new" cream of mushroom soup-based casserole that everyone is fixing these days. I must have been given ten recipes—each slightly different, but all good.

Of course it's popular. The cook can stir it up in 15 minutes. Kids will ask for seconds. And best of all, you can add to, take from, or substitute the ingredients—according to what you like and what you have on hand.

So, think of this recipe as a guide. Read over the alternative and additional ingredients and let your imagination be your guide.

SERVES 6

Vegetable oil cooking spray

1 (9-ounce) package baked tortilla chips, as many as needed

2 (10-ounce) packages fully cooked chicken slices or pieces, fajita flavored if you wish

1 (10-ounce) can cream of mushroom soup

1 (10-ounce) can cream of chicken soup

1 (10 to 14-ounce) can diced tomatoes and hot peppers, mild, medium, or hot, to your taste

½ cup frozen, diced green peppers

1 cup frozen corn

1 (14-ounce) can black beans, drained and rinsed

1 cup Cheddar cheese, grated

Alternative or additional ingredients:

3 to 4 boneless frozen or fresh chicken breasts, cooked and cubed, may be used in place of the already cooked chicken strips or pieces

1 cup of frozen vegetable gumbo mix (okra, corn, onions, celery, and red peppers) can be used in place of the corn

Sliced ripe or Spanish olives can be added to the mixture or sprinkled on top

Cookware needed: 9 x 13-inch baking dish or casserole, mixing bowl

Preheat the oven to 350 degrees.

Spray the inside of a 9 x 13-inch baking dish with vegetable oil cooking spray and crumble the tortilla chips in the bottom. Lay half the chicken over the chips.

Combine the soups, tomatoes and pepper, and the vegetables and beans in a mixing bowl. Pour half the soup mixture over the chicken.

Repeat the layering of tortilla chips, chicken, and soup mixture.

Crumble a few more tortilla chips over the final layer and sprinkle the Cheddar cheese on top.

Bake for about 30 minutes, or until the casserole is thoroughly hot and the cheese has melted.

PREPARATION TIME: *10 to 15 minutes*
TOTAL TIME: *approximately 30 to 40 minutes*

Old-Timey Tuna Casserole

I PROMISED to tickle your nostalgic taste buds. My generation's Mexican Chicken Casserole was the tuna casserole. I thought everyone still made it.

Then at a meeting of women ranging from their mid-30s to early-70s, I learned that some of the younger women had never had it, and some of the older ones had lost their old recipes. So here it is.

But like the Mexican Chicken Casserole, there are countless variations of tuna casserole. Garrison Keillor even gave his rendition of the recipe on a *News from Lake Wobegone* broadcast when telling a story about a city fellow who longed to return to his mom's kitchen for her "tuna hot dish" made from macaroni, tuna "out of cans," peas, and "cream of mushroom soup for sauce, and Lipton's dried onion soup for spice, and crunched potato chips on top for crunch."

That's why, I've listed some alternative or additional ingredients.

SERVES 8

1 (12-ounce) package egg noodles, wide or thin

1 (14-ounce) can cream of mushroom soup

1 (8-ounce) can Le Seur petite peas, or 1 cup frozen petite peas

1 or 2 (12-ounce) cans tuna, water-packed, of course, and well drained

½ to 1 cup milk

1 cup Cheddar cheese, grated

Pepper, to taste

Alternative or additional ingredients:

Additional cheese, either grated or a bottled type like Cheese Whiz or Velveeta can be stirred into the casserole mixture

½ cup (or more) slivered almonds or cashews can be added to the casserole mixture

Lipton's dried onion soup mix (à la Keillor)

Crumbled potato chips can be added to the grated cheese for a crunchy topping

Cookware needed: 8-quart pot, baking dish or casserole

Cook the egg noodles according to package directions.

Preheat the oven to 350 degrees.

When the noodles are done, drain them and combine them in a large baking dish with the cream of mushroom soup, peas, and tuna. Add the milk according to your preference for a creamier or drier casserole. Add pepper, to taste.

Top with the cheese, cover loosely with aluminum foil, and bake for 45 minutes, or until bubbly. You can remove the foil for the last few minutes to brown the top, if you wish.

PREPARATION TIME: *10 to 15 minutes*
TOTAL TIME: *approximately 60 minutes*

Chinese Tuna Casserole

ANOTHER version of tuna casserole that circulated back in the 1960s and early '70s was this "misnamed" recipe.

Obviously there's nothing "Chinese" about it, except the chow mein noodles. One night I decided to "dress it up" a little. I took a hint from the name and added some sliced water chestnuts. I have never heard the end of that fateful error.

My son, Langdon, really dislikes water chestnuts…a fact that seemed to have eluded me. To this day, he reminds me that I took a perfectly good recipe and (according to him) deliberately ruined it.

I beg to disagree. Still, you'll notice that I have not included any water chestnuts in the list of ingredients below. But you can!

SERVES 8

1 (8-ounce) can chow mein noodles

2 (10-ounce) cans cream of mushroom soup

½ cup milk

1 (12-ounce) can water-packed tuna, drained

½ cup chopped cashews

1 to 2 cups diced or sliced celery

½ cup frozen, diced onion

Salt and pepper, to taste

Cookware needed: baking dish or casserole

Preheat the oven to 350 degrees.

Combine all of the ingredients, except for ¾ cup of the chow mein noodles, in a baking dish.

After the ingredients are well mixed, top the casserole with the remaining noodles.

Cook for 30 to 35 minutes.

PREPARATION TIME: *10 minutes*
TOTAL TIME: *approximately 40 to 45 minutes*

Company All-in-One Tuna-and-Shrimp Casserole

IF YOU really like canned tuna, and I do, you may be looking for new and different ways to use it. This tuna and shrimp All-in-One Meal may surprise you—with its ingredients and its flavor.

Don't let the longer-than-usual list of ingredients frighten you away. They are mostly items you'll take straight from the freezer or shake from the spice jar.

Sage Advice

If you decide to prepare this really delicious casserole at the last minute, and you have everything except the biscuits, never fear. You can serve this over rice, on top of toasted English muffins, or even on waffles. Another note: I suggested using 2 or 3 cans of artichoke hearts. You can guess that I always make it three. I find that the slightly tart taste of the artichoke hearts adds tremendously to the flavor. Just as I take this liberty, so may you adjust the recipe as you wish. If you don't like artichoke hearts, omit them altogether, add a package of peas or broccoli, and toss in some capers. After all, cooking is supposed to be fun, and you should prepare food to your own liking.

SERVES 8

3 tablespoons butter

1 (10-ounce) package Picksweet seasoning blend, or a frozen, diced combination of onion and green pepper, and celery

1 (10-ounce) bag shelled and cleaned frozen shrimp

½ teaspoon dried tarragon

1 tablespoon dried thyme

1 (16-ounce) jar Ragú® Classic Alfredo or Roasted Parmesan Cheese Sauce

1 (12-ounce) can water-packed tuna, drained

1 (4- to 6-ounce) can sliced mushrooms, drained

2 or 3 (14-ounce) cans artichoke hearts, drained and quartered

1 tablespoon lemon juice

Salt and pepper, to taste

1 (8-ounce) package refrigerator biscuits

Cookware needed: skillet, baking dish or casserole

Preheat the oven to 375 degrees.

Melt the butter in a skillet and sauté the onion, pepper, and celery for about 3 minutes.

Toss in the shrimp, tarragon, and thyme and cook another 2 to 3 minutes.

In a large casserole or baking dish combine the Ragú® sauce, drained tuna, mushrooms, artichoke hearts, lemon juice, salt, and pepper; stir, and then add shrimp mixture and combine.

Arrange the biscuits on top of the casserole so they are not quite touching, to allow space to spoon out each serving.

Bake for 25 to 30 minutes, or until the biscuits are browned and the mixture is bubbling hot.

PREPARATION TIME: *10 to 15 minutes*
TOTAL TIME: *45 to 50 minutes*

Quickly Assembled Chicken Meal-in-One

Sage Advice
Young children in the finger-food stage really love this dish. All Mom or Dad has to do is to cut the chicken and potatoes into smaller pieces. And, oh, remember to pick out the peppercorns!

SOME recipes are so simple that all you are doing is assembling them. There's no stirring, mixing, or basting required. They can even be put together in a baking dish. Those are the ones I *really* like. Especially when they're yummy.

This quickly assembled chicken meal-in-one fits all of the above requirements. Mother fixed it regularly when I was in high school, and she was teaching school, so she had little time to prepare an evening meal. (This was way before the dawning of fast-food restaurants or the eating-out craze.) I, in turn, served it to my children every two or three weeks. My daughter now throws it together for her two young sons. It's become a three-generational family favorite.

The directions for making this recipe are really simple. The only decisions you'll have to make are how many chicken pieces to use and whether to go light or heavy on the whole peppercorns.

SERVES 8

Chicken parts: fresh or frozen chicken breasts, thighs, legs, whatever your family likes (enough for 8 servings)

2 (14-ounce) cans small, whole white potatoes, drained

1 (14-ounce) can sliced carrots, drained

2 (14-ounce) cans French-style green beans, with their liquid

Whole peppercorns, to taste

Cookware needed: rectangular baking dish or casserole

Preheat the oven to 375 degrees.

Assemble by putting the chicken pieces in the baking dish and then spreading the drained potatoes and carrots around them.

Last, add the French-style green beans with their liquid. Toss on a few (10 or 12), or a full handful of, whole peppercorns.

Cover the pan with aluminum foil and bake for 35 to 45 minutes, or until the chicken is done, or white all the way through.

PREPARATION TIME: *8 to 10 minutes*
TOTAL TIME: *50 to 60 minutes*

Quick Chicken Pie

WHEN you get a *From Storebought to Homemade* recipe from a real chef, you know you're on the right track!

Margaret Mullen Breison worked as a *sous*-chef in Atlanta before becoming the head cook for her husband and sons in Thomasville, Georgia. To keep her hand in, she comes up with quick ways to provide dishes with that "home-cooked" flavor.

This quick chicken pot pie is a Breison family favorite that is so good you can serve it to guests by following the hint in *The Finishing Touch!*

SERVES 4 TO 6

1 (9-inch) frozen pie crust

1 rotisserie chicken, skinned, meat removed from the bones

either

2 tablespoons butter

2 tablespoons flour

1 cup chicken broth, plus extra to adjust

1 cup half-and-half or milk

Salt and pepper, to taste

or

½ cup chicken broth

1 cup white or Alfredo sauce (this is how I make it)

1 cup peas and carrots, frozen, or other frozen vegetable mixture that includes diced potatoes and/or corn (optional),

1 egg, beaten

Cookware needed: mixing bowl, saucepan (optional), baking dish or casserole

Set the pie crust out to thaw.

Cut or tear the chicken meat into small pieces, and place in a mixing bowl.

Preheat the oven to 325 degrees.

If you wish to make your own white sauce: melt the butter over medium-high heat. Add the flour and cook, stirring, until it is golden, approximately 3 minutes.

Add the broth and milk and cook, stirring, until thickened, usually about 5 minutes. Season the sauce with salt and pepper and pour it over the chicken. Add more broth if it seems too thick.

To make it "my way," simply add ½ cup of chicken broth to 1 cup of already made Alfredo sauce and blend well.

Combine the chicken and sauce (and vegetables, if desired), stir, and pour the mixture into a baking dish.

Top with the pie crust, sealing edges well. Cut a few vent holes in the top with a sharp knife.

Brush the crust with the beaten egg, and bake for 20 to 30 minutes, or until the crust is golden brown.

PREPARATION TIME: *20 minutes*
TOTAL TIME: *50 to 60 minutes*

Sage Advice

Margaret says that this dish freezes well.

The
Finishing Touch

A friend tells me that one time when she dined at Oscar's, the famed restaurant at the Waldorf, she ordered a meat pie. When it was served, the crust was popped off and placed on her plate first; then the succulent pie was dished out on top of it. Try this technique for a small casual company dinner.

Chicken Stew

REMEMBER those stories your grandmother used to tell about how everyone looked forward to having chicken for Sunday dinner? Images of Norman Rockwell's family-meal paintings flashed before my eyes when I came upon another of my mother's recipes—this time, one for chicken stew.

Taking a lesson from Margaret Brinson's homemade (well, almost) Quick Chicken Pie, I decided to adapt Mother's recipe by using a rotisserie chicken, which would be juicy and have that home-roasted flavor. It works beautifully, and I highly recommend that you try it.

SERVES 6

2 (10-ounce) cans cream of chicken soup (or use 1 can cream of chicken and 1 can cream of mushroom soup)

1 cup thickly sliced celery (this is one time when you may not have to dice the celery pieces you buy from the salad bar!)

1 (1-pound) package frozen stew vegetable mix that includes potatoes, carrots, and onions

2 teaspoons dried ground sage

¼ teaspoon freshly ground pepper

1 rotisserie chicken, skinned, meat removed from the bones

Cookware needed: large saucepan or pot, with lid

The
Finishing Touch

To complete the Norman Rockwell scene around your own table, pass a bread basket filled with piping-hot, buttered biscuits. You can even pour the stew over an opened biscuit the way your great-grandfather used to do!

Pour the soup into a large heavy saucepan or pot and add the vegetables, dried sage, and pepper. Cook over medium or medium-low heat until the liquid is bubbly. Do not let the mixture stick or burn.

Meanwhile, tear or cut the chicken into small pieces. Stir the chicken into the vegetable soup mixture.

Continue to cook until the vegetables are cooked through, about 30 minutes, and adjust the seasoning to your taste.

PREPARATION TIME: *15 minutes*
TOTAL TIME: *approximately 45 minutes*

Sunday-Night Shrimp Casserole

I HAD FORGOTTEN about this simple dish Mother used to fix for Sunday-night supper, until I found it among her recipes. It was handwritten and included a note from her brother, Kenlon: "Hope you'll enjoy this as much as I have." These days, my son-in-law, Mike, is as crazy about the dish as Uncle Kenlon was.

It was easy to prepare in the 1960s, and is even easier to make today. With a little ahead-of-time grocery planning (I usually have either a package of frozen shrimp, *or* the slivered almonds on hand...but seldom both), this dish is a delicious family treat that's also suitable for a casual, relaxed company dinner any night of the week.

By the way, the almonds add an unexpected crunch, so do be sure to include them.

SERVES 6 TO 8

1 (1-pound) bag frozen, cooked medium-size shrimp (add some scallops or imitation lobster for additional flavor, if you wish, or substitute already cooked, diced chicken if seafood isn't to your liking)

1 (6- to 8-ounce) can sliced mushrooms, drained

½ cup frozen, diced combo of onion and green pepper

½ cup (or more) slivered almonds

1 ½ cups Ragú® Roasted Garlic Parmesean pasta sauce

½ cup sherry

1 cello package Ritz or other cheesy crackers, crumbled (approximately 30)

1 cup Parmesan cheese, grated

3 to 4 cups cooked rice

Cookware needed: baking dish or casserole

Preheat the oven to 350 degrees.

In a buttered baking dish, alternate layers of shrimp (or chicken), mushrooms, onion and green pepper (or only onion, if you prefer), slivered almonds, and sauce.

Repeat until all the ingredients are used.

Top with the crumbled Ritz crackers and sprinkle with the Parmesan cheese.

Bake for approximately 35 to 40 minutes, or until thoroughly bubbling.

Serve over hot rice.

PREPARATION TIME: *15 minutes*
TOTAL TIME: *50 to 60 minutes*

Reuben Casserole

ALTHOUGH cooking is one of Joan Sprinkle's favorite pastimes, she had to get used to serving her physician husband, Jim, and their four children when she, and they, were on the run. Plus, there just was not enough time in the day to garden, play tennis, sew, *and* cook.

Joan began fixing this great Reuben Casserole when Jim was in his medical residency. She continued making it through the kids' growing up years, and now she makes it when they come home—with grandchildren in tow.

This is one of those assemble-in-its-baking-dish meals that should be at the top of the list for anyone who has limited cooking space and who dislikes clean-up time.

SERVES 6 TO 8

2 (10-ounce) cans sauerkraut, drained

2 medium tomatoes, sliced

½ cup Thousand Island dressing (if not on hand, combine mayonnaise, ketchup, and pickle relish to equal this amount—until it looks right, a nice dark pink)

2 tablespoons butter

8 ounces corned beef from the deli, sliced very thin

1 (8-ounce) package Swiss cheese, grated

1 (8-ounce) can flaky buttermilk biscuits

8 crisp rye crackers, crushed

1 teaspoon caraway seeds

Cookware needed: baking dish or casserole

Preheat the oven to 425 degrees.

Spread the sauerkraut in the bottom of an 8-inch baking dish.

Top with the tomato slices and dot with the dressing and butter.

Cover with the corned beef and sprinkle with the cheese.

Bake for 15 minutes.

Remove from oven.

Separate each biscuit into 3 layers and slightly overlap the biscuit layers on top of the casserole to form three rows. Sprinkle with the crackers and caraway seeds.

Bake 15 to 20 minutes, or until the biscuit topping is golden brown.

PREPARATION TIME: *15 minutes*
TOTAL TIME: *approximately 45 minutes*

Quick Ham and Cheese Bake

Sage Advice

I prefer slightly crunchy Brussels sprouts, but Mike likes his more thoroughly cooked. According to your taste (and their size), you may want to add the Brussels sprouts a little later in the baking process.

MY PENNSYLVANIA son-in-law, Mike Hultzapple, loves Brussels sprouts. So do I. But we're the only two in the family who do. Sometimes I cook them just for the two of us. Other times I simply slip those "little cabbages" into this casserole, then give everyone else one Brussels sprout, while piling the remainder on Mike's plate and mine.

SERVES 6 TO 8

1 (10-ounce) can cream of celery soup

½ cup milk

½ cup frozen, diced onion

1 cup diced potatoes (I take them from the frozen, hash-brown potato bag)

1 cup Cheddar cheese, grated

1 (2-ounce) jar pimiento, drained (optional)

1 (10-ounce) package frozen Brussels sprouts

2 cups diced and cooked ham

Cookware needed: baking dish or casserole, with lid

Preheat the oven to 350 degrees.

Combine all the ingredients in a large baking dish, cover, bake for 30 minutes. Remove the cover and continue to cook uncovered 10 to 15 minutes longer, until bubbly.

PREPARATION TIME: *10 minutes*
TOTAL TIME: *approximately 45 to 50 minutes*

The Picky Eater's Beef Stew

I KNOW all about picky eaters.

If a contest were held, my husband, Bob, would be among the finalists. He's getting better, gradually. Meanwhile, though, I moan, groan, and complain as I try to accommodate the few foods he loves to my see-food (if I see food, I'll try it, well, almost always) ways.

This later-life experience of living with a picky eater (Bob and I were married in 1996) has made me sympathetic toward cooks who have to try to please the limited preferences of others.

But what happens when the picky eater is the cook? That's what young Maggie Forgèt admitted when she gave me her recipe for beef stew.

"Since I'm not a big vegetable fan, this is how I make it—beef and juices—and just serve it over rice," Maggie apologized. "But, you *could* add veggies," she conceded.

So here's a veggie-free beef stew that's ready to serve with a side salad, unless the veggie-free eaters dislike salad too.

The mushroom gravy mix provides all the flavorful spices you'll need. That's a boon to today's cook, who wants to use fresh beef but doesn't want to spend the time gathering and preparing the onions and other spices we used to include when we fixed beef stew (also without the veggies), served it over rice, and gave it the fancy name, Boeuf à la Bourguignon. The rich, dark color of the gravy even makes it unnecessary to brown the meat first.

Sage Advice
These words come from Maggie, a busy young wife and mother. "Be sure to buy stew beef that has already been cut into small cubes. These will be much more tender than the large stew beef pieces."

SERVES 6
■ ■ ■ ■ ■ ■ ■ ■

1 (10-ounce) can cream of mushroom soup

1 package Knorr's mushroom gravy mix (formerly called Hunter's Sauce)

2 pounds cubed stewing beef

1 cup red wine

Cookware needed: large pot, or Crock-Pot

Combine the mushroom soup and gravy mix in the cooking pot.

Add the meat. If using a Crock-Pot, cook on high for 7 to 9 hours. If cooking on top of the stove, simmer gently for 3 to 4 hours.

Stir in the wine approximately 1 hour before serving

■ ■ ■ ■ ■ ■ ■ ■

PREPARATION TIME: *5 minutes*
TOTAL TIME: *3 to 9 hours*

Quick-Quick Brunswick Stew

"**IS YOUR** Brunswick Stew as good as your mother's?" my long-time family friend Adele Clement asked me. "We couldn't have a church bazaar without your mother's Brunswick Stew."

After a thirty-eight-year absence, I had returned to Danville, Virginia, the town where I grew up, and before I could even unpack my pots and pans, my culinary talents were being challenged!

Adele's question brought back fond memories of hours Mother and I had spent together in the kitchen, talking all the time we boiled the hens and peeled and chopped the onions and potatoes. If it was summertime, we even shelled fresh lima beans and cut corn off the cob to make this Southern delicacy.

Then we stirred the stew for hours on end, careful to keep it from sticking to the bottom of the pan. And, oh yes, there was the constant tasting of the concoction throughout the stirring time to add exactly the right amount of flavoring—our favorite part, of course.

But Adele's question also put me on the spot, because it had been years since I'd made Brunswick Stew from scratch.

"You'll have to taste mine to decide for yourself," I told her—not wanting to reveal my secret.

Several days later, once I had found my trusty can opener and unpacked my heaviest 8-quart pot, I went to work. In just a matter of minutes, I whipped up a big mess (as we call it in the South) of Brunswick Stew and ran it by Adele's house. (Neither my house, nor I, was ready for dinner guests.)

"You have your mother's touch," she raved, after tasting it. "Now, about the church bazaar..."

You too can have delicious "homemade Brunswick Stew" that everyone will rave about—thanks to Mrs. Fearnow's canned product, which provides the perfect chicken base to which you add your homemade touch.

Sage Advice

If you like larger pieces of tomato, you will want to use the stewed tomatoes. On the other hand, if you prefer your stew to have a soupier consistency, you'll reach for a can of crushed tomatoes.

SERVES 12

1 (14-ounce) can chicken broth

1 cup frozen lima beans (any variety from small to Fordhook will do)

1 cup frozen corn (traditionally yellow, but a mix of yellow and white will work)

1 (14-ounce) can crushed or stewed tomatoes (either works perfectly well—see *Sage Advice*)

1 to 2 cans tomato and jalapeño mix (either 10-ounce Rotel, or 14-ounce house brand)—see the recipe directions below

2 (40-ounce) cans Mrs. Fearnow's Brunswick Stew

Cookware needed: large 8-quart pot with lid

Bring the chicken broth to a boil and add the lima beans and corn. Cover, reduce the heat to a simmer, and cook for 5 to 10 minutes. (Note: Fordhook limas are large and will take longer to cook.)

Add the crushed or stewed tomatoes and one can of the tomato and jalapeño mix, stir, and cook for about 5 minutes to blend the flavors.

Add the already prepared Brunswick Stew, stir well, and cook on medium-low heat for 15 to 20 minutes.

At this point, do what Mother and I always did. Taste it. If you want a spicier stew, open another can of the tomato and jalapeño mix and add more to taste, always allowing a couple of minutes for the flavors to blend before making your final judgment as to whether to add more.

PREPARATION TIME: *15 to 20 minutes*
TOTAL TIME: *35 to 45 minutes, but it will hold on low heat until you are ready to serve it*

The
Finishing Touch

Brunswick Stew is one of my favorite foods. In the South, we serve it with piping-hot ham biscuits any time of day and call it dinner. But you may wish to add a salad to your menu. This is the perfect dish for a casual get-together, especially if you have an attractive pot to serve it from— whether in the kitchen or in the dining room. And if you don't have ham biscuits, don't fret. A good storebought cheese bread, or one of the Jiffy mix corn breads (see pages 228–230) will be just as tasty.

Quick Brunswick Stew

UNFORTUNATELY, Mrs. Fearnow's Brunswick Stew is not available throughout the country. But it can be ordered, either by e-mail (www.snows.com/lovstew/mailorder.html) or by phone (1-800-222-7839).

For those who love this Southern delicacy, but not the making of it (and if you can't get the canned product to use as a base), here's a short-cut recipe that begins with a rotisserie chicken instead of a raw fryer.

SERVES 12

4 (15-ounce) cans chicken broth

4 cups water

6 medium potatoes, peeled and diced, or a package of the ready-to-cook variety for hash-brown potatoes

1 (32-ounce) bag frozen lima beans (any variety from small to Fordhook will do)

1 (32-ounce) bag frozen corn (traditionally yellow, but shoepeg is good)

2 whole rotisserie chickens, skinned, meat removed from the bones

1 cup frozen, diced onion, thawed

3 (15-ounce) cans crushed or stewed tomatoes (either works perfectly well—see *Sage Advice* on page 210)

1 to 2 cans tomato and jalapeño mix (either 10-ounce Rotel, or 14-ounce house brand)—see the recipe directions below

1 (6-ounce) can tomato paste (optional)

Cookware needed: large 8-quart pot with lid

Bring the chicken broth and water to a boil and add the potatoes. Cook 5 minutes, then add the lima beans, corn, and onion. Cover, reduce the heat to a simmer, and cook for another 15 minutes, or until the lima beans are tender.

Tear or cut the chicken meat into small pieces.

To the pot, add the chicken, the crushed or stewed tomatoes, and the tomato and jalapeño mix. Stir, and cook on medium-low heat for about 30 minutes to blend the flavors and until the mixture begins to thicken.

Now adjust the seasoning and the consistency to your liking by adding another can of the tomato and jalapeño mix and/or a can of tomato paste.

PREPARATION TIME: *30 minutes*
TOTAL TIME: *about 1 hour, but it will hold on low heat until you are ready to serve it*

Baked Pasta

"WHERE DO YOU get all your recipes from?" I'm often asked.

By now you've figured out that, like your recipes, mine come from all over—from friends, strangers in airports, family, old cookbooks and magazines, my kids, out of my own head, and often a combination of all the above. These days you can add yet another source to the list—the Internet.

Almost every food company has a score of recipes posted on their Web pages. But who has the time, or who wants to, spend hours surfing the Net looking for a timesaving recipe. (Sounds self-defeating to me!)

Still, these companies' kitchens offer excellent recipes, like this 10-Minute Baked Ziti recipe from Ragú/Lipton, which really exemplifies the concept of *From Storebought to Homemade*. I became familiar with it when I became good phone friends with some of the Ragú folks after discovering Ragú's line of Cheese Creation sauces.

These sauces are delicious, great time-savers, and give a real pick-me-up to many casseroles and entrées. In fact, they have become as much a staple in my kitchen as Campbell's cream soups were in my mother's. For example, I use Ragú's Roasted Garlic Parmesan Cheese sauce instead of the usual cream of mushroom soup in several of my older chicken and shrimp dishes.

But most people associate Ragú with pasta, and here, to save you the time of turning on your computer, are a couple of quick *From Storebought to Homemade* dishes to serve in your home, courtesy of my new-made friends.

"The conscientious housewife of yesteryear rolled out her noodle dough every morning and hung it up to dry in sheets behind the stove. There are still a few old-fashioned wives who make noodles in the old manner, but most people think the manufactured noodle of today is as good as its handmade ancestor."

—SILAS SPITZER,
"EVERYBODY LOVES
SPAGHETTI," 1951

10-Minute Baked Ziti

SERVES 8

1 (26-ounce) jar Ragú® Pasta Sauce (your favorite tomato-based flavor)

1 ½ cups water

1 (15-ounce) container ricotta cheese

¼ cup Parmesan cheese, grated

1 (8-ounce) package mozzarella cheese, grated

1 (8-ounce) box ziti

Cookware needed: 9 x 13-inch baking dish or casserole, mixing bowl

Preheat the oven to 400 degrees.

Combine the sauce and water in a mixing bowl.

Stir in the ricotta, Parmesan, and ½ the mozzarella cheese, then the uncooked ziti.

Spoon the mixture into a 9 x 13-inch baking dish and cover it with foil.

Bake for 55 minutes.

Remove the foil, sprinkle with the remaining mozzarella, and bake uncovered for an additional 5 minutes.

PREPARATION TIME *10 minutes*
TOTAL TIME: *1 hour and 10 minutes*

IF YOU'RE looking for an alternative to the tomato-based ziti, try this variation which uses Ragú's® Cheese Creations!™ Parmesan and Mozzarella Sauce. My assistant, Charlotte, suggests that you try other types of quick-cooking pasta, such as curly rotini, bow ties, or angel hair—even some of the tri-colored varieties of these pastas—to vary the look of this meat-free, but very satisfying All-in-One Meal. It's good served with a salad.

SERVES 8

1 ½ (16-ounce) jars Ragú® Parmesan and Mozzarella Sauce

1 cup water

1 (15-ounce) container ricotta cheese

¼ cup Parmesan cheese, grated

1 (8-ounce) package mozzarella cheese, grated

1 (8-ounce) box ziti, or one of the other pastas mentioned above

2 eggs beaten

Cookware needed: 9 x 13-inch baking dish or casserole, mixing bowl

Sage Advice
When preparing this dish, you can add more sauce if you so wish.

Preheat the oven to 400 degrees.

Combine the sauce and water in a mixing bowl.

Stir in the ricotta, Parmesan, and ½ the mozzarella cheese, then follow with the uncooked ziti, or other pasta.

Spoon the mixture into a baking dish and cover it with foil.

Bake for 55 minutes.

Remove the foil, sprinkle with the remaining mozzarella, and bake uncovered for an additional 5 minutes.

PREPARATION TIME: *10 minutes*
TOTAL TIME: *1 hour and 10 minutes*

3-Cheese Spaghetti Pizza

AND HERE, especially for when the kids in the house are clamoring for pizza, but you are determined not to call for home delivery one more time this week, is a 3-Cheese Spaghetti Pizza. If you like this recipe, refer to the Hot Cheese Pie on page 52, which also becomes a "pizza," thanks to the cheese and eggs that cook into a crust.

Just as I suggested you could add some meat to that recipe, you can try the same with this one.

SERVES 6 TO 8

1 (8 ounce) box spaghetti

1 (15-ounce) container ricotta cheese

2 eggs, slightly beaten

Salt and freshly ground pepper, to taste

1 (16-ounce) jar Ragú® Parmesan and Mozzarella Sauce

¼ cup Parmesan cheese, grated

Cookware needed: mixing bowl, 10-inch pizza pan

Preheat the oven to 375 degrees.

Cook the spaghetti according to the package directions.

Combine the spaghetti, ricotta, and eggs in a large bowl. Add the salt and pepper, to taste.

Spread this mixture evenly in a greased 10-inch pizza pan.

Spread the Ragú® Parmesan and Mozzarella Cheese Sauce evenly on top.

Bake for 30 minutes or until bubbling.

Let stand 5 minutes before serving.

PREPARATION TIME: *10 minutes*

TOTAL TIME: *40 to 45 minutes*

Lazy Boy Lasagna

THERE are those times when you open the freezer and find you don't have the ready-to-serve meal you thought you had. That's when you turn to the pantry and the refrigerator.

Among the items usually in my pantry is a package of lasagna noodles...the regular pasta that has been available for years. Nowadays, "no boil" lasagna noodles can be found on the shelves of every supermarket. But my son, Langdon, discovered this "no boil" trick years ago when he didn't have the time, or the patience (or probably both) to boil the lasagna noodles first.

He just started layering the ingredients in the baking dish, and when he finished assembling it all, he stuck it in the oven. To his amazement, it worked. He hasn't boiled a lasagna noodle since.

SERVES 10 TO 12

1 teaspoon olive oil
3 to 4 cloves garlic
½ cup frozen, diced onion
1 pound lean ground beef
approximately 48 ounces Ragú® Pasta Sauce (your favorite flavor)

2 (15-ounce) containers ricotta cheese
1 (8-ounce) package mozzarella cheese, grated
10 to 12 lasagna noodles/regular
¼ cup Parmesan Cheese, grated
Cookware needed: skillet, baking dish or casserole

Heat the oil, add the garlic, and sauté briefly to release the flavor and aroma.

Add the onion and ground beef and brown. Drain and set aside.

Preheat the oven to 350 degrees.

Spread a thin layer of the sauce in a baking dish, followed by layers of lasagna noodles, ricotta cheese, meat, a sprinkling of the mozzarella cheese, and more sauce.

Repeat the layering twice more, ending with the noodles and sauce.

Cover the pan with foil and bake the lasagna for 45 minutes.

Remove the foil, add the remaining mozzarella and Parmesan cheese, and bake about 10 to 15 minutes longer, or until the top cheese has melted.

PREPARATION TIME: *15 minutes*
TOTAL TIME: *1 hour and 10 to 15 minutes*

Sage Advice

Langdon says that cooking is like chemistry. You take the ingredients you have, mix them together, and see what happens. So if he doesn't have enough Parmesan cheese for the top, he uses grated Romano. And as far as the specific number of lasagna noodles goes, he says, "however many fit in the baking dish. Break them up, if need be." And, of course, sometimes he uses more or less sauce. So it comes as no surprise that his sage advice is this: "Read the recipe first, check the ingredients you have on hand, and then relax, use what you have, and have fun." Incidentally, by following his directions for assembling the lasagna, you only dirty one skillet and the baking pan. You spoon the rest of the ingredients directly from their containers.

Zippy
Breads

*"**OUR SUPPER** was very good: only bread was lacking; but inquiring of us what sort we wanted, in an hour's time they served us what we had asked for."*

—The Marquis de Chastellux, traveling in America in the 1780s

How well I remember the hours I spent kneading and rolling, punching down and pinching off bits of dough, in those long-ago days when I thought it was necessary to make homemade bread.

Occasionally, those hours were well spent and generously rewarded when I turned out the perfect loaf. But more often my time was wasted when, for some unknown reason, the bread rose on one side only, or was sad in the middle, or didn't rise at all.

I never thought about it at the time, but I was doing something our ancestors had done since time immemorial—trusting my hard-spent labor to external conditions (heat and humidity) that were out of my control and could, in turn, cause that carefully blended flour and yeast and water to flop in the twinkling of an eye. All of which is why the first real convenience food has to have been bakery-baked bread.

What housewife, after all, had the time to man the special oven required for baking bread in ancient days? (If she had one, that is.) That is why there were *bakeries* in ancient Greece (first) and Rome (by the second century B.C.). A tradition that continues today.

Truth be told, in most homes, homemade bread is a recent indulgence—thanks to the newfangled bread machines!

So, under the circumstances, I choose to buy loaves of bread from the store. But I do thoroughly enjoy mixing up a quick batch of muffins or corn bread or even cheese biscuits.

That's why I'm including only a few recipes for breads. But the ones that are here will add zip to your entire meal and, when served, will make everyone think you could always bake bread...if you wanted to!

"Everybody is always out of bread," Mrs. Grace Townsend

wrote in **The Star Cook Book** *back in 1895.*

"Prevent it if you can."

A well-stocked traditional breadbasket fills the bill, and one with a loop handle makes for easy passing. A simple rattan or straw-type basket with a checkered or colorful napkin liner is great for informal meals and buffets, but for more formal occasions, a silver or brass basket lined with a damask napkin adds real pizzazz to the table.

Sage Advice

In one of mother's dog-eared cookbooks, there were numerous newspaper clippings with all kinds of kitchen advice. Most of them would be worthless to today's cook, who uses a microwave and food processor as a matter of course. But this one on how to grease a loaf pan or muffin tin is as relevant today as ever. "Margarine and oil can be absorbed into the dough or batter and even make the bread stick to the pan. Always use shortening to grease pans."

Beer Bread

FOOD historians have long pondered the question, which came first—the bread or the brew?

Historians believe that prehistoric man heated water to boiling and then added grain kernels to make an early version of gruel or mash. But, if left alone in the water—which eventually cooled down—the grain fermented, making brew.

Beer bread combines grain and beer in a quick-and-easy loaf that even I can make! The result—-great aroma from the kitchen, a true *From Storebought to Homemade* bread, and raves from the table.

MAKES 1 LOAF

½ cup sugar
2 cups self-rising flour
12 ounces beer (not light)

1 stick butter, melted
Cookware needed: loaf pan

Preheat the oven to 350 degrees.

Combine the sugar, flour, and beer, and transfer the dough to a greased loaf pan.

Allow the dough to stand for about 10 minutes (this can be while the stove pre-heats).

Bake for 50 minutes.

Pour the melted butter over the top of the bread as soon as it comes out of the oven.

PREPARATION TIME: *5 minutes*
TOTAL TIME: *approximately 60 minutes*

Sage Advice

This is a sweet, moist bread that should be eaten immediately after cooking. For a less sweet bread, use as little as 3 tablespoons of sugar, or for a really sweet bread, use up to a full cup.

Ice Cream Muffins

THIS IS ONE RECIPE you aren't going to believe.

Meredith Maynard Chase, one of the authors of *Caterin' to Charleston*, shared it with me in the mid-1980s when I was living in Raleigh and my former husband was president of Saint Mary's College.

Read the recipe, and then there's more.

MAKES 12 MUFFINS

2 cups self-rising flour or Bisquick

2 cups softened vanilla ice cream

Cookware needed: mixing bowl, 12-cup muffin tin

Preheat the oven to 425 degrees.

Combine the flour and ice cream until smooth. Add a little more ice cream, if necessary to make it creamy.

Grease the bottoms of 12 muffin cups and then fill ¾ full with the batter. Bake for 25 minutes, or until golden.

That's it! Meredith actually recommended sprinkling the muffins with cinnamon and sugar before serving, but that's not necessary.

This recipe isn't just easy. It also has endless possibilities.

When my grandson, Benjamin, was going through his two-or-more-bananas-a-day stage, I made banana-nut bread muffins. Other times I have turned the recipe into strawberry bread muffins, and even rum-raisin muffins.

The secret is to use the best, richest, creamiest ice cream you can find. For the banana-nut bread muffins I used Breyer's Homestyle Butter Pecan ice cream and Bisquick, to which I added ½ cup chopped pecans and three overripe bananas. Benjamin and I ate them for breakfast, lunch, supper, and snacks.

PREPARATION TIME: *5 minutes*
TOTAL TIME: *25 minutes*

Marmalade Muffins

ARE YOU ONE of those folks who loves ketchup, but doesn't like tomatoes?

I'm one who loves oranges but will usually pass up marmalade, if I have the choice between a berry preserve (usually strawberry or raspberry, but even blackberry or gooseberry) *or* marmalade.

That's why I particularly enjoy these quick and delicious marmalade muffins. There's no "berry" choice to compete with their delicious orange flavor. Further, these slightly sweet muffins are a great addition to that special breakfast, or even dinner when chicken, ham, or pork is being served.

MAKES 12 MUFFINS

2 cups Bisquick
2 tablespoons butter, melted
3 heaping tablespoons sugar
½ cup orange juice

2 eggs, lightly beaten
½ cup orange (or lemon) marmalade
Cookware needed: mixing bowl
12-cup muffin tin

The
Finishing Touch

Consider baking these sweet muffins in miniature muffin tins. These minimuffins are delicious with afternoon tea. If you do this, they will bake a little more quickly, in approximately 12 or 15 minutes, and will yield 24 muffins.

Preheat the oven to 400 degrees.

Grease or spray the bottoms of 12-muffin cups.

Measure 1 cup of the Bisquick into a mixing bowl.

Combine the melted butter with the sugar and stir the mixture into the Bisquick.

Add the orange juice and the eggs and stir.

Now add the rest of the Bisquick and mix just enough to moisten.

Lightly stir in the marmalade.

Fill the muffin cups ⅔ full, and bake for 15 to 20 minutes, or until golden brown.

PREPARATION TIME: *10 minutes*
TOTAL TIME: *30 minutes*

Miniature Pineapple Cupcakes

FOR ANOTHER SWEET, dainty treat, try these pineapple muffins that are so sweet you can even call them cupcakes.

MAKES 48 MINIATURE MUFFINS

1 box orange or yellow cake mix

4 eggs

1 (15-ounce) can crushed
pineapple

Cookware needed: mixing bowl, 2
24-cup miniature muffin tins

Preheat the oven to 325 degrees.

Combine all the ingredients.

Fill 48 greased miniature muffin cups ⅔ full, and bake 12 to 15 minutes, or until brown.

PREPARATION TIME: *10 minutes*
TOTAL TIME: *approximately 25 minutes*

The
Finishing Touch

To turn these into real "tea" muffins, shake powdered sugar over them when they are cool.

"Do you remember the mouth-watering aroma of homemade bread baking over a slow fire—the memorable sight of steaming bread fresh from the oven—the exquisite taste of each delicious slice...the kind you haven't had since grandmother's day?"

—A NOTE FROM MARGARET RUDKIN OF PEPPERIDGE FARM, 1962

Incredibly Quick Cheese Biscuits

USED to be that no Southern lady could have a party without serving paper-thin, crispy cheese straws. If she made them herself, she would have practiced for years to perfect the technique of pushing them through a cookie press with just the right pressure and to just the right length. Otherwise, she had to buy them (for a pretty penny) from other enterprising ladies who had learned that these delicacies were essential party fare.

These incredibly quick miniature cheese biscuits are a great substitute for those labor-intensive cheese straws, and they're so easy to make that you will want to serve them to your family, not just to the ladies.

Sage Advice

If you're going to be pressed for time, mix the batter the day before and store it overnight in the refrigerator.

MAKES 48 BISCUITS

1 (8-ounce) package sharp Cheddar cheese, grated

2 sticks butter, melted

1 (8-ounce) container sour cream

2 cups self-rising flour

½ teaspoon cayenne pepper or garlic powder (optional)

Cookware needed: mixing bowl, 2 24-cup miniature muffin tins

Preheat the oven to 350 degrees.

Combine the cheese and melted butter. Cool for 2 minutes, then add the sour cream and mix well. Stir in the flour.

For variety, add ½ teaspoon cayenne pepper or ½ teaspoon garlic powder to the flour before it is added to the cheese, butter, and sour cream mixture.

Fill 48 greased miniature muffin cups ⅔ full.

Bake for 18 to 22 minutes.

PREPARATION TIME: *10 minutes*
TOTAL TIME: *approximately 30 minutes*

Blue Cheese Nibbles

THE FOLLOWING is one of those recipes that made me ponder, "Where should I put it?"

The Blue Cheese Nibbles that Shirley Duncan was kind enough to share with all of us work equally well as a cocktail party treat, an unexpected and delicious indulgence served with soup at lunch, or as a bread passed at a dinner party. With so many options, I concluded they belong under Zippy Breads.

MAKES 32 NIBBLES

1 (8-ounce) can refrigerator biscuits, cut into quarters

½ stick butter (not margarine)

¼ cup blue cheese, crumbled

1 teaspoon Worcestershire sauce

Cookware needed: 9 x 13-inch cake pan, small saucepan or microwave-safe bowl

Preheat the oven to 400 degrees.

Arrange the biscuits in a 9 x 13-inch cake pan so they touch each other.

In a small saucepan or microwave-safe bowl, melt the butter and cheese together.

Add the Worcestershire sauce, and mix well.

Pour the cheese mixture over the biscuits.

Bake for 12 to 15 minutes or until golden brown.

Serve hot.

PREPARATION TIME: *5 minutes*
TOTAL TIME: *20 minutes*

No-Mess Quick Biscuits

"You know you can't write a cookbook without including
biscuits in it," a neighbor said, chastising me.
"Biscuits!" another friend, who was along with us, moaned.
"I'm tired of getting flour all over my kitchen."
"You won't if you make those quick biscuits made with
mayonnaise," another friend chimed in.
"Or the ones made with sour cream," said yet another.

If you, and your friends and neighbors, are still making biscuits the old-fashioned way...

Or, if you depend on some of the delicious frozen biscuits now available, but have that urge to mix and stir up a batch of homemade biscuits...

Try one of the following three-ingredient, no-mess recipes.

Mayonnaise Biscuits

MAKES 12 BISCUITS

1 cup Bisquick or self-rising flour
½ cup milk
3 tablespoons mayonnaise

Cookware needed: mixing bowl, 12-cup muffin tin

Preheat the oven to 400 degrees.

Combine the three ingredients until smooth.

Spoon the batter into 12 greased muffin cups, filling them about ½ full.

Bake for about 10 to 12 minutes.

PREPARATION TIME: *10 minutes*
TOTAL TIME: *approximately 20 minutes*

Sour Cream Biscuits

MAKES 24 BISCUITS

½ stick butter

1 cup Bisquick

½ (8-ounce) carton sour cream

Cookware needed: mixing bowl, 24-cup miniature muffin tin

Preheat the oven to 425 degrees.

Melt the butter in the microwave or over very low heat.

Stir in the Bisquick and sour cream and mix thoroughly.

Fill 24 miniature muffin cups half to ⅔ full.

Bake for 10 to 12 minutes, or until the tops are well browned.

PREPARATION TIME: *10 minutes*
TOTAL TIME: *approximately 20 to 25 minutes*

Bread should be broken, never cut.

Pastry should be broken and eaten with a fork.

Fish must be eaten with the fork.

Peas and beans require the fork only.

Potatoes, if mashed should be mashed with the fork.

Green corn should be eaten from the cob,

held with a single hand only.

Eat slowly for both health and manners.

Never eat all there is on your plate, nor attempt to do so.

—TABLE ETIQUETTE, FROM *THE STAR COOK BOOK*,
BY MRS. GRACE TOWNSEND, 1895

Cornmeal Biscuits

Oh, and just in case you find those recipes too much trouble, but you're determined to bring a *From Storebought to Homemade* biscuit to your table, try this trick: Separate the biscuits from a can of refrigerator biscuits and roll them in cornmeal, then bake them according to the package directions.

Corny Corn Bread

Being a Southerner, I like my corn bread made from coarse-ground yellow cornmeal, water, eggs, and a little "grease"—be it butter or bacon fat or shortening. But I'm in the minority these days.

My kids like corn added to their cornbread. If that's what you like, you'll want to try these three updated versions of an old-timey favorite.

Corn Bread Plus

SERVES APPROXIMATELY 8

1 (8-ounce) box Jiffy corn bread mix

1 (15-ounce) can whole kernel corn, drained

3 tablespoons butter or, if you have it on hand, bacon grease

Cookware needed: square baking dish

Preheat the oven to 400 degrees.

Prepare the corn bread mix according to the directions on the package.

Stir in the corn.

Melt the butter or bacon grease in square baking dish over very low heat and spread it all around.

Pour the corn bread mixture on top and bake for 40 minutes or until brown.

PREPARATION TIME: *5 to 6 minutes*
TOTAL TIME: *approximately 45 to 50 minutes*

Sage Advice

Charlotte Sizer, my trusty assistant, says that Jiffy corn bread mix is always dependable.

The Finishing Touch

You can dot the bread with pats of butter when you remove the pan from the oven. The butter will melt while you cut the bread into squares to serve immediately.

Sweet Pepper Corn Bread

SERVES APPROXIMATELY 8

1 (8-ounce) package Jiffy corn bread mix

1 (15-ounce) can whole kernel corn with sweet peppers, drained

¼ cup frozen, diced combo of onion and green pepper

3 tablespoons butter or, if you have it on hand, bacon grease

Cookware needed: square baking dish or casserole

Preheat the oven to 400 degrees.

Prepare the corn bread mix according to package directions.

Add the corn and the onion and green pepper combo.

Melt the butter or bacon grease in the square baking dish over very low heat and spread it all around.

Pour the corn bread mixture into the baking dish and bake for 40 minutes or until brown.

PREPARATION TIME: *5 to 6 minutes*
TOTAL TIME: *45 to 50 minutes*

Jalapeño Corn Bread

HERE we go again! Just start with the Jiffy corn bread mix and add ingredients to your taste buds' delight. What makes this bread different from the previous two is that it is more like a spoon bread that you dish out at the table than a bread you cut ahead of time and serve in the traditional "pass the bread" way.

By the way, my son, Langdon, says this is his "pick" of these recipes. He is crazy about it. It can even take the place of a potato, rice, or pasta dish.

Sage Advice

When you add the meat, this bread becomes almost a meal in itself, albeit a very rich one. It's delicious when served with a taco salad and refried beans. I like to prepare it without the meat when I'm having guests in for a casual chili and salad buffet.

SERVES 10 TO 12

- 1 (8-ounce) package Jiffy corn bread mix
- ¼ cup melted butter or bacon drippings
- 1 (8-ounce) can cream-style corn
- ½ cup frozen, diced combo of onion and green pepper
- ½ cup Cheddar cheese, grated (or one of the cello-pack cheese mixtures that you have on hand)
- 1 to 3 tablespoons diced canned jalapeño peppers
- ½ to 1 pound ground meat, either mild sausage or hamburger, cooked and drained (optional)
- **Cookware needed:** 2-quart baking dish or casserole

Preheat the oven to 400 degrees.

Prepare the corn bread mix according to package directions.

Pour a little of the melted butter or drippings into the bottom of the 2-quart baking dish to grease it.

Add the remaining butter or drippings to the corn bread mix along with all the other ingredients, and pour the batter into the baking dish.

Bake for 45 to 50 minutes, or until set and brown on top.

PREPARATION TIME: *5 to 6 minutes, add 10 minutes if cooking meat*
TOTAL TIME: *50 to 60 minutes*

Anything-Goes Crescent Rolls

One of the most versatile items in the grocery store is a can of refrigerator crescent rolls. You can create just about any bread by adding a favorite spice, meat, or herb. The ones that follow run the gamut from sweet to salty and can be served at a variety of meals.

Tomato Basil Crescents

SERVES 8 (OR MORE AS APPETIZERS)

1 (8-ounce) can refrigerator crescent rolls

1 (3-ounce) jar pesto sauce (with olive oil base)

1 (5-ounce) jar sun-dried tomato tapenade

Cookware needed: baking sheet

The Finishing Touch

For appetizers, or smaller appetites, the rolls can be cut in half before baking—they rise into a lovely knot. This applies to all the refrigerator crescent recipes.

Unroll the triangles of dough and, onto each one, spread 1 scant teaspoon of pesto sauce and 1 heaping teaspoon of sun-dried tomato tapenade. Re-roll the crescents and place them on a baking sheet.

Bake according to package directions. Wrap in aluminum foil to reheat.

PREPARATION TIME: *5 minutes*
TOTAL TIME: *17 to 25 minutes*

Cinnamon Crescents

SERVES 8

1 (8-ounce) can refrigerator
crescent rolls

8 tablespoons superfine
granulated sugar

Cinnamon

3 tablespoons melted butter
(optional)

Cookware needed: baking sheet

Unroll the triangles of dough and, onto each, sprinkle 1 teaspoon of sugar. Dust them all generously with cinnamon and re-roll the crescents.

Bake them on a baking sheet according to package directions. Wrap in aluminum foil to reheat.

Add a yummy touch to this sweet bread by brushing the crescents with the melted butter just before removing them from the oven.

PREPARATION TIME: *5 minutes*
TOTAL TIME: *17 to 25 minutes*

Ham Biscuits in a Flash

SERVES 8

¼ pound sliced ham (if you want to be authentic, use Smithfield or Virginia Country Ham)

2 tablespoons olive oil

or

½ (8-ounce) jar deviled Smithfield ham

1 (8-ounce) can refrigerator crescent rolls

Cookware needed: mixing bowl, baking sheet

If using sliced ham, combine it with the olive oil and mince it in a blender or food processor.

Unroll the triangles of dough and spread about 1 tablespoon of the ham mixture onto the upper third of each one.

Re-roll the triangles and put them on a baking sheet. Bake according to package directions. Wrap in aluminum foil to reheat.

PREPARATION TIME: *5 minutes (plus 5 more if grinding the ham)*
TOTAL TIME: *17 to 30 minutes*

"It is not mere chance or legend which gives the Smithfield ham honorable acclaim throughout the world. The rich, pervading flavor of the slices is quite unlike anything else in the way of pork. Something more than a hundred years ago, Queen Victoria of England ordered for Buckingham Palace a shipment of six hams a week from Smithfield, Virginia. The order has never been canceled. The shipments have never been interrupted, even in times of war."

—MORRIS MARKEY, "THE TASTY PIG," 1949

Easy Sausage Swirls

YIELDS 40 SWIRLS

2 (8-ounce) cans refrigerator
crescent rolls

2 tablespoons hot mustard

1 pound bulk hot pork sausage

Cookware needed: baking sheet

Separate the rolls into four rectangles and spread each one with mustard.

Spread each rectangle with a thin layer of sausage.

Re-roll and chill the crescents until ready to bake.

Thinly slice each roll (10 swirls to a roll) and place the rounds on an ungreased baking sheet.

Bake according to package directions.

PREPARATION TIME: *5 minutes*
TOTAL TIME: *17 to 25 minutes*

Seeded Bread Sticks

SERVES 8 OR MORE

1 (8-ounce) can refrigerator
crescent rolls

Vegetable oil cooking spray

Poppy seeds

Sesame seeds

Sea salt

Dried onion (optional)

Cookware needed: baking sheet
or large pizza stone

Unroll and lay the crescent roll dough out in one single layer on a baking sheet, or shape to fit a large pizza stone, pressing all the perforated edges together to seal them.

Spray the surface of the dough with vegetable oil spray.

Sprinkle both kinds of seeds over the entire surface of the dough. Then sprinkle with salt and onion, less generously than with the seeds.

Bake according to package directions.

Remove from the oven and cut into sticks about 1 inch wide and 3 inches long.

PREPARATION TIME: *5 minutes*
TOTAL TIME: *17 to 25 minutes*

Sage Advice

A pizza cutting wheel comes in handy when cutting the bread sticks.

Fabulous Finales

THOSE TRAYS the waiters bring around at the end of a meal with a slice of triple chocolate mousse topped with raspberry sauce; a crimped lemon galette prepared with zest of lemon; a plum tart with swirls of dried apricots and toasted almonds; and a mocha torte with toffee drizzled over the top are, well...*over* the top.

Never underestimate the appeal of a sweet to round out the perfect meal, but a good dessert need not require a double boiler, a candy thermometer, and a pastry tube to be delicious. Take my experience last Thanksgiving.

While looking through the pile of cookbooks that are always by my side of the bed, I came upon a dessert recipe for "Sin." How could I resist?

This is what I read, "Mix [chocolate wafer] crumbs and melted butter. Press into bottom of 13 x 8-inch pan. Chill until firm."

Hhmmmm, I thought. I can cut out that step. I'll just use a storebought Oreo Cookie crust.

For the filling, I was supposed to "Crush chilled [toffee] candy bars and mix together with [vanilla] ice cream."

Now let's see. After doing all that, I'm going to end up with butter brickle ice cream. Why not just buy a quart, I concluded.

Finally, whip...

"Or, just buy an aerosol can of whipped cream," I said out loud.

So that's what I did. I bought an Oreo Cookie crust; filled it with butter brickle ice cream, and squirted a fancy border of whipped cream around the edge—Sinful Butter Brickle Ice Cream Pie (page 257).

Thanksgiving dinner came and went and it was dessert time. I brought out slices of homemade (for real) brownies, Old-Fashioned Lemon Chess Pie (it's so simple I've included it in the book, page 250), and *From Storebought to Homemade* Sinful Butter Brickle Ice Cream Pie.

"I'll have some of that ice cream pie," my daughter piped up. "Me too," "me too," "me too," everyone around the table chimed in.

No one touched a single one of those other desserts I had taken the time to prepare.

Not only was the last slice of ice cream pie gobbled up, there wasn't even a crumb of storebought Oreo Cookie crust left on a single plate.

The moral of the story is this: Simple, easy desserts work just fine.

Fruit Platter

EVERY TIME you walk into a well-lighted, cheerful grocery store, I'll wager that you stroll by the fruit display just to enjoy the beautiful array of pears, apples, grapes, and berries. It's a feast for the eyes...and for the palate as well.

Somehow, in these days of layered cakes and fancy tortes, we seem to have forgotten how succulent and satisfying a simple arrangement of fresh fruits can be at the end of a meal. Next time you're having guests over, make a pretty centerpiece of nothing but fruit on a platter. Then, when dessert time comes around, pass a fruit plate, followed by a bowl of flavored cream. You'll be amazed how much everyone will enjoy this traditional, but seldom served dessert.

SERVINGS VARY WITH FRUITS USED
(QUANTITY GIVEN FOR APPROXIMATELY 8 PEOPLE)

Sage Advice

For an even simpler fruit tray, arrange small grape clusters and apple wedges (sprinkled with lemon juice as described) on a plate. On a separate plate, put ½-inch slices of French bread and wedges of Brie, blue, and Camembert cheese. Garnish the bread and cheese tray with two or three flower blossoms or a few plump blueberries and mint leaves for color.

2 red and 2 green apples

Juice of 1 lemon

4 large seedless oranges
(or tangerines, a can of
mandarin oranges, or a jar
of orange sections)

A combination (your choice) of
1-pint containers of blueberries, blackberries, raspberries

1 quart strawberries

½ pound seedless grapes

2 or 3 kiwi

Almonds, toasted

Flavored Whipped Cream
(recipe follows)

Caramel and/or chocolate sauce
(optional)

Cookware needed: medium bowl,
platter

Wash and core the apples. Slice them into wedges and put them in a bowl. Or use the one-step apple corer/slicer that can be found in most grocery stores.

Squeeze lemon juice, or, if using bottled lemon juice, dribble the juice over the apples to keep them from discoloring. Refrigerate.

Peel and section the oranges or tangerines, or drain if using fruit from a can or jar.

Wash and pat dry the grapes. Snip small clusters from one bunch to be used to decorate the platter.

Rinse the berries and allow them to dry in a strainer or on paper towels.

Peel the kiwi, and slice them into rings.

To arrange the platter, put one or two large clusters of grapes in the center of a round platter. Surround them with a circle of apple wedges, kiwi slices, smaller grape clusters, and orange or tangerine sections.

These can be arranged in like groups—placing together all the red apples, all the kiwi circles, etc. or interspersed—apple slice, orange section, kiwi slice, grape cluster, apple slice, orange section, and so forth.

Sprinkle berries and almonds on top.

Pass the platter with a serving spoon and fork and follow it with a dish of Flavored Whipped Cream and, depending on how decadent you feel, bowls of hot caramel and chocolate sauce.

■ ■ ■ ■ ■ ■ ■ ■

PREPARATION TIME: *approximately 20 minutes,*
depending on the amount of fruit
TOTAL TIME: *same*

The Finishing Touch

Any time you are serving fruits for dessert, it is nice to have a small bowl or dish of storebought chocolates on hand for the serious chocoholic. Chocolate covered raspberry or orange sticks, chocolate covered nuts, or even chocolate covered miniature pretzels will do nicely.

"Strawberries, and only strawberries, could now be thought or spoken of."

—JANE AUSTEN

Flavored Whipped Cream

YIELDS APPROXIMATELY 3 CUPS

1 pint whipping cream

3 tablespoons confectioners' sugar

one of the following flavorings: a vanilla or almond extract, or a

liqueur such as crème de menthe or crème de cocoa

Cookware needed: stainless steel or copper mixing bowl

Pour the carton of whipping cream into a prechilled stainless steel or copper mixing bowl. Begin to beat on high with an electric mixer. Add the confectioners' sugar slowly and continue to beat until soft peaks form (be careful that you don't beat too long, or the cream will yellow and turn to butter!). Stir in the flavoring (begin with 1 tablespoon and add more to taste).

PREPARATION TIME: *10 minutes*

TOTAL TIME: *10 minutes*

Flan

IF, when you read "flan," you're expecting to have to pull out the dreaded double boiler, think again.

Instead, next time you're at the grocery store, pick up as many packages of Kozy Shack or other ready-to-serve flans as you need and try this trick.

SERVINGS VARY ACCORDING TO NUMBER OF GUESTS

Ready-to-serve flan

1 jar whole berry preserves

Cool Whip or whipped cream

Mint leaves or fresh fruit for a garnish

Cookware needed: individual dessert plates or ramekins

Turn the flans out onto individual dessert plates or suitable ramekins.

Top them with a spoonful of your favorite whole berry preserves and a dollop of Cool Whip or whipped cream. Garnish them with mint leaves or fresh fruit to complement the preserves (strawberries, blueberries, blackberries, whatever).

PREPARATION TIME: *5 minutes*

TOTAL TIME: *5 minutes*

Pots de Crème

JUST as easy to assemble is this *From Storebought to Homemade* version of Pots de Crème, which is a fancy way of saying cream in a pot (small, individual, and very fancy pots though they be).

SERVES 4

1 box instant vanilla pudding mix, or 4 ready-to-serve individual cups of pudding

A nice liqueur such as Cointreau or Grand Marnier, Amaretto, or Framboise

Cookware needed: mixing bowl

If using instant pudding mix, prepare the pudding according to package directions. Stir ¼ cup of liqueur into the pudding and then put it into individual dessert dishes (demitasse cups or small bowls work very well for this).

Garnish each serving with a complementary fruit—mandarin oranges for Cointreau or Grand Marnier, roasted almonds for Amaretto, and raspberries or strawberries for Framboise.

PREPARATION TIME: *5 minutes*
TOTAL TIME: *5 minutes*

Baked Tipsy Apples

SERVINGS VARY

Stouffer's Escalloped Apples, frozen (as needed)

toasted, sliced almonds for a garnish

½ cup brandy

1 (12-once) jar caramel sauce

Cookware needed: baking dish or casserole, mixing bowl

Before baking the apples according to package directions, sprinkle with ¼ cup of brandy.

While the apples are baking, combine a jar of caramel sauce with another ¼ cup of brandy.

To serve, heat the brandy sauce in the microwave, or on the stovetop. Either put some of the sauce on the plate, place the apples on top, and garnish with toasted sliced almonds, or, put the apples on the plate, garnish it with the almonds, and drizzle the sauce over the top of the apple.

Serve with whipped cream.

PREPARATION TIME: *10 minutes*
TOTAL TIME: *50 minutes*

Frozen Oranges

I'VE NEVER seen frozen oranges served in a restaurant, and I've had them only a couple of times at dinner parties. Don't ask me why. They are the best and the absolutely perfect way to end a summertime dinner.

SERVINGS VARY, 1 ORANGE PER GUEST

Seedless oranges—as many as you need.

Cookware needed: a knife—that's the joy of this recipe!

Wash and dry the oranges. Slice off the top third and replace it.

Put the oranges in the freezer for the day or overnight. Just before serving dinner, take them out, remove the tops, and they'll be ready to eat (with a spoon) when it's time for dessert.

PREPARATION TIME: *5 minutes, unless you add a Finishing Touch*
TOTAL TIME: *same*

Sage Advice

When selecting the oranges, choose those with a flattened base so they'll sit up well on the plate. If available, blood oranges are best because of their vibrant color.

The Finishing Touch

Garnish each orange with a swirl of whipped cream, a sprig of fresh mint, or a few fresh raspberries. Serve them with your favorite cookies (my choice would be Milanos, orange-flavored thins, Pirouettes, or even a chocolate-covered orange candy) or splurge and get a really rich chocolate cake or torte from a local bakery or the bakery department of your grocery store.

Here's a great opportunity to pull out the squirt bottle, fill it with chocolate sauce, and make a design on the plate before placing the orange. Or, if, in one of your "I'm-going-to-fix-a-fancy-dish" moments you bought a kitchen torch, now's the chance to use it. Sprinkle the orange with granulated sugar and caramelize it.

The Basic Poached Pear

NEED an unusual, even elegant, dessert to dress up an ordinary meal? Try pears.

I've yet to figure out why pears are seldom served, when they are so delicious and so easy to prepare in such a wide variety of ways. Oh yes, did I mention that they are also good for you?

Begin with either fresh or canned pears. (If you choose fresh pears, you will want to poach them, but that's a simple task.) Combine with a flavored juice, garnish with an already made or fresh topping, and you're through.

Read through these options and see which ones tickle your taste buds. Then try one or two. I'll wager that pears will begin appearing more often around your house.

Sage Advice

Whether using fresh or canned pears, add either mint leaves, or 2 or 3 cloves and a cinnamon stick, or even a little flavored complementary fruit liqueur to the liquid. For example, to orange juice, add 1 to 2 tablespoons of Grand Marnier, or to Welch's wild raspberry blend, add Kirsch.

SERVES 4

Pears—if fresh, select firm (not quite ripe) Bosc or other pears that are in season, or canned

Some suggested flavored juices are:

cranapple juice

orange juice

juice drained from any canned cocktail fruits

your favorite mixed or blended fruit drink that you have on hand (see page 18)

If using canned pears:

Cookware needed: large bowl or baking dish or casserole

Drain the pears and place them in a bowl. Pour enough liquid (your choice) over them to cover. (Though it's not necessary, if you quickly heat the liquid in the microwave before pouring it over the pears, the pears will absorb the flavor more readily.)

Refrigerate for at least 2 hours. Serve with some of the liquid on individual dessert plates.

PREPARATION TIME USING CANNED PEARS: *5 to 10 minutes*
TOTAL TIME: *10 minutes, plus 2 hours to chill*

If using fresh pears:

Cookware needed: large bowl or saucepan or baking dish or casserole

Peel 4 whole pears. If you wish to leave them whole with the stem on, do so. Otherwise, halve the pears and remove the core.

Pears can be poached on top of the stove (in a saucepan), in a microwave, or in the oven (in a baking dish). The result is just about the same, so do what is most convenient for you. To poach on the stovetop, bring the liquid (see below) to the boiling point and then add the pears. But if microwaving or baking, place the pears in the dish, and then add the liquid.

Use approximately 2 cups of one of the suggested juices for every 4 whole pears or 8 halves.

If poaching on the stovetop, simmer the pears for approximately 15 minutes, or until they begin to soften. Microwaving takes about 10 to 15 minutes.

If baking, cook them at 350 degrees for approximately 30 minutes, basting occasionally for a richer taste.

Once the pears have cooked, chill them, juice and all, for about 4 hours. Serve with some of the cooking liquid on individual dessert plates.

■ ■ ■ ■ ■ ■ ■ ■ ■

PREPARATION TIME USING FRESH PEARS: *15 to 20 minutes*
TOTAL TIME: *varies with cooking method from 15 to 30 minutes, plus 4 hours to chill*

The
Finishing Touch

Add a few small berries—raspberries, blueberries, or sliced strawberries—to each dish for color and flavor. Mint leaves are another pretty addition. A dollop of rich vanilla ice cream is a delicious accompaniment, as is a liberal dousing of ready-to-serve boiled custard from the dairy section. And if you're feeling really indulgent, top it all off with a little chocolate—shaved, a prepared topping, or even a piece or two served on the side.

Cheesy Chocolate Pears

HERE is yet another way to serve up a quick pear dessert. It combines three delicious flavors—pear, cheese, and chocolate. Since it is "assembled" on the dessert plates themselves, there isn't even a bowl to clean up.

SERVES 4

8 well-shaped canned, pear halves, drained

Lemon juice

4 ounces cream cheese, softened—a fruit flavor, if you wish, or a more sophisticated creamy cheese such as chèvre

Chocolate sauce, your favorite commercial brand

½ cup nuts (pecans, chopped walnuts, or slivered almonds)

Cookware needed: just the serving utensils

Place 2 pear halves on each dessert plate.

Squeeze a little lemon juice on the pears for flavor.

Spoon some cream cheese into the cavity of each pear. Drizzle chocolate sauce over and around the pears and sprinkle the nuts around them.

PREPARATION TIME: *10 minutes*
TOTAL TIME: *10 minutes*

The
Finishing Touch

Thawed frozen berries, or even a gourmet preserve that is filled with large pieces of fruit, can be substituted for the chocolate sauce.

Fruit Pizza

SPEAKING of easy fruit desserts, this fruit pizza is one that daughter Joslin brought back from a trip to visit her Pennsylvania in-laws. Kelly Seiler, Mike's stepsister and a busy young mother herself, made it by gathering the fruits from a salad bar. I suggest that you do too, but as a guide the following list of ingredients includes canned or jarred fruits.

SERVES 6 TO 8

For the pizza:

1 (16-ounce) roll slice-and-bake sugar cookies

1 (8-ounce) package cream cheese, softened

1 (8-ounce) can pineapple chunks, drained

1 (11-ounce) can mandarin orange slices, drained

1 (8-ounce) can apricot halves, drained, juice reserved

2 cups halved green grapes

1 (6-ounce) jar maraschino cherries, drained

For the glaze:

½ cup reserved apricot juice

1 tablespoon cornstarch

¼ teaspoon cinnamon

Cookware needed: 14-inch pizza pan

Sage Advice
Have fun with this dessert pizza! Try substituting slice-and-bake chocolate chip cookie dough and/or a flavored cream cheese. You can also use an apricot jam (heated in the microwave for 30 seconds) instead of the glaze.

Preheat the oven to 350 degrees.

Pat sugar cookie dough into a 14-inch pizza pan.

Bake for 7 to 10 minutes or until golden brown.

Cool completely.

Spread the cream cheese over the crust.

Layer the fruits over the cream cheese in the order they are listed.

Combine all the glaze ingredients in a small saucepan and cook over medium heat until syrupy. Cool thoroughly.

Spoon the glaze over the fruit.

Chill the pizza and serve cold.

The Finishing Touch
This pizza can be topped with Cool Whip or whipped cream before serving.

PREPARATION TIME: *15 minutes*
TOTAL TIME: *approximately 20 minutes to bake and cool the cookie crust, plus a few hours to chill thoroughly*

Let Them Eat Pie!

Thank goodness my daughter has a wonderful mother-in-law who loves to bake. My poor child has been cake-deprived ever since her first birthday in 1971.

Trying to be a good mother, I had invited several friends with infants and toddlers over for a proper birthday celebration. But when the big day arrived, Joslin refused to take a morning nap and her brother, three year-old Langdon, dragged Kirk and Rodney, the little boys from next door, in to play—in the middle of the kitchen floor, of course.

Did I get aggravated? No. I simply put the eggs back in the fridge and the flour sifter back in the cabinet. For on that fateful day I took the path of no aggravation—I bought Joslin a birthday cake from the nearest grocery store. It was a great party and a family tradition was born. In our house, birthday cakes are storebought. Even today.

Unfortunately, though, my easy way out backfired the year Langdon was eight or nine and he went to his friend David Moore's birthday party. As he was leaving, Langdon made a point (I'd threatened him with no cartoons for a week if he forgot) of thanking Mrs. Moore for the nice party.

"That was great cake," he chirped, adding, "Did you buy it at the A&P?"

"Langdon!" his hostess replied, "aren't you ashamed! That was a homemade cake."

"I meant it as a compliment," Langdon replied. "Mother has tried them all. Kroger. Food Lion. Winn Dixie. A&P makes the best birthday cakes of all!"

These days, when I scoot up to Richmond, Virginia, to see Joslin and Mike and the two grandsons, I can always tell if Nancy Sweger, Mike's mom, has been there. The remains of a fabulous, home-baked cake are the telltale signs.

Me? I prefer pies. You don't have to worry about them rising (or falling) or trying to get the icing to just the right consistency.

It is sinfully easy to buy a ready-to-fill pie shell right off the grocer's shelf and then spend a minimum amount of time making a delicious filling for it. That's enough to take care of my creative dessert urges when Nancy's not around to bake cakes for everyone to enjoy!

Lemonade Pie

ONE of my earliest cooking memories is of making this frozen lemon dessert in our un-air-conditioned kitchen. There were no ready-made graham cracker pie shells, or food processors then, so my job was to crush the graham crackers. Thank goodness that's all changed!

SERVES 12 OR MORE

1 (14-ounce) can condensed milk

1 (16-ounce) container Cool Whip

1 (6-ounce) can frozen lemonade

2 graham cracker pie crusts

Cookware needed: mixing bowl

Chill the can of milk for an hour or so. Then combine it with the Cool Whip and lemonade and beat with an electric mixer until frothy.

Pour or spoon the mixture into the pie shells.

Refrigerate the pies for several hours or until well set before cutting.

PREPARATION TIME: *15 minutes*
TOTAL TIME: *several hours for the chilling*

The Finishing Touch

In those pre-ready-to-fill graham cracker crust days, we made the crust by combining the crumbled graham crackers with a little melted butter and a sprinkle of sugar. We would save some of this concoction to use as a topping for the pie. It was awfully good. So, if you have the time, make up a little of this topping and everyone will think you even made the crusts!

Old-Fashioned Lemon Chess Pie

EARLY ON, in the Appetizers and Hors d'oeuvres chapter, I mentioned how compiling these recipes has taken me on a sentimental journey through my family's lives. And I've mentioned all sorts of relatives, blood kin and step-kin.

Funny, but whenever I think of Lemon Chess Pie, I remember my former sister-in-law's now former husband (how's that for a distant relation!) and how much Buddy loved this pie. He always asked me to fix it for family dinners, and I did, although not without mentioning that it would be a lot of trouble, but I'd do it "just for him."

In truth, if you can read a recipe and hold an electric mixer, you can make this pie that is guaranteed to please!

SERVES 6 TO 8 PEOPLE

1 teaspoon flour
1 ½ cups sugar
2 lemons
3 large eggs, well beaten

1 teaspoon butter, melted
1 cup milk
1 unbaked, prepared pie shell
Cookware needed: mixing bowl, small bowl

Preheat the oven to 350 degrees.

Combine the flour and sugar.

Squeeze the lemons into a small bowl, making sure to get all the juice and remove the seeds—which is why it is wise to do this separately.

Grate as much of the lemon rind as possible into the flour and sugar mixture and then add the lemon juice, the eggs, and the butter, stirring well.

Gradually add the milk and continue to mix well.

Pour the filling into the pie shell and bake for 45 minutes or until firm, lightly browned, and thoroughly set in the middle.

PREPARATION TIME: *15 to 20 minutes*
TOTAL TIME: *approximately 1 hour*

Chocolate Chess Pie

ANOTHER old-fashioned favorite, and as easy as the previous one (maybe even easier because you don't have to squeeze the lemons or grate them) is this Chocolate Chess Pie.

SERVES 6 TO 8 PEOPLE

2 large eggs

1 stick butter, softened (not melted)

2 cups sugar

2 tablespoons flour

4 tablespoons cocoa

Pinch of salt

1 (5-ounce) can evaporated milk

2 teaspoons vanilla extract

1 unbaked, prepared pie shell

Cookware needed: mixing bowl

Preheat the oven to 350 degrees.

Beat together the eggs, butter, sugar, flour, cocoa, and salt, until well blended.

Add the evaporated milk and vanilla, and, when thoroughly combined, pour the mixture into the pie shell.

Bake for 40 minutes or until firm and thoroughly set in the middle.

PREPARATION TIME: *10 minutes*
TOTAL TIME: *approximately 45 minutes*

The
Finishing Touch

To "gild the lily," so to speak, garnish the pie with Cool Whip or whipped cream, and ½ cup pecan pieces or some grated chocolate.

Brownie Pie

CHOCOLATE AND NUTS. Reminds me of brownies... which is exactly what this next pie is...Brownie Pie. It was a favorite dessert in North Carolina in the late 1970s, but like so many delicious foods, it doesn't seem to have been around lately. With all the chocoholics there are these days, it's time to resurrect it!

SERVES 6 TO 8 PEOPLE

1 cup sugar

½ cup flour

2 large eggs, beaten

½ cup butter

1 cup chopped or broken pecans

1 cup chocolate chips

1 teaspoon vanilla extract

1 unbaked, prepared pie shell

Cookware needed: 1 mixing bowl, small bowl or saucepan to melt the butter

Preheat the oven to 350 degrees.

Combine the sugar and the flour and add the eggs.

Melt the butter and allow it to cool slightly, then stir it into the egg mixture, followed by the pecans, chocolate chips, and vanilla.

Pour the filling into the pie shell and bake for 45 minutes.

PREPARATION TIME: *10 minutes*

TOTAL TIME: *approximately 1 hour*

Coconut Fruit Pie

IT'S HARD to beat a chocolate pie, but this fruit and nut pie, and Millionaire's Pie (page 254), are awfully good, and so ridiculously easy to prepare that you can make them at the drop of a hat. This one needs to be baked, the other chilled, which may help you decide which one to try first.

SERVES 6 TO 8 PEOPLE

1 stick butter

2 large eggs, lightly beaten

1 cup sugar

½ cup flaked coconut

½ cup pecans

½ cup raisins (I like the golden ones, or a mixture)

1 teaspoon distilled white vinegar

1 unbaked, prepared pie shell

Cookware needed: mixing bowl

Preheat the oven to 350 degrees.

Melt the butter, allow it to cool, and then, one at a time so they will be well blended, stir in the eggs, then the sugar, coconut, pecans, raisins, and vinegar.

Pour the filling into the pie shell and bake for 35 to 40 minutes.

PREPARATION TIME: *15 minutes*
TOTAL TIME: *1 hour*

Millionaire's Pie

THIS LUSCIOUS, silky pie calls for a baked pie shell, and the flaky contrast with the gooey filling is really good. But if you're running short on time, you can substitute a graham cracker crust to eliminate that step. Do remember to chill the pineapple, though. Simply put the can in the refrigerator as soon as you bring it home from the grocery store.

SERVES 6 TO 8 PEOPLE

1 fully baked pie shell, or graham cracker crust

1 (8-ounce) package cream cheese, softened

2 cups confectioners' sugar

1 cup chilled crushed pineapple, drained

1 (12-ounce) container Cool Whip, softened, at room temperature

½ cup chopped pecans (optional)

Cookware needed: mixing bowl

If using a traditional pastry shell, bake it according to package directions.

Combine the cream cheese, sugar, pineapple, and Cool Whip and blend well.

Transfer the filling to the pie shell and, if you wish, sprinkle the top with chopped pecans.

Cover and chill for several hours.

PREPARATION TIME: *10 minutes*
TOTAL TIME: *4 to 5 hours for chilling*

Brown Sugar Pie

IF YOU LOVE pecan pie, and who doesn't, this is an excellent, ever-so-slightly different version of that Southern favorite. This recipe comes in really handy if you don't happen to have the Karo syrup that you need to make true pecan pie.

SERVES 6 TO 8 PEOPLE

1 cup brown sugar

½ cup granulated sugar

1 egg

½ eggshell milk

1 unbaked, prepared pie shell

½ to 1 cup pecans, halved or broken (optional)

Cookware needed: mixing bowl, electric mixer

Preheat the oven to 325 degrees.

Combine the sugars, the egg, and the milk, and pour the mixture into the pie shell.

If you cover the top with nuts, most people will think they're eating a pecan pie—and they are, almost.

Bake for 50 to 55 minutes, or until completely set in the middle.

PREPARATION TIME: *10 minutes*
TOTAL TIME: *approximately 1 hour*

"Eggs can be kept for some time by smearing the shells with butter or lard, then packed in plenty of bran or sawdust, the eggs not allow to touch one another; or coat the eggs with melted paraffin."

—*THE WHITE HOUSE COOK BOOK* BY HUGO ZIEMANN
AND MRS. F. L. GILLETTE, 1926

Sage Advice

Did the measurement of "½ eggshell milk" catch your eye? I almost translated this into its "1 tablespoon" equivalent, as is typically done in today's cookbooks, but then you would miss the fun surprise of finding yourself measuring milk using this natural cup. And why dirty the plastic or metal variety if you don't have to?

The Finishing Touch

Not only do I recommend adding the pecans, I suggest that you top the pie with whipped cream or hard sauce and sprinkle cinnamon or chocolate shavings over it. Let's face it. If you're going to be eating this much pure sugar, a little more indulgence won't kill you.

Almost Sugar-Free Pie

BACK to that old question, "You don't eat like this all the time, do you?" The answer, "No, of course not!" hasn't changed, either.

One reason I don't indulge in these wonderful rich desserts at every meal is that my husband, Bob, has diabetes, just like almost everyone else in his father's family. It is inherited. So I watch his diet like a hawk.

Ironically, one of my father's relatives was Dr. Elliott Joslin, founder of the famed Joslin Diabetic Clinic in Boston, but I know of no diabetes in our family, so I've had to learn all about this far-reaching problem.

One thing I've learned is that more and more people, diabetic or not, are watching their sugar intake seriously. That makes this very good pie a great alternative to sugar-filled ones. I try to have it when offering more than one dessert, but oftentimes I serve it to everyone and no one suspects it is almost "sugar free," with only a few grams of sugar in the pie crust and natural sugars in the fruit (if you add no-sugar-added fruits to the mix).

Read through the recipe and decide what fruit flavor you're in the mood for—strawberry, cherry, lemon, raspberry, whatever, then buy complementary Jell-O and yogurt.

SERVES 6 TO 8 PEOPLE

1 (3-ounce) box sugar-free Jell-O (your favorite flavor)

1 cup hot water

½ cup cold water

1 (8-ounce) container sugar-free yogurt (a flavor to complement the Jell-O)

1 (8-ounce) container Cool Whip, softened, at room temperature

½ cup canned fruit in natural juices, drained and/or chopped nuts of your choice (optional)

1 graham cracker pie crust

Cookware needed: mixing bowl

Prepare the Jell-O using the hot water and the cold water. Allow it to partially jell in the refrigerator—about 30 minutes.

Stir in the yogurt and Cool Whip and, if you wish, fruit and/or nuts.

Pour the filling into the graham cracker crust and chill, or freeze.

PREPARATION TIME: *10 minutes*
TOTAL TIME: *allow for jelling and then chilling*
or thawing time, approximately 3 to 4 hours

Sinful Butter Brickle Ice Cream Pie

"TELL ME again exactly how you made that butter brickle ice cream pie," the eager young bride asked when I told her the story (included in the introduction to this chapter) of how I converted the complicated recipe for "Sin" into a 3-step sinfully easy new recipe. Just for the record, it goes like this.

SERVES 6 TO 8 PEOPLE

1 pint butter brickle ice cream or Coffee HEATH® Bar crunch ice cream

1 Oreo cookie pie crust

1 can whipped topping

Cookware needed: None

Soften the ice cream just enough to spread it in the pie shell. Cover the pie with plastic wrap or aluminum foil and put it in the freezer. Just before serving, add a frilly border of whipped topping.

PREPARATION TIME: *10 minutes*
TOTAL TIME: *1 to 2 hours to chill*

Easy Enough Crème de Menthe Pie

EASY ENOUGH? Once you've practiced on the "sinfully" easy pie above, you'll be ready to move up to this equally easy Crème de Menthe Pie, which is wonderful in the summertime.

SERVES 6 TO 8 PEOPLE

1 pint whipping cream

1 (7-ounce) jar marshmallow cream

¼ cup Crème de Menthe

1 Oreo cookie pie crust

Cookware needed: 2 mixing bowls

Whip the cream and set aside.

Whip the marshmallow cream and Crème de Menthe together and fold the mixture into the whipped cream.

Pour the filling into the pie shell, cover the pie with plastic wrap, and freeze for at least 3 hours.

PREPARATION TIME: *15 minutes*
TOTAL TIME: *3 hours minimum freezing time*

Angels to the Rescue

I still remember the day my mother tried to make an angel food cake. What I don't remember is *why* she tried to do it. We'd bought angel food cakes many times from the grocery store and the bakery.

Knowing Mother, she probably did it for the same reason some people climb mountains—just to prove she could. But she couldn't. The cake was a disaster, and she was still talking about "all those egg whites" for days on end.

I've never even tried to make an angel food cake, but many times a store-bought angel food cake has saved the day. That's why I've called these various angel food cake desserts "Angels to the Rescue"—they involve all the complexity of purchasing an angel food cake and selecting the finishing flavor that will best complement your meal.

Hawaiian Angel

SERVES 8 TO 12

1 (8-ounce) container Cool Whip, softened, at room temperature

3 tablespoons sugar

½ teaspoon vanilla extract

¼ cup maraschino cherries, quartered

1 (8-ounce) can crushed pineapple, well drained

1 cup minimarshmallows

1 (2-ounce) package chopped walnuts

1 angel food loaf cake

Cookware needed: mixing bowl, serrated knife

Empty the Cool Whip into a mixing bowl and fold in the remaining filling ingredients, then chill the mixture for about 20 minutes.

Using a serrated-edge knife, cut a 1-inch horizontal slice from the top of the cake, then cut out a ring 2 inches wide and 2 inches deep from the inside, leaving a hollow.

Fill the cake with the chilled filling. Replace the top slice.

Frost the top and sides of the cake with additional Cool Whip or whipped cream and chill.

Slice to serve.

PREPARATION TIME: *15 to 20 minutes*
TOTAL TIME: *at least 1 hour to chill*

Angel Creams

MAKES APPROXIMATELY 16 CREAMS

1 angel food loaf cake

1 (16-ounce) container sour
cream

8 tablespoons light brown sugar

Food coloring (optional)

Cookware needed: cookie sheet,
serrated knife

Using a serrated-edge knife, cut the cake in half horizontally, then crosswise into bars or squares. Separate the individual cakes, laying them out on a cookie sheet or a plate.

Combine the sour cream and brown sugar. If desired, divide the mixture into 2 or 3 portions and tint each one with a different food coloring.

Ice the top of each cake, and place the cakes in the refrigerator to chill until serving time.

PREPARATION TIME: *15 to 20 minutes*
TOTAL TIME: *about 40 minutes to chill*

Strawberry Angel Short Cake

FOR this delicious summer dessert, buy a cake, slice it, and top with sweetened fresh sliced strawberries and a dollop of Cool Whip or whipped cream. Or, try this variation on the theme:

SERVES 8 TO 12

1 (10-ounce) package frozen strawberries in heavy syrup

1 angel food tube cake

1 package strawberry Jell-O

¾ cup hot water

1 (12-ounce) container Cool Whip, softened, at room temperature

Cookware needed: saucepan, mixing bowl

Set out the strawberries to thaw while you slice the cake into three horizontal layers.

Once the strawberries have thawed, pour the syrup into a measuring cup and add enough water to equal ¾ cup.

Dissolve the strawberry Jell-O in the hot water and add the ¾ cup syrup mixture.

Chill about 30 minutes, or until partially set.

Fold ½ of the Cool Whip and the strawberries into the partially set Jell-O. If necessary, chill a little longer until the mixture is a good consistency to spread.

Spread the strawberry mixture between the layers of cake, then frost it with the remaining plain Cool Whip.

Refrigerate until ready to serve, then slice.

PREPARATION TIME: *15 to 20 minutes*
TOTAL TIME: *at least 1 hour to chill*

Chocolate-Glazed Angel Food Cake

SERVES 8 TO 12

3 cups sifted confectioners' sugar

¼ cup unsweetened cocoa

¼ cup plus 1 ½ tablespoons hot water

1 angel food cake

Cookware needed: mixing bowl

In a bowl, combine the first three ingredients and stir until smooth.

Drizzle the glaze over the angel food cake and serve as is, or with ice cream or an accompaniment of raspberry or strawberry sherbet.

PREPARATION TIME: *10 minutes*
TOTAL TIME: *10 minutes*

Sugar-Topped Angel Food Cake

SERVES 8 TO 12

1 ½ cups sifted confectioners' sugar

2 tablespoons milk

½ teaspoon vanilla extract

1 angel food cake

Cookware needed: mixing bowl

In a bowl, combine the first three ingredients. Drizzle the topping over the angel food cake and serve.

PREPARATION TIME: *10 minutes*
TOTAL TIME: *10 minutes*

Lemon Delight

SERVES 8 TO 12

1 angel food cake

1 jar lemon curd sauce

1 (16-ounce) container Cool Whip, softened, at room temperature

Cookware needed: 3 knives—one to cut, one to spread, one to frost

The Finishing Touch

Garnish the cake with yellow pansies or lemon curls, if you wish.

Using a serrated edge knife, cut the angel food cake into three horizontal layers and spread the lemon curd sauce on each layer, reassembling the cake as you go.

Frost with the Cool Whip, and chill until ready to serve.

PREPARATION TIME: *10 minutes*

TOTAL TIME: *about 40 minutes to chill*

Ice Cream Cake

THIS is a fun cake because you can do anything with it—as Kathryn Wyatt did in the 1950s. Try different ice cream flavors and pick a complementary sauce. Include nuts, candies, or sauce in the cake, or not. If you're having a special party at Christmas, St. Patrick's Day, or the Fourth of July, for example, you can carry your party theme through to the end by using an appropriate mold and tinting the icing to match the occasion.

For an unusual dessert, use pistachio and peppermint ice cream. But experiment...try chocolate and pistachio with hot fudge in the middle, vanilla ice cream and orange sherbet in the summer, or vanilla and strawberry with strawberry sauce on top. The possibilities are endless.

SERVES 8 TO 12

- 1 angel food tube cake
- 2 flavors (½ gallon containers) ice cream of your choice
- 1 (16-ounce) container Cool Whip, softened, at room temperature
- Nuts of your choice
- Sauces of your choice
- **Cookware needed:** nonstick mold (ring or another shape), or a bundt pan

Break up the angel food cake into chunks about the size of a half-dollar.

Cover the bottom of the mold with a layer of cake, then add scoops of one ice cream flavor, another layer of cake, and the other ice cream flavor, alternating until you have filled the pan. Or fill it any way you like, mixing cake and ice cream together or adding sauce or nuts to the layers.

Freeze the cake for about 2 hours, then remove it from the pan by running a knife around the edge and turning it out onto a plate.

Return the cake to the freezer to harden, then ice it with Cool Whip.

Serve the cake with a bowl of hot fudge or a fruit sauce.

PREPARATION TIME: *15 minutes to assemble, 5 minutes to ice*
TOTAL TIME: *add about 2 hours to freeze*

Sage Advice

This is a good do-ahead dessert. You can assemble the cake in the mold a day or two before your party and cover it with plastic wrap. Unmold it the morning of the party, return it to the freezer, then quickly ice the cake at serving time.

The
Finishing Touch

Decorate your cake with live flowers in the summer, or with traditional ice cream toppings such as chocolate syrup or caramel sauce, M&Ms, crushed cookies, candy bars, nuts, or a dusting of colored sugar.

Allison's Vanilla Crisps

ALLISON MOORE started baking these cookies when she was about six years old. She's now all of twelve and on her way to becoming a great cook (a talent she has inherited from her father, Jeff, according to her mother, Cyndee).

Allison found the recipe in one of her grandmother's old cookbooks (printed in 1947). Together, they made some modifications (used self-rising flour instead of all-purpose flour, cut back on the vanilla, etc.), which resulted in this updated recipe.

This revised old-fashioned treat is such a simple recipe that from the start Allison was able to make the batter herself, although Grandma helped with the oven. Now Allison makes them any time the family is in the mood for something sweet.

By the way, her family considers them the most delicious cookies in the world. What better recommendation could you ask for?

MAKES ABOUT 5 DOZEN ABSOLUTELY DELICIOUS COOKIES—AND THAT'S A QUOTE

1 stick butter

1 cup sugar

2 eggs, beaten

1 teaspoon vanilla extract

1 ⅓ cups self-rising flour

Cookware needed: mixing bowl, cookie sheet

Preheat the oven to 400 degrees.

Soften the butter and blend in the sugar. Add the eggs and beat the mixture until fluffy.

Stir in the vanilla and the flour.

Drop the cookies from a tablespoon onto a nonstick cookie sheet.

Bake for 8 minutes, or until slightly brown around the edges.

PREPARATION TIME: *15 minutes*
TOTAL TIME: *approximately 45 minutes*

Chinese Chews

I HADN'T made Chinese Chews since I was home for Christmas vacation when I was in college. In truth, I had forgotten all about them. Then Gaenell Stegall reminded me of them.

Immediately, I began plotting how my grandchildren, Benjamin and Matthew, could help me make these delectable treats for Christmas in just a year or so. But wait. That's a couple of years down the road. I can't wait that long, and neither should you.

MAKES 2 TO 3 DOZEN CHEWS

1 (12-ounce) package
    butterscotch morsels

½ cup peanut butter

1 (8-ounce) can salted peanuts

1 (5-ounce) can chow mein
    noodles

Cookware needed: saucepan

Stir the butterscotch morsels and the peanut butter together in a saucepan over medium heat, until the butterscotch is melted. Or melt the mixture in a microwave.

Add the peanuts and the chow mein noodles and stir until well blended.

Drop the mixture by spoonfuls onto wax paper and set the chews aside to cool.

Variation:

Use 1 (6-ounce) package butterscotch morsels and 1 (6-ounce) package chocolate chips.

PREPARATION TIME: *15 minutes*
TOTAL TIME: *about 1 hour to cool*

English Trifle

JUST the name alone is enticing—English Trifle. Actually, I've been told it should be Scottish Trifle, but on this side of the Atlantic, I wouldn't think the exact origin mattered much.

What *does* matter is that this time-proven favorite, which used to take hours to prepare, can now be turned out in a matter of minutes. No longer must the pudding be made in a double-boiler and the cake made from scratch. Thank goodness!

Something else that does matter is the inclusion of spirits—in this case, usually sherry. This is the sort of dessert into which, in olden days, even a teetotaler would manage to slip a little "spirit" for that once-a-year holiday treat. It absolutely brings all the flavors to life.

SERVES 10 TO 12

½ cup (or more) sherry

1 ½ cups prepared vanilla pudding or boiled custard

1-pound Sara Lee or other frozen, pound cake

½ (12-ounce) jar strawberry or raspberry preserves

Slivered almonds (toasted are best)

2 cups whipped cream

Cookware needed: mixing bowl

Add the sherry to the vanilla pudding and stir well.

Slice the pound cake while still slightly frozen.

Spread each slice with the strawberry preserves.

Lay a bottom layer of cake in a pretty crystal bowl. Sprinkle the cake with almonds. Top with the sherry and pudding mixture and a layer of whipped cream. Repeat until all the ingredients have been used. (Save a few almonds to sprinkle on the top.)

PREPARATION TIME: *10 to 15 minutes*
TOTAL TIME: *20 to 30 minutes (if you toast the almonds at the time)*

Lazy Woman Peach Cobbler

GAENELL STEGALL, who reminded me of Chinese Chews (page 265), cooks like I do. She uses every shortcut and convenience food available to turn out excellent *From Storebought to Homemade* dishes while expending a minimum of time and effort. This Lazy Woman Peach Cobbler is a good example. It also fills the house with wonderful "baking" aromas while you assemble the rest of the meal from already prepared items.

SERVES ABOUT 8

1 stick butter
1 cup all-purpose flour
1 cup milk

1 (15-ounce) can (or more) peaches, lightly drained
Cookware needed: baking dish or casserole

Preheat the oven to 350 degrees.

Melt the butter in the baking dish you are going to use.

Combine the flour and the milk, and pour the mixture over the butter.

Add the peaches and some juice and bake for 30 minutes.

PREPARATION TIME: *10 minutes or less*
TOTAL TIME: *approximately 40 minutes*

Sage Advice

You may substitute half-and-half for the milk for a much richer cobbler. Adding a little more of the peach juices will add additional flavor. Remember, too, these days canned peaches aren't just canned peaches... there are variations, like cinnamon-flavored peaches or harvest peaches that have spices already included. Try using some of these more richly flavored varieties in this easy dish, or doctor up the basic recipe by adding your own sprinkle of cinnamon or a dab or two of brown sugar. Also, remember to experiment. Try blueberries or cherries or blackberries, for example. There are many ways to make a "fruit" cobbler.

Serendipity Pumpkin Cake

WANT TO START a conversation? Read a cookbook in public.

That's what happened the day in the Houston airport that I was reading *Lagniappe,* the cookbook published by the Beaumont, Texas, Junior League.

"What are you cooking?" the attractive young woman who sat down beside me asked, as she peeped over my shoulder.

"Just checking out a recipe I was told is wonderful—and easy," I answered.

That was all she needed to hear.

"Let me tell you about the best recipe I've ever cooked," she offered. "Everyone always raves about it. And it's so easy!"

In no time, this friendly stranger was rattling off the recipe, finishing it up just as the final boarding announcement for her flight was being called. In the rush, I barely got her name, Laurie Harlow ("like the actress," she said). But I got the recipe!

Laurie was right. This recipe *is* something to rave about, and a perfect dessert to have around the holidays when time is at a premium. I've decided to call it Serendipity Pumpkin Cake in honor of our fleeting meeting.

SERVES APPROXIMATELY 12

For the cake:

1 (30-ounce) can pumpkin pie filling

1 box yellow cake mix

1 (2.5-ounce) package slivered almonds, toasted

1 stick butter, melted

For the frosting:

2 tablespoons confectioners' sugar

1 teaspoon vanilla extract

1 (8-ounce) package cream cheese, softened

1 (12-ounce) container Cool Whip, softened, at room temperature

Cookware needed: mixing bowl, 9 x 13-inch baking dish or casserole

Preheat the oven to 375 degrees.

Line a 9 x 13-inch baking dish with wax paper.

Prepare the pumpkin pie filling as directed on the can, or use one that is already flavored and ready to go into the pie crust, and spread it evenly on the wax paper.

Distribute the yellow cake mix (your choice—Pillsbury, Duncan Hines, a store brand, whatever, Laurie said) over the pumpkin mixture.

Sprinkle the almonds over the cake mix and drizzle the butter over all.

Bake for 30 minutes, or until set.

Remove the pan from the oven, allow the cake to cool, then turn the pan upside down, and pull off the wax paper.

To make the frosting, combine the confectioners' sugar, the vanilla, and the cream cheese. Mix this into the Cool Whip, and frost the cake.

▪▪▪▪▪▪▪▪

PREPARATION TIME: *30 minutes*
TOTAL TIME: *1 hour and 10 to 15 minutes*

Sage Advice
Laurie said she first made this cake when she was living in Hawaii, and used crushed Macadamia nuts instead of the almonds. Almonds, walnuts, Macadamia nuts—the choice is yours.

John Josselyn, an ancient ancestor of mine on my father's side, wrote about what he found in New England when he arrived there in 1663. Included in his book, *New England Rarities Discovered* (London, 1672), is this instruction on how the housewives cook pumpkins. Once "stewed," they would then add butter, vinegar, and spice "as Ginger, &c" to make it "tart like an Apple," and serve with fish or meat.

"...When ripe, and cut them [pumpkins]

into dice, and so fill a pot with them of two or

three Gallons, and stew them upon a gentle fire a

whole day, and as they sink,...fill again with

fresh Pompions [pumpkins], not putting any

liquor [water or broth] to them; and when it is

stew'd enough, it will look like bak'd Apples...."

Bread Pudding

"**OLD FASHIONED** bread pudding, that's what I miss these days," a friend of mine said with a sigh, as he turned away the dessert menu in a fancy California restaurant.

So I was thrilled, many years later, when the nice young waitress at the very elegant Thomasville, Georgia, antiques show's Patrons' Dinner asked our table, "And would you like some bread pudding?" A unanimous YES resounded!

"Bread pudding has to be the world's oldest dessert," my host, John Breison, remarked.

Which reminds me of yet another comment a friend of mine made about bread pudding last Christmas.

Tony Muncey, a fabulous chef and CIA (Culinary Institute of America) graduate, joked that if there had been really *good* bread pudding in New Orleans the British would never have allowed themselves to be defeated there.

With bread pudding apparently on so many people's minds, I decided to include a basic recipe you can throw together in just a few minutes, with a *Finishing Touch* idea to dress it up a little if you choose.

The thing to remember about bread pudding is that it truly is delicious and very filling. It makes the perfect ending to any meal—formal or casual, company or family, seated or buffet. And, best of all, if you end a meal of rotisserie chicken, deli-mashed potatoes, and cello-bag lettuce salad with this long-favored "homemade" dessert—everyone will think you made the whole meal from scratch!

SERVES 8

4 cups French bread, preferably
  day-old, cubed

1 cup sugar

3 cups milk

2 eggs, beaten

2 cups raisins or currants

2 cup chopped pecans (optional)

1 tablespoon lemon zest, or even
  Cointreau

3 tablespoons vanilla extract

½ teaspoon cinnamon

1 recipe Hard Sauce (recipe
  follows), or 1 recipe Whiskey
  Sauce (page 272)

Cookware needed: 2-quart
  baking dish or casserole

Preheat the oven to 350 degrees.

Place the bread in a 2-quart baking dish.

Combine the sugar, the milk, and the eggs.

Add the raisins, pecans, lemon zest or Cointreau, vanilla, and cinnamon.

Pour the mixture over the bread.

Bake the pudding for 1 hour 15 minutes.

Serve hot with Hard Sauce or warm with Whiskey Sauce, if you wish.

PREPARATION TIME: *15 minutes*
(plus more if you make the Hard or Whiskey Sauce)
TOTAL TIME: *1 hour and 30 minutes*

The
Finishing Touch

*For a special occasion,
turn bread pudding into
a Queen of Puddings. Do
this by spreading your
favorite jelly (black
cherry is good) over the
pudding after it is baked
and still warm. Then
make a meringue from
scratch (see page 273)—
supper was a whiz, so you
have time to do this— or
use Sauer's Egg White
Magic. Apply the
meringue in peaks to the
pudding. Return it to the
oven, set at 400 degrees,
until the jelly is warmed
and the meringue is
nicely "tanned" and set,
about 15 minutes.*

"Food,

glorious food!"

—FROM *OLIVER*

Hard Sauce

MAKES ABOUT 1 ½ CUPS

Sage Advice

Many recipes call for whiskey in Hard Sauce, but since the Whiskey Sauce is given next, I've stuck with the vanilla here. Because Hard Sauce is hard and cold, serve it on a piping hot dessert—like bread pudding. It's like putting butter or sour cream on a baked potato.

5 tablespoons butter, softened

1 cup confectioners' sugar, sifted

Pinch of salt

1 tablespoon vanilla extract

½ cup half-and-half or heavy cream

Cookware needed: mixing bowl

To the butter (soft, not melted) gradually add the sugar, beating until well blended.

Add the pinch of salt and the vanilla, blending well.

Add the cream and beat continuously until the sauce is smooth, then refrigerate until it becomes "hard."

PREPARATION TIME: *5 to 6 minutes*
TOTAL TIME: *10 minutes plus the hardening time*

Whiskey Sauce

MAKES ABOUT 1 ⅓ CUPS

Sage Advice

You can prepare the Whiskey Sauce before dinner, up to adding the egg yolk. Cover the saucepan to keep it warm. When you are ready to serve, return the saucepan to very low heat and finish the sauce.

1 cup confectioners' sugar

½ stick butter

3 tablespoons half-and-half or heavy cream

1 egg yolk, lightly beaten

¼ cup whiskey (bourbon), the better the quality, the better the taste

Cookware needed: saucepan, mixing bowl

Combine the sugar, butter, and cream in a saucepan.

Cook over low heat until the sugar dissolves, stirring often with a wooden spoon.

Remove from the heat.

Put about ¼ of the hot sauce in a mixing bowl, and add the egg yolk, beating with a whisk until it is well blended.

Add this to the remaining sauce in the saucepan and whisk well.

Cool slightly (4 to 5 minutes), then stir in the bourbon. Serve over the warm pudding.

PREPARATION TIME: *10 minutes*
TOTAL TIME: *10 minutes*

Homemade Meringue

Whip 2 egg whites till frothy. Add ¼ teaspoon cream of tartar and continue to whip until curvy peaks form. You do not want to beat the egg whites until they are so dry that they are overly stiff. Add 4 tablespoons of confectioners' sugar, ½ to 1 teaspoon at a time. Finally add ½ teaspoon vanilla extract and beat just long enough to blend, and it's ready to use.

What's-in-It Ice Cream Dessert

MY LIFELONG FRIEND Anne Geyer should have written this book. I've told her so, but she's busy doing other things—like having casual dinner parties that are always relaxing and enjoyable. Why?

We should all learn from Anne's secret. She puts her emphasis on her guests and serves them delicious, but easily prepared dishes, like this wonderful ice cream dessert that I always hope will be on her menu when we're on her guest list. Thing is, I couldn't quite figure out exactly what the ingredients were.

Naturally, I asked Anne for her recipe. But rather than taking credit for it herself, Anne 'fessed up and said she must give credit where credit is due.

Anne got the recipe from her eldest daughter, Elizabeth—a busy wife, mother of two, and businesswoman in Athens, Georgia. In the Southern tradition, Elizabeth enjoys taking this dessert to friends who've had new babies, an illness or sadness in the family—or for just no reason at all.

When Elizabeth shared the recipe with her mother a few years ago, Anne admits, "I took it and ran!"

You will too—right to the grocery store to grab up the ingredients.

SERVES 12 OR MORE

12 to 16 ice cream sandwiches

1 (18-ounce) container Cool Whip, softened, at room temperature

1 pint vanilla ice cream

Chocolate sauce in a squeezable container

1 cup slivered almonds, toasted

2 ounces Kahlua

Cookware needed: large crystal bowl

"**Ice**" the interior of a crystal bowl large enough to hold the ingredients by putting it in the freezer till frost crystals appear, for a well-dressed appearance.

Cut the ice cream sandwiches in thirds for a good fit.

Now, begin to layer as follows: ice cream sandwich, Cool Whip, ice cream.

Spoon the Cool Whip and ice cream evenly over the sandwiches—the amount of each is up to you.

Drizzle chocolate sauce over the first layer, followed by almonds and Kahlua.

Start the layering over with more sandwiches and build several layers until you've reached the top, ending with lots of chocolate, almonds, and Kahlua on top.

Cover with plastic wrap and freeze for at least 8 hours, or for several days.

PREPARATION TIME: *15 minutes*
TOTAL TIME: *15 minutes, plus at least 8 hours "freezing" time*

You'll-Never-Guess-It's-Made-with-Cookies Icebox Dessert

AS FATE would have it, no sooner had Anne Geyer given me the recipe for What's-in-It Ice Cream Dessert, than my daughter said she'd just learned of an "icebox dessert," adding, "and you'd never guess it's made with cookies."

What's great about this dessert is that you can use whatever cookies you already have on hand, even though most of us would go with the chocolate variety.

It's as easy to make as Anne's dessert, and since it doesn't have the Kahlua, it's more of a family treat.

SERVES 8 OR MORE

1 cup milk

1 (21-ounce) package Keebler chocolate chip cookies (or another of your choosing)

1 (8-ounce) container Cool Whip, softened, at room temperature

¾ cup mini chocolate chips

¾ cup chopped pecans

Cookware needed: mixing bowl, deep casserole dish

Sage Advice
This is a wonderful recipe to prepare with the help of children. But be ready to fish an occasional cookie out of the milk, and to lose at least one or two cookies to the eager helpers themselves.

Pour the milk into a wide-mouthed measuring cup or bowl.

Dip approximately 10 cookies, one by one, into the milk for 5 to 6 seconds and then place them in the casserole. (At the end, you may need to break a cookie to fill in the corners.)

Cover this bottom layer with ⅓ of the Cool Whip, followed by ⅓ of the chocolate chips and ⅓ of the pecans.

Dip another 10 cookies and repeat this process another time.

Spread the third and final cookie and Cool Whip layer. At this point, crumble 4 or 5 additional cookies (dry—not dipped in milk) over it, then add the final ⅓ chocolate chips and pecans.

Cover the dessert with plastic wrap and chill for at least 8 hours.

PREPARATION TIME: *10 to 15 minutes*
TOTAL TIME: *15 minutes, plus 8 hours for chilling*

Cake Mix Cookies

MOST writers will tell you their most often-asked question is, "What made you write your book?"

Scores of people have asked me that very question about *From Storebought to Homemade.* When my son, Langdon, is around, he interjects, "Not *what.* Who? It was Barney. Remember those cookies he made. I've never seen you so mad in all your life, Mom."

Let me explain.

My former husband was a college president, and we used the school's catering service for many large events. Once, we were having the freshman class over for a picnic. For dessert I suggested to Barney (not his real name) that we might have really good homemade cookies—a special treat, I figured.

We got cookies all right. Cookies that the kids found worked better as Frisbees. They were the biggest and the worst cookies I've ever tasted. And ugly to boot.

"Next time," I vowed, "I'll make them myself."

And I did...but by the old time-consuming method of creaming the butter, adding the flour, vanilla, and sugar. You know the routine.

I had always looked for quick-and-easy recipes, but as the college president's wife, with so much entertaining to do—and never knowing exactly what I'd get from the catering service—I learned lots of ways to turn storebought items into "homemade" specialties.

If only I'd had Nancy Sweger's recipe for Cake Mix Cookies back then!

One thing is for sure—these days, when I come to the end of the Cake Mix Cookie dough, I always roll one extra-large cookie, about the size of a Frisbee, and mutter, "Barney, this one's for you!"

MAKES APPROXIMATELY 2 ½ DOZEN COOKIES

1 box cake mix of your choice
(see *Sage Advice*)

2 eggs, beaten

1 (8-ounce) container Cool Whip,
softened, at room temperature

1 cup confectioners' sugar

Cookware needed: mixing bowl,
cookie sheet

Sage Advice
The hardest part of this
recipe is trying to decide
what flavor cake mix to
use—Lemon Supreme,
Chocolate, White, or
another one of your
favorites.

Preheat the oven to 350 degrees.

Mix the cake mix, the eggs, and the Cool Whip together with a fork.

Roll the dough into balls the size of a nickel, and roll them in the confectioners' sugar.

Place the cookies on a cookie sheet, allowing room for them to spread.

Bake for 10 minutes.

Let the cookies sit for 1 minute, then remove them to an airtight container.

PREPARATION TIME: *30 minutes*
TOTAL TIME: *40 to 60 minutes*

Brunch for the Bunch

IF FONDUE has made a comeback, then brunches can't be far behind.

I've always liked brunches—both as a hostess and a guest.

One reason I particularly enjoy having a brunch is that you can serve almost any food you can think of—from egg and cheese dishes to tenderloin.

When I began thinking about which of my favorite dishes I usually prepare for this late-morning or noontime gathering, I realized that I serve a wide variety of selections—from Crab Imperial (page 99, usually an entrée but served on toast, rather than rice, for a brunch) to Cheese Garlic Grits (page 192), which appears in the Salads, Vegetables, Potatoes and Rice chapter.

So I decided to include the more traditional brunch dishes here, but also to provide a short list of recipes that appear in other chapters that work equally well for a brunch. That list appears on page 300.

Brunch provides the host or hostess with a perfect opportunity to serve a wide variety of jellies and condiments. Most farmers' markets and quaint stores have all kinds of berry jellies and preserves, and grocery store shelves are filled with vast numbers of pickles and relishes that I'm always dying to try.

If you're worried about what to serve these goodies in, don't be. You can buy unmatched saucers, that long ago lost their cups, for only a few cents at most flea markets and yard sales. Gather up a collection and have them on hand for your next brunch or buffet. The array of the condiments and colorful saucers will add charm and interest to your table.

"Condiments are like old friends— highly thought of, but often taken for granted."

—MARILYN KAYTOR, *LOOK*, JANUARY 29, 1963

Not-Just-for-Brunch Casserole

IF YOU haven't fixed this casserole, you must be the *only* person who hasn't!

Of all the recipes shared with me when I mentioned *From Storebought to Homemade*, this was the one I received most frequently. Interestingly, unlike many casseroles that have been around for some time (I first made it when the kids were about 8 and 10, so that was some 23 years ago now), this is one that has never been forgotten. To this day I make it for our Christmas breakfast.

But it isn't just a party or special-occasion recipe. Should you be a busy mother worried about feeding your children a good hot breakfast—or dinner for that matter—try preparing this for them. The leftovers reheat well too.

SERVES 10 TO 12

10 slices bread, cubed (crusts removed if you wish—I don't)

1 pound bulk sausage (hot or mild), cooked and crumbled, or for a quicker version, 1 (8-ounce) package cooked, diced ham

1 (8-ounce) package Cheddar cheese, grated (or a cheese mixture)

8 eggs, beaten

4 cups milk

Salt and pepper, to taste

Cookware needed: skillet, mixing bowl, deep baking dish or casserole

Put the bread cubes in a greased deep baking dish.

Add the sausage (or the ham if you're using that) and the cheese to the baking dish.

Combine the eggs, milk, and salt and pepper and pour the mixture over all, making sure it doesn't overflow.

Cover and refrigerate the casserole overnight, or for at least 8 hours, so the custard is absorbed.

When ready to bake, preheat the oven to 350 degrees. Bake the casserole for 45 to 50 minutes

PREPARATION TIME: *10 minutes (plus 10 more minutes if you use the sausage)*
TOTAL TIME: *a little more than 1 hour, plus at least 8 hours to chill*

A Side of Beans

WILL CHILDREN be at the brunch? This ready-in-no-time dish will satisfy them if they turn up their noses to your other offerings—if the grownups leave any, that is.

SERVES 4 TO 6 (OR MORE CHILDREN)

1 (13-ounce) can B&M baked beans

1 tablespoon apple cider vinegar

2 tablespoons water

1 (16-ounce) package cocktail franks

⅓ cup Cheddar cheese, grated

Cookware needed: baking dish or casserole

Preheat the oven to 350 degrees.

Combine all the ingredients, or reserve the grated cheese to sprinkle on top, and pour the mixture into a lightly greased baking dish.

Bake for 20 to 30 minutes, or until bubbly.

PREPARATION TIME: *5 minutes*
TOTAL TIME: *approximately 35 minutes*

The
Finishing Touch

This is a dish that bene-fits from the crunch of some crumbled potato chips sprinkled on top with the cheese.

Eggnog Pancakes

EARLY ONE December morning, when the season and the weather screamed for pancakes, I discovered I had used my last egg the day before. It was then I remembered the trick for making Ice Cream Muffins (page 221). Ice cream would work here too I reasoned. But, while reaching into the refrigerator for some bacon, I saw a carton of Southern Comfort eggnog, a uniquely flavored nog, but without the spirits.

That morning we had the richest, fluffiest pancakes ever. They were so good, in fact, there was no reason to pass the syrup, just the butter.

Sage Advice

If using all eggnog is too rich for your taste, or your cholesterol, use half eggnog and half milk. These eggnog pancakes will be very fluffy, so be forewarned if you like thin, flat pancakes.

SERVES 4 TO 6

2 cups pancake mix

1¾ to 2 cups eggnog, preferably Southern Comfort

Cookware needed: mixing bowl, skillet

Stir the pancake mix and eggnog together and drop the batter by spoonfuls onto a hot nonstick griddle or skillet.

PREPARATION TIME: *3 minutes*

TOTAL TIME: *10 to 15 minutes*

Baked Egg, Shrimp, and Cheese Delight

ONCE, when I served this casserole, a guest asked me what was in it. I began answering, "shrimp, Worcestershire sauce, cheese, garlic sauce...."

"Well!" she interrupted me. "Anything would be good with shrimp, Worcestershire sauce, cheese, and garlic in it!"

I have to agree.

SERVES 4 TO 6

1 cup Ragú Roasted Garlic Parmesan sauce

Cayenne pepper

Worcestershire sauce

2 cups medium, cleaned and cooked shrimp (either from the fresh seafood counter or from the frozen food section)

1 cup Cheddar cheese, grated

6 hard-boiled eggs, chopped

Cookware needed: baking dish or casserole

Sage Advice

If you have the Egg Wave™ gadget to hard boil the eggs, you avoid the tedious task of shelling them after they are cooked. But if you don't have a microwave oven, or the Egg Wave™, you can buy already hard-boiled eggs from the salad bar the same way you buy sliced celery.

Preheat the oven to 375 degrees.

Season the sauce generously with the cayenne and Worcestershire. (You can do this right in the measuring cup.)

Combine the sauce with the shrimp, cheese, and eggs in a buttered baking dish.

Bake until piping hot, about 35 minutes.

PREPARATION TIME: *15 minutes*
TOTAL TIME: *approximately 50 minutes*

Your Mother's Basic Quiche Recipe

Quiche has suffered a bad rap since your mother or grandmother used to make it. You know, the "real men don't eat..." tag line.

But as I said, if fondue can have a comeback, then brunches can't be far behind. And how can you have a brunch without quiche?

When quiche was all the rage, several "instant" varieties were available in the milk or freezer bins at the grocery store. Those can be hard to find these days. But, actually, it takes no more time to stir up the egg and milk base to make a quiche than it does to open a carton of "instant" quiche mix to pour into your frozen pie shell. Your mother will tell you (or you may remember yourself) that the time-consuming part of making a quiche was grating the cheese—but already grated cheese packs have taken care of that.

So try making a "homemade" quiche using the following formula. (It might even satisfy your "closet chef" yearnings for a while.)

The basic quiche recipe is as simple as remembering *1 to ¼—one large egg per quarter cup of milk.*

This translates into 2 large eggs and ½ cup of milk per pie shell (9-inch, not deep dish) for most quiches. But if you want to make several different quiches to put out, just the way you might make several different pies for a dessert buffet, or if you prefer to use a deep-dish pie shell, mix the eggs and milk to make the "custard" in one large batch, and pour the desired amount over whatever fillings you use.

The Proof Is in the Pie Crust

Nancy Sweger, my daughter's mother-in-law, is the only person I know who always makes her own pie crusts. The rest of us use frozen pie shells or the refrigerated pie doughs. Whichever you use—from scratch to ready-to-cook—while preparing the custard and ingredients, prepare the pie crust as follows:

- Preheat the oven to 350 degrees.
- Separate the white of one of the eggs to be used in the custard and beat it lightly. Pour the leftover egg white(s) into the quiche mixture.
- Brush a pie shell with a little of this egg white, using a pastry brush.
- Prick the bottom and sides of the pie shell with a fork.
- Bake the crust for 5 minutes (just about the amount of time it will take you to prepare the quiche for baking).

(Incidentally, you do not have to defrost a frozen pie shell.)

Sausage Quiche

THE SIMPLE QUICHE that combines those three breakfast favorites, eggs, sausage, and cheese, is a good recipe to start with.

SERVES 6

1 9-inch pie shell
3 large eggs, beaten
¾ cup milk
Salt and pepper, to taste
Cayenne pepper, to taste

1 pound cooked (hot or mild) bulk sausage
1 ½ cups Cheddar cheese, grated—*sharp* is best
Cookware needed: skillet, mixing bowl

Prepare the pie shell according to the directions above.

Do not turn off the oven.

Combine eggs, milk, and seasonings and beat lightly until well blended.

Stir in the sausage and pour the mixture into the prepared pie shell.

Distribute the cheese on top and bake for 40 to 45 minutes.

PREPARATION TIME: *15 minutes*
TOTAL TIME: *approximately 60 minutes*

Broccoli and Ham Quiche

MANY a mother has persuaded her children (even the boys) to eat their broccoli by preparing this broccoli and ham quiche. It works just as well as a brunch dish for grown-ups.

Sage Advice

Did you notice that the egg to milk and sour cream ratio comes out to 6 eggs to 1 ½ cups—the 1 to ¼ formula?

SERVES 6

1 9-inch pie shell

6 large eggs, beaten

1 cup milk

½ cup sour cream

Salt and pepper, to taste

¾ cup broccoli florets, frozen or fresh

¼ to ½ cup small diced ham bits (these are available in vacuum sealed packages, as well as at the salad bar)

½ cup Cheddar cheese, grated

Cookware needed: mixing bowl

Prepare the pie shell according to the directions on page 285.

Do not turn off the oven.

Combine the eggs, milk, sour cream, and seasonings and beat lightly until well blended.

Stir in the broccoli, ham, and cheese, and pour the mixture into the prepared pie shell.

Bake for 40 to 45 minutes.

PREPARATION TIME: *5 minutes*
TOTAL TIME: *approximately 50 minutes*

The Finishing Touch

Bacon can be substituted for the ham, or, to make this a vegetarian quiche, omit the meat and use drained, canned mushrooms. Spinach can also be used in place of the broccoli.

Fancy Crabmeat Quiche

THIS SOPHISTICATED and rich quiche uses whipped cream in place of milk (which makes for a different egg to liquid proportion), Swiss rather than Cheddar cheese, and fills a deep-dish pie shell. The recipe does call for sautéing the bacon, but the taste makes it worth it.

SERVES 6 TO 8

1 deep-dish pie shell

4 strips bacon

½ cup frozen, diced onion

1 (8-ounce) package Swiss cheese, grated

1 (6-ounce) can crabmeat

4 large eggs, beaten

1 ½ cups whipped cream

2 tablespoons dry sherry

¼ teaspoon nutmeg

Salt and pepper, to taste

Cookware needed: skillet, mixing bowl

Prepare the pie shell according to the directions on page 285. For this larger size, bake 8 to 10 minutes.

Sauté the bacon, remove it to a paper towel to drain, and reserve the drippings in the pan.

Sauté the onion in the bacon drippings. Crumble the drained bacon.

Sprinkle 1 cup of the grated Swiss cheese in the bottom of the pie shell.

Layer the crabmeat over the cheese, followed by the crumbled bacon and the onion.

Combine the eggs, cream, sherry, and seasonings, and pour the mixture into the shell.

Top with the remaining Swiss cheese.

Bake for about 40 to 45 minutes.

PREPARATION TIME: *20 minutes*
TOTAL TIME: *approximately 1 hour and 10 minutes*

No-Pie-Shell Quiche

SHOULD you not have a pie crust handy, or if you happen to have extra "custard," try this version of quiche that makes its own crust.

SERVES 8

3 eggs

1 stick butter

1 ½ cups milk

½ cup Bisquick

¼ teaspoon salt

Dash pepper

1 cup Cheddar or Swiss cheese, grated (or a combination to your liking)

½ cup chopped ham (or use bacon or sausage)

1 (10-ounce) bag frozen, chopped broccoli, defrosted

1 (4-ounce) can sliced mushrooms, drained

Cookware needed: blender; pie pan, baking dish or casserole

Preheat the oven to 350 degrees.

Put the eggs, butter, milk, Bisquick, salt, and pepper in a blender.

Blend well, stir in the cheese, and pour half the mixture into a greased pie pan.

Press the broccoli, mushrooms, and ham into the cheese and custard mixture.

Top this layer with the remaining cheese and custard mixture.

Bake for 45 minutes.

Turn off the oven and allow the quiche to set for 10 minutes.

PREPARATION TIME: *10 minutes*
TOTAL TIME: *a little more than 1 hour*

Sage Advice

Once again, the ingredients you choose to put into this quiche can be determined by your personal preference. Frozen asparagus pieces might be substituted for the broccoli, for example, or you can leave out the mushrooms but toss in some toasted almonds.

Legendary Cheese Pie

MY FRIEND ANNE GEYER and I belong to some of the same civic groups and clubs, and invariably we are called on to "bring a dish" to a luncheon meeting or reception. While I'm fretting over what to take, Anne is at home whipping together her Legendary Cheese Pie. And when she doesn't bring it, I'm always disappointed.

Like many cheese-and-egg–based dishes, this one is very versatile and can be served at a brunch, for a formal luncheon, or, cut into small pieces, as an appetizer at a cocktail party.

SERVES 8 (OR 24 AS AN APPETIZER)

10 large eggs

½ cup flour

1 teaspoon salt

1 stick butter, melted

1 (8-ounce) package Monterey Jack cheese, grated

1 (8-ounce) package sharp Cheddar cheese, grated

1 (16-ounce) container small curd cottage cheese

1 (4-ounce) can chopped green chili peppers, drained

Cookware needed: mixing bowl, 9 x 13-inch baking dish or casserole

Preheat the oven to 350 degrees.

Beat the eggs until light in color.

Add the flour, salt, butter, cheeses, and chili peppers, and stir to blend.

Pour mixture into a lightly greased 9 x 13-inch baking dish.

Bake for 35 to 40 minutes.

Cool slightly before cutting.

PREPARATION TIME: *10 minutes*

TOTAL TIME: *approximately 45 minutes*

Quick Breakfast Ring

THIS LONG-TIME favorite is sweet, and probably one that you may be familiar with. Read through the basic recipe given below, but before making it, check out some of the possible variations in *Sage Advice*. You may prefer one of those.

SERVES 16 TO 20

¼ cup brown sugar, packed

6 tablespoons butter or margarine, melted

2 tablespoons pecan halves

6 maraschino cherries, cut in half

½ cup granulated sugar

2 teaspoons cinnamon

2 (8-ounce) cans refrigerator biscuits

Cookware needed: 10-inch ring mold

Preheat the oven to 425 degrees.

Mix the brown sugar with 2 tablespoons of the butter. Spread the butter and sugar into the bottom of a 10-inch ring mold.

Arrange the nuts and cherries, cut side up, on the brown sugar.

Combine the granulated sugar and the cinnamon.

Dip each biscuit into the remaining melted butter. Then roll it in the sugar-cinnamon mixture.

Arrange the biscuits in the mold so that they are slightly overlapping.

Bake for 12 to 15 minutes.

Unmold onto serving plate immediately. The butter usually prevents the mold from sticking, but if it does stick, loosen with a knife or spatula.

PREPARATION TIME: *15 minutes*
TOTAL TIME: *30 minutes*

Sage Advice

For some variety, try these combinations for the topping: substitute 1 cup walnuts, or almonds for the pecans (without the cherries, this variation is similar to the well-known favorite, "Monkey Bread"); use a granola mixture instead of the pecans and cherries; instead of cherries, use grated orange peel.

Ham-Stuffed Apples

YOU MAY HAVE read in the Introduction my suggestion for using a fruit or vegetable as an individual serving dish. These ham-stuffed apples do just that, and they don't take very long to prepare, especially if you're having only a few guests. But I wouldn't undertake making a dozen or so of these.

SERVES 6

6 large, red unpeeled apples

8 ounces ready-to-serve cooked ham cubes or bits

2 tablespoons butter, melted

⅓ cup raisins, brown or golden

⅓ cup chopped pecans

3 tablespoons brown sugar

½ to 1 cup apple juice

Cookware needed: mixing bowl, baking dish or casserole

Cut the tops off the apples and scoop out the core with some of the fruit, but be sure to leave a thick shell to hold the stuffing.

Preheat the oven to 350 degrees.

Put approximately 1 cup of the removed apple fruit in a mixing bowl and combine it with the ham, butter, raisins, pecans, and brown sugar, mixing the ingredients well.

Spoon this mixture into the cored apples and place them in a baking dish.

Pour the juice over the apples and bake for 35 to 40 minutes, basting occasionally with the juice.

PREPARATION TIME: *30 to 40 minutes*
TOTAL TIME: *approximately 1 hour and 15 minutes*

Sausage-Apple Ring

THIS MAKE-AHEAD Sausage-Apple Ring is good any time of the year, but my Raleigh, North Carolina, friend, Judy Root, says it is particularly good to have during the Christmas season. So good, in fact, that her daughter, Susan Jordan, who lives in Paris, even dares to serve it there.

Incidentally, because you don't have to cook the sausage first, this dish is easily and quickly assembled.

SERVES 6 TO 8

Pam, or other vegetable cooking spray

2 pounds bulk sausage, hot or mild, or a combination of the two

1 cello-pack saltines (approximately 42), crushed

½ cup milk

1 cup peeled and diced apples

3 eggs, lightly beaten

Cookware needed: mixing bowl, ring mold, or if you have one, a bundt pan

Preheat the oven to 350 degrees.

Spray, or grease, a ring mold well, even if it is nonstick.

Combine the ingredients and spread the mixture evenly in the pan.

Bake for 1 hour.

Turn the pan upside down to drain on a plate covered with paper towels. (Obviously you don't want the grease draining on your countertop.)

Use a spatula to loosen the edges of the ring and unmold it onto a serving plate (or, if planning to reheat, onto an ovenproof or microwaveable plate) and serve at once, or refrigerate it until you are ready to reheat it.

PREPARATION TIME: *10 minutes*
TOTAL TIME: *1 hour and 15 minutes*

Sage Advice

Susan insists that this dish is even better the second day, so she makes it up, cooks it, and then reheats it to capture its full flavor. If using the microwave, cover the ring loosely with a paper towel and heat it on high for about 8 minutes. However, for the best results, reheat in a 350 degree oven, uncovered, for about 30 minutes.

The Finishing Touch

If serving this at Christmas, garnish the outer rim of the sausage ring with greens or holly sprays, the way they decorated the suckling pig back in olden days.

Parmesan Asparagus

IN THE LIST of additional recipes suitable for brunches (page 300), you will find several fruit or vegetable dishes from the Salads, Vegetables, Potatoes and Rice chapter (page 128). But this simple Parmesan Asparagus makes such a nice presentation on a buffet table that I have included it here.

SERVES 4 TO 6

2 (10-ounce) boxes frozen asparagus

2 tablespoons butter, melted

¼ cup dry white wine

¼ teaspoon freshly ground pepper

½ to ¾ cup Parmesan cheese, grated, or more, to taste

Cookware needed: baking dish or casserole

Preheat the oven to 400 degrees.

Cook the asparagus according to package directions, being sure not to overcook them.

Drain and place them in a shallow baking dish.

Drizzle the butter and wine over the asparagus and sprinkle them with the freshly ground pepper.

Cover all with the Parmesan cheese, adding more if you wish.

Bake for about 10 minutes, or until the cheese melts.

PREPARATION TIME: *15 minutes*
TOTAL TIME: *25 to 30 minutes*

The
Finishing Touch

For a variation, arrange slices of large, ripe tomatoes in the baking dish and top each one with 3 or 4 asparagus spears. Follow with the rest of the ingredients to make individual servings of this nice vegetable dish.

Queenly Chicken Salad

WHEN QUEEN ELIZABETH II visited the University of Virginia, my alma mater, she was served a chicken salad fit for royalty, complete with green grapes and slivered almonds. But it's the curry powder and soy sauce, plus the pineapple, that make this a special delicacy indeed.

Ever since then, this very unusual, and definitely delicious Queenly Chicken Salad has been a favorite for brunches and special luncheons.

SERVES 5

2 cups Time Trimmer, or other ready-to-serve chicken pieces, unflavored

¾ cup mayonnaise

2 teaspoons lemon juice

1 teaspoon curry powder (optional)

2 teaspoons soy sauce

1 (5-ounce) can sliced water chestnuts, drained

½ pound seedless grapes, halved

½ cup chopped celery

½ cup toasted slivered almonds

1 (8-ounce) can pineapple chunks, drained

Cookware needed: mixing bowl

Set the chicken pieces out to thaw, if necessary.

Combine the mayonnaise with the lemon juice and other seasonings.

Toss thoroughly with the chicken and remaining ingredients.

Chill in the refrigerator for 2 to 3 hours.

PREPARATION TIME: *15 minutes*
TOTAL TIME: *approximately 3 hours*

The
Finishing Touch

Treat your friends and family like royalty and serve this on a pretty leaf of lettuce topped with extra slivered almonds or a swirl of lemon peel. Garnish the plate with a small bunch of grapes. And always remember to wear your very best jewelry.

Coke-Cooked Dogs

LOOKING FOR SOMETHING you can do at the last minute for a casual brunch or backyard picnic? Many's the time I've surveyed a table set with storebought fried chicken, a big bowl of homemade Pickled Cole Slaw (page 131), a casserole of delicious Jalapeño Corn Bread (page 230), and panicked.

That's when it's time for Larry Aaron's Coke-Cooked Hot Dogs, a recipe he learned from his mom, Evelyn Groff Aaron. They're a little like my favorite, Everyone's Favorite... Meatballs (page 65) appetizer. They're cooked in a secret ingredient (in this instance the Coke) that adds an unidentifiable zing and keeps everyone guessing, "What makes them so good?"

SERVES 8 TO 10 (OR MORE IF USED AS AN APPETIZER)

1 (12-ounce) can or bottle
Coca-Cola

1 tablespoon ketchup or
barbeque sauce

1 pound hot dogs
Cookware needed: skillet

Combine the Coke and ketchup or barbeque sauce in a skillet.

Prick the hot dogs with a fork.

Simmer the hot dogs in the liquid for about 5 minutes or until thoroughly hot.

PREPARATION TIME: *5 minutes*
TOTAL TIME: *10 minutes*

The
Finishing Touch

Just serve in a warm bowl or on a platter, with a basket of buns and small dishes of the usual condiments nearby, or cut into small pieces and spear with toothpicks.

Open House Shrimp, Virginia-Style

TRUST ME! Don't let the long list of ingredients or the instructions frighten you off. This is a wonderful recipe that will make a hit at your next large party. Furthermore, as I suggest, you can kill two birds with one stone by preparing this recipe—food for your party and Christmas remembrances for your friends. Read on!

Kaye Anne Davis Aikins has eaten or served her mother's pickled shrimp every Christmas Eve since she was tall enough to reach the dining-room table. "No matter where we were living, Mother always cooked what she called her Virginia pickled shrimp," Kaye Anne fondly remembers. "And now I'm fixing it for my grandchildren." That makes this a four-generation Davis-Aikins family favorite.

It is so much a tradition, in fact, that it was served to the 400-plus guests at her family's Sea Island, Georgia, home when Kaye Anne's father, Bill Davis, celebrated his 95th birthday.

Of course, when Kaye Anne's mother, Alice Davis, was fixing her Virginia pickled shrimp, it took hours and hours to shell those succulent sea creatures we all love so much.

Thank goodness we can now buy the packages of frozen, shelled, and deveined raw shrimp (with tails left on) that make this family recipe a real cinch.

This is an easy recipe, but you will need a large jar to hold the ingredients. And, as I suggested at the outset, because it yields more shrimp than you can possibly use at one party, and because it can be made 4 or 5 days in advance, it's a great way to make neighborhood Christmas gifts *and* party food with a minimum of effort.

Sage Advice

Do not use already cooked shrimp as a shortcut. The shrimp need to be freshly cooked and still hot to absorb the flavor of the pickling sauce while they are cooling.

SERVES A HOUSE FULL OF SHRIMP-LOVING GUESTS!

For the Pickling Juices:

7 teaspoons salt

3 to 4 teaspoons pepper, cracked or freshly ground

2 teaspoons confectioners' sugar

2 teaspoons dry mustard

A pinch of cayenne pepper

1 cup distilled white vinegar

2 cups olive oil

2 cups water

Juice of 2 lemons

For Shrimp preparation:

10 cups water

5 pounds frozen, uncooked, peeled and deveined, ready-to-cook shrimp

2 (12-ounce) bags frozen, diced onion, defrosted and drained on paper towels (or 10 to 15 small onions, sliced or diced)

2 ounces whole bay leaves

Cookware needed: mixing bowl, 10-gallon pot, very large jar

The Finishing Touch

Serve with Ritz crackers and fancy toothpicks nearby. There's no need to have a cocktail sauce for these spicy treats.

Thoroughly mix the first 5 ingredients with the vinegar. Combine the olive oil, water and lemon juice, then add—*very* slowly—to the vinegar mixture, stirring to blend thoroughly. Set aside.

Bring the 10 cups of water to a boil and add the shrimp.

When the water comes back to a boil (after a minute of two), pour it off immediately. Do not allow the shrimp to boil or sit in the water.

In a very large jar, assemble the following layers immediately (this must be done while the shrimp are still warm in order for all the flavors to be absorbed): (1) shrimp; (2) onions; (3) bay leaves.

Repeat the layers until all the ingredients have been used.

Stir the vinegar and oil mixture again and slowly pour it over the ingredients in the jar.

Tightly screw on the top of the jar and place it in the refrigerator.

At least 3 times a day, turn the jar over to be sure all the shrimp are being properly "pickled."

To serve, empty the contents of the jar into a bowl. With a slotted spoon, scoop up the shrimp and whatever onions cling to them, and place them in a large serving dish.

PREPARATION TIME: *30 minutes*
TOTAL TIME: *2 to 3 days minimum to become really flavorful*

Lynda Bird Johnson Robb's Hot Spinach Casserole

WHEN LYNDA ROBB was a guest in our home, my Republican daughter, Joslin, was most excited. Not because Lynda was President Johnson's daughter, or Senator Robb's wife, but because her recipe for a hot spinach casserole had long been one of Joslin's favorite company dishes. You see, Lynda has long lived in Virginia, where her husband was a senator, and her recipe is a favorite among Virginians.

Lynda says that even people, who don't like spinach ask for seconds of this spicy dish.

Your guests will too...whatever state they live in.

Sage Advice

Have no fear, this casserole is a favorite of Democrats and Republicans alike.

SERVES 6 TO 8

2 (10-ounce) packages frozen, chopped spinach

2 to 3 tablespoons frozen, chopped onion

4 tablespoons butter

2 tablespoons all-purpose flour

1 (5-ounce) can evaporated milk

Freshly ground black pepper, to taste

¾ teaspoon celery salt

¾ teaspoon crushed garlic

1 teaspoon Worcestershire sauce

Small dash cayenne pepper

1 (6-ounce) roll jalapeño cheese, cut into small pieces

Croutons

Cookware needed: medium saucepan, skillet, baking dish or casserole

Preheat the oven to 350 degrees.

Cook the spinach according to package directions. Drain well, reserving ½ cup of the cooking liquid.

Sauté the onion in the butter. Add the flour and mix well.

Stir in the evaporated milk and the reserved spinach liquid (a whisk is a good tool for this).

Season the mixture with the pepper, celery salt, garlic, Worcestershire sauce, and cayenne pepper. Add the jalapeño cheese and stir until the cheese is melted.

Add the cooked spinach and blend well.

Pour the mixture into a baking dish and top it with the croutons.

Bake for 30 minutes or until bubbly.

PREPARATION TIME: *20 minutes*
TOTAL TIME: *50 minutes*

Oranges Vermouth

BY NOW you know that many of these *From Storebought to Homemade* recipes were given to me by friends and acquaintances, but the other day someone asked me *why* people give away their favorite recipes.

Her question brought back memories of the occasional time when I've asked someone for a recipe—a compliment because the dish was so delicious—only to have my request refused. Or worse, to be given the recipe, but with an essential ingredient omitted. Either way, those few experiences have left a bad taste in my mouth, so to speak.

Her question also brought to mind the wonderful comment made by my friend Mina Wood when I told her about this cookbook. She said, "Oh, I'd like to share a couple of my recipes in your cookbook so my daughters-in-law, who are wives, mothers, and career women, and other young girls like them, can have them."

I can't imagine a more generous thought. To me it exemplifies sharing the best you have with those you love in order to enhance their lives.

So, for Alex, Lalla, and Anne Wood, and for others like them, here's a wonderful dessert recipe that makes a light and delicious finale for a fancy dinner party, a family gathering, or a brunch.

The Finishing Touch

Serve the orange sections in pretty crystal dishes and garnish each serving with raspberries, strawberries, or a few seedless green grapes for complementary taste and color. Orange or raspberry chocolate candies, or orange-flavored Milano cookies, are also nice accompaniments.

SERVES 4

⅓ cup sugar
½ cup vermouth
2 whole cloves

4 large seedless oranges, or a jar of orange sections
Cookware needed: mixing bowl

Combine the sugar, vermouth, and whole cloves in a covered bowl.

Carefully peel the oranges and separate the sections, if using fresh. Place the oranges in the bowl, cover, and refrigerate overnight. Remove the cloves and serve.

PREPARATION TIME: *10 minutes, less if using bottled orange sections*
TOTAL TIME: *overnight for chilling*

Among the many other dishes in this book suitable for brunches are the following:

- Almost any recipe in Appetizers, especially Dressed Up English Muffins (page 53) and Curried Chicken Bits (page 63)
- Individual cups or mugs filled with a chilled or hot soup, including Love Apple Fromage (page 77), Chilled Strawberry (page 81), or Virginia Cream of Peanut Soup (page 80)
- Either beef or pork tenderloin, served cold and thinly sliced, or the Wild Rice and Sausage entrée (page 119), or Crab Imperial recipe (page 99), all in Easy Entrées
- A colorful jelled salad, such as Avocado or Tomato Aspic (page 143 or page 148) or the Mango Soufflé (page 146) is always a good choice
- And for the accompaniments, try a grits dish (pages 192-193), Scalloped Corn (page160), or a Baked Fruit dish (pages 176-177)

■ ■ ■ ■ ■ ■ ■ ■

I'VE BEEN GIVEN this recipe many times, and by many names—Life's a Cake, the Happiness Cake, and the Cake of Human Kindness, for starters. But the first time it was shared with me was when I was giving a talk in Bartlesville, Oklahoma, many years ago. No matter what its name, it rings as true now as it did when it was first written:

1 cup good thoughts	**2 cups sacrifice**
1 cup kind deeds	**2 cups well-beaten faults**
1 cup consideration for others	**3 cups forgiveness**

Mix thoroughly. Add tears of Joy, Sorrow and Sympathy.

Flour with Love and Kindly service.

Fold in Prayer and Faith.

Pour all into your daily life. Bake with the heat of Human Kindness. Serve with a Smile. Serves all the Starved Souls who hunger.

Index